the fuel
and the flame

the fuel
and the flame

ten keys to ignite your college campus for
Jesus Christ

STEVE SHADRACH

FOREWORD BY JOE WHITE

Authentic

Authentic Publishing
We welcome your questions and comments.

USA   1820 Jet Stream Dr., Colorado Springs, CO 80921
          www.authenticbooks.com
India   Logos Bhavan, Medchal Road, Jeedimetla Village, Secunderabad
          500 055, A.P.

The Fuel and the Flame
ISBN: 978-1-884543-85-2

Cover design: projectluz.com

Printed in the United States of America

what christian leaders are saying

"Now I don't need to write the book I wanted written! This is a unique resource. Nothing like it has been written for years. There is not a book out there that is this practical, but also principle oriented. I am very enthusiastic about us using this. I have seen God's hand on Steve's life in reaching, equipping, and mobilizing college students to labor a lifetime for Christ. His life message lends credibility to this written work."

—Mike Hearon
Director
Campus Outreach
Augusta, Georgia

"Steve Shadrach has taken his own passion for students to become reproducing disciples for Jesus Christ and translated it into a practical, hands-on tool to be used by students to do the same."

—John D. Brooks
President
FOCUS International
(Friends of College and University Students)

"I read every word. I couldn't put it down. I've been looking for something to train my key students, and this is perfect. If you really want to do campus ministry, you have to get this book."

—Derrick Moore
Georgia Tech Football Team Chaplain
Fellowship of Christian Athletes

"Steve Shadrach is an excellent writer and diligent worker. He understands the university and knows how to impact campuses with the Good News. *The Fuel and the Flame* is an excellent in-depth, practical, and interactive resource tool that will help equip students and workers for ministry on today's college and university campus."

—Dennis Gaylor
National Director
Chi Alpha Campus Ministries, USA

"This is a great resource I'm going to take my whole staff through. Steve has done a great job explaining the basics of ministry philosophy and how to succeed in ministering to students. Thanks!"

—**Isaac Jenkins**
Ole Miss Campus Director
Campus Crusade for Christ

"Here is a book to take off the shelf and into the heart (the fuel). Then, walk it on over to the campus (the flame). Steve is a strategist, but he is also a practitioner. There is theory here, but it is tried and tested theory. There is motivation. There is vision. There are ideas and tools. Having known Steve for years, I know that he is a man who is a synthesizer of the best and the most practical. If you are asking the question, "How can I be used in this generation to glorify God and see His kingdom spread from the campus to the nations?" then this might just be the catalyst to ignite a fire that will burn to the ends of the earth."

—**Mark Lewis**
Southwest Regional Director
The Navigators

"I first met Steve Shadrach in my sorority house as he led a "Love and Dating" Bible study. That message rocked my world, and it was the beginning of a tidal wave of change for me. The Shadrachs not only shared the gospel message with me, but they shared their lives too. Living with them, I laughed, cried, shared, and prayed more times than I remember. Eighteen years later from my first encounter with Shad, he is still at it and going strong on the college campus. He has a passion for God and for college students that just won't quit. It's about time he wrote this book. If you want to make a difference on your campus, read it. He knows his stuff."

—**Kim Vollendorf**
Women's Ministry Staff
Student Mobilization
University of Arkansas

"Steve Shadrach has compiled a heavy stack of explosive principles into a controlled burn. This book enables campus workers to apply Jesus' Great Commandment and Great Commission."

—**Greg Fritz**
President
Initiative 360

"I have known Steve since he was a student at the University of Arkansas, and I was his pastor. We brought him on staff, and I was able to observe him up close. I know no man who would surpass him in his intense dedication and compassion to link college students to a vision of reaching the world. From his founding of Student Mobilization to the content of this book, I can say no heart beats more fervently with the mandate of Jesus to go, win, and disciple."

—Dr. H. D. McCarty
Senior Pastor, Emeritus
University Baptist Church, Fayetteville, Arkansas

"Steve Shadrach is changing the world. This book will help you change yours—starting with your life and quickly spilling over to your campus. I heartily recommend it."

—Mike Woodruff
Director
Ivy Jungle Network

"I am deeply grateful to Steve for *The Fuel and the Flame*. Herein is some tremendous help for university students and their leaders."

—Max Barnett
Former Director
Baptist Collegiate Ministry, University of Oklahoma

"Steve Shadrach is my mentor. As a college student my life was changed by living out the principles that Steve teaches in this book. *The Fuel and the Flame* is a catalyst for every young adult seeking to take the Christian life seriously. From beginning to end Steve draws you in as he offers incredible insight on how to change your world."

—Todd Ahrend
International Director
The Traveling Teams

"I pray that The Fuel and The Flame will be mightily used to start fires of renewal on hundreds, even thousands of campuses. It is an honor to be a colaborer with you in these momentous times of unparalleled spiritual harvest."

—Dr. Bill Bright
Founder
Campus Crusade for Christ

"Steve is one of the few who trains his staff to walk onto a college campus with a vision for the nations! If your heart beats for the college campus AND the nations, read this book! Join Steve and others who are pursuing God's glory through the campus to the nations."

—**Bob Sjogren**
President
UnveilinGlory Ministry
Author of *Missions Mobilizer* **and** *Cat and Dog Theology*

"Steve Shadrach is a passionate man who has impacted thousands through his multiplication ministry to students. The reach of his ministry and the fruitful evidence of the timeless principles in this book can be seen throughout the world. In *The Fuel and the Flame*, Steve releases a strong dose of this passion along with principles and practical helps for student ministry that have been proven over the test of time. Read and catch a vision for what God has done and will do through students reached with the gospel and empowered to change the world."

—**Doug Nuenke**
Director of Metro Ministries
The Navigators
Colorado Springs, Colorado

about the author

Steve Shadrach has a passion for raising up laborers for Christ from the university campuses of the world. Even though he grew up attending Fellowship of Christian Athletes and Highland Park Presbyterian Church in Dallas, Texas, he didn't commit his life to Christ until age eighteen. During his college years at the University of Arkansas, he worked with Campus Crusade and the Navigators and spent his summers as head counselor at Kanakuk Kamps. After graduating from Dallas Theological Seminary in 1983, Steve became pastor of students and missions at University Baptist Church in Fayetteville, Arkansas—with over 800 students involved. Having received training at the U.S. Center for World Missions in 1985, he began teaching *Perspectives* courses and leading Haystack Missions Conferences.

In 1986 Steve founded the campus ministry Student Mobilization, which focuses on evangelizing and discipling college students in the south central United States. After he and his family spent a year in Ukraine, helping to establish a campus ministry, Steve helped launch the *Day of Discovery* World Missions Seminars (now called *NVision*) and the nationwide missions mobilization effort called The Traveling Teams. He holds a Doctorate of Ministry in Church and Para Church Executive Leadership from Denver Seminary and has been published in numerous magazines and journals.

Steve and his wife, Carol, along with their five children, live in Arkansas, where he served for years as an elder in his local church. They have always lived next to a college campus and have ministered to and had students living with them. Steve is now the Director of Mobilization for the U.S. Center for World Mission, spearheading an effort to educate and energize one million believers in North America to give of their time, talent, and treasure to reach the unreached people groups of our world. He is also president of The BodyBuilders, a ministry committed to building up the body of Christ through the development of ministry tools, seminars, and publications. Steve and his team provide teaching, training, and consulting for churches, campus ministries, and Christian organizations around the world.

Related web sites:

Student Mobilization	stumo.org
The Traveling Teams	thetravelingteam.org
U.S. Center for World Mission	uscwm.org
Perspectives on the World Christian Movement	perspectives.org
The BodyBuilders ministry	thebodybuilders.net
The Fuel and the Flame	fuelandtheflame.com

# in appreciation

To my wife, Carol:
You are my cherished teammate in life and ministry.
Thanks for sticking with me! I love you.

To my children, Marietta, Spencer, Trey, Clark, and KK:
I love you with all my heart and believe God has great things in
store for each of you. It is a joy to be your dad.

To the ministry and staff of Student Mobilization and
The Traveling Teams:
You have laid your lives down for Jesus Christ,
and it has been a privilege to colabor with you.

To the ministry and staff of The BodyBuilders:
You have worked hard to make this project a reality.
You are a godly team of servants.

To Brian Klotz, John Patton, Kim Vollendorf, Amy Gerke,
Joy Ernst, Josh Johnson, and Darren Huckey:
You have labored behind the scenes to put this book
in people's hands. May God bless you richly!

To all the people and ministries who are listed in this book:
You have impacted my life and millions of others.
May your tribe increase!

contents

part 1: the fuel
five keys to your personal preparation

part 2: the flame
five keys to your ministry implementation

foreword

I spell Steve Shadrach with four words—*vision, passion, discipline,* and *risk.* Since hiring him (to work at Kanakuk) as a college student many years ago at the University of Arkansas, I've seen one of God's precious few true platoon leaders, in a vast army of believers, who has truly stepped out on faith to change the university climate . . . and a nation . . . and a world.

Author and speaker Dr. Ian Thomas said, "Faith is stepping out so far that God has to do a miracle to keep you from falling." Steve is a man of faith, and, like other truly great books, *The Fuel and the Flame* exudes just such vision, passion, discipline, and risk on every page.

This book will help pour the fuel of the Holy Spirit upon the flame of any willing believer's heart. Hopefully, God will use it to ignite a raging fire that will burn out of control so that our university campuses might be aflame for Christ forever.

Dr. Joe White
President, Kanakuk Kamps
Branson, Missouri

introduction

t his book is for the multitude of student leaders, staffers, and volunteers involved in the church and parachurch collegiate ministries around the world who want to ignite their campuses for Jesus Christ.

I want to be honest. This book is not for the faint of heart. We're not interested in just having a small and ineffectual ministry, content with merely finding our little niche for God. No, our heart beats to saturate the campus with the gospel of Jesus Christ and to raise up workers who will take His name to the ends of the earth.

Our family knows full well that many collegians come from broken homes, are hurting, and need healing. But, after having students living with us for twenty years now, we have come to a conclusion: one of the greatest things we can do for *any* student is to help give him or her an outward focus, instead of the inward one that most bring with them to college. When students take their eyes off themselves and their own problems and lift their gaze toward Jesus Christ and His purposes on earth, amazing things happen!

Many Christian bookstores are chock full of self-help books and romance novels to further our self absorption and the love affair we have with ourselves and our needs. I think you would agree that we're definitely a pampered, indulged generation. In this text we are seeking to motivate you in "forgetting what lies behind and reaching forward to what lies ahead" (Philippians 3:13). I want you to "press toward the goal for the prize of the upward call of God in Christ Jesus" (Philippians 3:14).

You may be a young Christian student, a brand new staff person, or an adjunct volunteer who's feeling very inadequate right now. Don't despair: you've got to start someplace! Zechariah 4:10 encourages us not to despise the day of small beginnings. We start out slow and spend the first half of this book talking about your personal preparation and the resources you have in Jesus Christ, showing how, if your life will provide the fuel, God will produce the flame. We *all* have such a long way to go, including me. I thought about including a list of all the mistakes I've made in campus ministry, but that would have taken another whole volume!

As you read and digest what is before you, there will be some things you disagree with or are uncomfortable with. As you read and wrestle through each section, pray and consider what's valuable for your life and ministry, and what's not. Also, if your ministry primarily measures your success by how many people come to your weekly large group meeting, you might be frustrated. We do have an appendix item on the whats, whys, and hows of large group meetings, but the heart and soul of this book deals with the Great Commission as contained in our four E's: Evangelism, Establishing, Equipping, and Exporting student laborers to the world.

You might be searching for some hip, new clichés or techniques to wow your college students. You probably won't find them here. I purposely used language that would not go out of style with this generation. We touch on a few forms (methods) here and there, but we chose to focus on principles that you can apply to *many* settings in *many* cultures for *many* years to come. Jim Peterson with the Navigators said, "Over time, forms outlive original functions. Forms then become an end of themselves and the functions can get lost." Where there's a will, there's a way; and if you desire to reach the campus in order to reach the world, you'll always be coming up with better forms to fulfill that function. More power to you!

My desire, though, is to serve all the campus ministries. I have relationships with staff in most of the major collegiate ministries around the country and have included numerous stories of how students' lives have been permanently marked by those groups. I personally have been impacted by Campus Crusade, the Navigators, Kanakuk Kamps, Campus Outreach, InterVarsity Christian Fellowship, Student Mobilization, and University Baptist Church in Fayetteville, Arkansas. Also, Southwestern, Dallas, and Denver

Theological Seminaries, the *Perspectives on the World Christian Movement* course, and the U.S. Center for World Missions have contributed to my life and vision. There are so many other ministries, churches, and individuals that I would like to list (and thank!) for helping to shape and to form me.

You see, I've never really had an original thought in all my life! *Everything* I've ever thought, known, written, or spoken about has been because God and others placed it in my mind. So many of the truths, principles, and even pithy sayings in this book belong to others. All I can take credit for is arranging all these unoriginal thoughts into something that will hopefully make sense. If you come across something and say, "Hey, I was the one who came up with that!" and I did not list you or your ministry as the source, please forgive me. Let me know, and I will include it in the next printing.

Finally, this book is designed for you to go through with other staff members, student leaders, or volunteers to discuss and to make applications at the end of each chapter. As you begin, stop and pray, asking God to help you put your hand to the plow, and make a lifetime commitment to know Christ and to make Him known. The most strategic avenue I've found to do that? The winning, building, and sending of college students for the glory of God and the evangelization of the world. May God be with you!

part 1
the fuel
five keys to your personal preparation

chapter 1

lay your foundation

eric grew up in a good, moral family that went to church most Sundays, said grace before dinner, and even sang in the Easter choir. Through most of his teenage years this level of religiosity seemed normal for any self-respecting person in a church-saturated small town in southern California. That is, until he became a Christian. It wasn't until the summer before his freshman year in college that someone told him he couldn't be good enough to get into heaven, and that Jesus came to begin a *personal* relationship with him. A light clicked on in his mind and heart, and he determined to serve God zealously with every waking moment.

Now on campus—and having already earned the reputation for being a fun but perpetually busy person—he threw himself into every imaginable spiritual activity. He dropped in on different campus ministry meetings each week, attended multiple Sunday school classes, joined the church choir, and even served on the soup line at the local homeless shelter. He was trying to fill his schedule with a whirlwind of religious activities, thinking that it was what God expected of him. He didn't let people get too close to him, and deep down he *knew* his Christian walk was a mile wide and only an inch deep.

Eric yearned to know his Lord in a more intimate way and to help his many friends experience the life-changing transformation that only Christ can give. Only one problem—he didn't know how! It was now his junior year in college, and time and opportunity were slipping away. Feeling desperate, he set up a lunch appointment with one of the campus ministry staff guys and poured out his heart. It felt like his soul was being cleansed as he confessed, "I feel like such a fake. Everybody *thinks* I'm such a great Christian, because I show up at everything ready to help and with my smile plastered on. I've been here for two and half years, and I've never asked anyone to disciple me, never led a single person to Christ, and I'm lucky to squeeze in one quiet time per week. I'm sorry to dump all this on you, but I'm serious about making some changes. Would you be open to helping me?"

Of course *any* ministry or church leader with even an ounce of vision, dreams and prays for students like Eric to ask them for spiritual help. In fact, there are hundreds of thousands of church and parachurch staff, student leaders, and volunteers around the world who are anxious to pour themselves into students who want to make a difference for Jesus Christ. And like Eric, they realize the college years are the *best* time in life to build the essential knowledge, skills, character, and vision to prepare effectively for another forty, fifty, or sixty years of walking with God and leaving a legacy of changed lives.

> **college** (*Webster's* definition) an independent institution of higher learning offering a course of general studies leading to a bachelor's degree

> **college** (my definition) a four (or more!) year window in a person's life when God has maximum opportunity to build a foundation into a life lived for Him

If life is defined as the preparation for an eternity lived with one's Maker, then college is the ideal time of prepping for *this* life. It's a small window in life where the Lord can reach down into your heart and turn it toward Himself. College is the ideal time because you're no longer under the protective wing of Mom or Dad, and you get a chance to figure out what *you* really believe. It's the perfect period for God to lay down some long-term tracks in your life, because you don't yet have to face the rush of responsibilities that follow after graduation. Dr. James Dobson, founder of Focus on the Family, says that a critical decade exists between the ages of sixteen and twenty-six where "most of the decisions that will shape the next fifty years will be made, including the choice of occupation, perhaps the decision to marry, and the establishing of values and principles by which life is governed. What makes this period even more significant is the impact of early mistakes and errors in judgment. They can undermine all that follows."

If a deep and solid foundation can be built during your college years, there is a much better chance that, later in life, you will withstand the pressures of the world, continue to walk with the Lord, and impact others. Let's look at two foundations that any Christian college student needs. First we will focus on building a personal and spiritual foundation for your life and ministry. Then we will take a look at some of our predecessors in order to learn from the life-changing lessons of students who have touched the world for Christ.

Your Own Personal Foundation

I grew up in Dallas but went to college in Fayetteville, Arkansas. Whenever I came home for a visit, I would cruise through downtown just to see the new buildings that were going up. One day I heard a lot of heavy earth-moving equipment. I got out to look but could not see anything due to the tall, wooden wall the construction workers had built around the site. The only thing I could be sure of was that they were digging a hole—a very deep hole.

Each time I came home that year, I looked in on the building project. My curiosity compelled me to search for a crack in the fence where I could stand on my tiptoes and peer through. For almost a year they did nothing but dig a deep foundation for that building. In fact, I think it took them longer to lay the foundation than to construct the entire ninety-story skyscraper!

In the midst of my fascination, I realized that the taller the building was, the deeper the foundation it needed. If *I* had been the contractor, having no knowledge of construction, I probably would have scratched my head, looked to see if the ground was level, turned to the work crew, and said, "Okay boys, let's get started on the first floor!" I might be proud of completing my edifice of steel and glass, but I'm sure the people working on the eighty-seventh floor would be quite surprised the first time a gust of wind came along and the whole building toppled over!

My construction philosophy might work for a one- or two-story structure, but certainly not for anything with real height to it. The question I pose to you today is, Do you want to be a giant skyscraper for Christ or a little one-story bungalow? It's *your* decision what kind of man or woman of God you become.

FUTURE
HEALTH
FINANCES
COMMUNITY ACTIVITIES
CHURCH AND MINISTRY
HOUSE THINGS
KIDS
SPOUSE
JOB
FOUNDATION

Do you want to have a deep and abiding lifelong walk with the Lord, where you are drawing many others to the Savior? Then begin at once on your personal excavation project! You will *never* again have as much time and opportunity to lay the groundwork required to become the beacon of light for Jesus Christ you desire to be. On the other hand, if you're unwilling to invest your time, talent, and treasure in the things of God, you will be trading these critical foundation-building years for lesser, more temporal pursuits. Write this down: The depth of the foundation you build in college will determine the strength and height of your building in the years to come.

This is your life! If you can build a deep, spiritual foundation before the major responsibilities of life are piled on, you will be more likely to stand firm, not just surviving, but thriving in the midst of the pressures. If a proper foundation is not laid, a hairline fracture can develop and cause a collapse. Available time and energies are reduced as the pyramid gets taller. College is the time to deepen the base.

Are you willing to pay the price now to become what you aspire to be five, ten, twenty-plus years in the future? If you want to be a towering force for Christ, you're going to have to spend years digging and laying the foundation. You may have to say no to a lot of fun and exciting things, maybe even some Christian activities that everyone is doing. Why? In order to focus on the foundation. Sit down right now, team up with God, and draw up a game plan that forever alters the course of your life. You'll be glad you did!

One Decision I Made in College

It seemed like it was just yesterday I was a freshman in love. Yes, I was a Christian as was she, but our emotions were more wrapped up in each other than in Jesus Christ. I kept getting a gnawing feeling that the Lord wanted us to break up with each other, but I wouldn't listen. I thought, "All my Christian friends have girlfriends, and certainly all my fraternity brothers do; why shouldn't I?" I carried this heavy load of rationalization around with me until the end of my fall semester. We finally got enough courage to bring up the subject, talk about it, and make a decision. We broke up because both of us felt it was God's will.

In Luke 6:47–49 Jesus tells us the wise man is the one who built his house upon the rock, and it was able to withstand the winds and the rain. The fool built it upon the sand, and it was destroyed by the wind and rain.

That night I went and hid out in an empty classroom and cried for three hours. I didn't feel sad or jilted—instead I felt like hundred-pound weights had been taken off my shoulders! I'm not very emotional, but that night I had a steady stream of joyous tears signaling I was finally free! I had fully obeyed and was now willing to do anything and everything God wanted me to do. This gave me the courage to make another important decision that night. I resolved that for the rest of my college years I would develop only friendships, not romances, with other Christian girls. Making a commitment not to date may sound radical and unrealistic for some, but for me, it was one of the best decisions I ever made. I'm not prescribing this step as God's will for you, but I am saying that you may have to make some fundamental changes in your priorities to make room in your life for what's really important.

Even though I'd been a Christian for over nine months, it was at this juncture that my spiritual life really accelerated. I had fully submitted my life to the Lordship of Jesus Christ, and I could now pursue Him with unhindered zeal. My love for Christ and my desire to spend time with Him took massive steps forward! I searched for gaps in my schedule where I could steal away for some intimate fellowship with the Lord and drink deeply from the Scriptures. Early each morning I found a dark, lonely place among the discarded furniture in the third-floor attic of my fraternity

the fuel and the flame ♦

house to get on my knees, worship God, and intercede for the souls of all the men in my chapter.

On Friday and Saturday nights while the other guys were out with their dates, I would lock my door and click off the overhead lights, turn on my little desk lamp, spread out my Bible and concordance, and spend huge chunks of time just soaking in the Word. It may sound weird or fanatical, but God and I were spending hour after hour, month after month, digging, digging, and digging a deep foundation in my life. I was finding a secret joy and fulfillment in my ever-increasing love relationship with the Lord and Savior of my life. Understanding that He was all I would ever need, I sought to find my satisfaction in Him—and in Him alone.

Late night prayer walks on campus became my routine. Many times I would cry out to God, "Whom have I in heaven but You, and besides You, I desire nothing on earth" (Psalm 73:25). Yearning to be abandoned to His purposes, I sensed that God was preparing me—that He wanted to use me mightily. My great-grandfather had studied on the same campus almost eighty years earlier, but I realized the Lord had placed me there for more than just academic purposes. He wanted me, a lowly college student, to impact the world for Jesus Christ.

"We're not saying the college campus is special in and of itself, just that our hearts are there. Our roots are there. Our calling is there. And our desire, like you, is to see God's name magnified in this collegiate generation."

**Louie Giglio,
Passion Ministries**

The Powerful Percent

We don't have to look far to see the incredible potential of college students. Even though only one percent of the world's population are collegians, they are a powerful one percent! This small sliver of humanity is, and will be, the leader of every facet of society. Every country sends their best and brightest to the university for education and training. Focusing our evangelistic and multiplication efforts on this one percent is a *very* strategic way to expand the kingdom of God and fulfill the Great Commission. Almost one-fourth of the world's college students reside in North America, and they represent the most reachable, recruitable, trainable, and sendable category of persons on the planet. It's true what Dr. Bill Bright of Campus Crusade says, "If we can win the university today, we will win the world tomorrow."

> *"There are about 3,300 colleges in the United States. There are about 25,000 around the world. Despite the efforts of so many groups, more than a third of the world's college campuses do not have any contact with full time Christian workers."*
>
> **Patricia Burgin, author of *The Powerful Percent***

There is a growing openness among college students worldwide toward the gospel. Being a current events buff, I'm always clipping newspaper articles about student protests and rallies in other nations. My observation is that students are more open than ever to the West, to new ideas and technology, and to philosophies and beliefs that are different from their ancestors'. Who and what will fill that gap? Will it be other world religions, cults, secularism, or the life-changing gospel of Jesus Christ? We're living in an amazing period of history, and as I travel to different countries, I see that students want to meet Westerners. They want to learn English and listen to the personal, political, and spiritual ideas we present. Never before has God opened the hearts of so many students worldwide to allow English speaking Christians from North America to have impact. This unprecedented opportunity for sharing the gospel with students globally also brings an undeniable obligation. We have been blessed. Why? To be a blessing to others!

Ecclesiastes 3:11 puts it like this: "He has made everything beautiful in its time. He has also set eternity in the hearts of men"(NIV).

Raw idealism, unrestrained aspirations, and the belief that God may just be big enough to pull off what He says He will are in the hearts of today's college students. Before they get out into the so-called real world and have their godly hopes and passions snuffed out, we need to prepare them to be God's kind of leaders.

Take a Look Back

Now it's time to take a look at our historical foundation. Students have always been strategic. The apostle Paul thought so. Check this out:

> And he entered the synagogue and continued speaking out boldly for three months, reasoning and persuading them about the kingdom of God. But when some were becoming hardened and disobedient, speaking evil of the Way before the multitude, he withdrew from them and took away the disciples, reasoning daily in the school of Tyrannus. And this took place for two years, so that all who lived in Asia heard the word of the Lord, both Jews and Greeks. (Acts 19:8–10)

Now, I'm not assuming that the listeners at this school were exclusively students. Paul picked this location not only for its availability but for its strategic location as well. He realized that to set up shop in one of the main learning centers of the great city of Ephesus was going to produce not only addition but multiplication. Many of these students he reasoned with caught the vision and worked with Paul to spread the gospel throughout Asia. The apostle's investment during those twenty-one months paid off—he mobilized these students to reach the entire known world!

Wherever missionaries went

"College students are idealistic, energetic, and active. They comprise one of the greatest reservoirs of manpower for the cause of Jesus Christ in the entire world."

**Dennis Gaylor,
national director
of Chi Alpha**

throughout the centuries, they sought to win the students in that locale. Many times when Christian groups started ministries in a certain country, they would set up hospitals and schools. In the 1500s, for example, it was the Society of the Jesuits who founded a chain of universities from Ireland to Japan as a means to reach the world. As for our own country, Rice Broocks, founder of Every Nation Campus Ministries, tells us that "106 out of our country's first 108 colleges were founded on the Christian faith. At the time of the Civil War, non-religious universities could be counted on one hand. College presidents were almost always clergymen up until about 1900." We've strayed just a bit since then, haven't we?

Eleven Students Who Changed the World

I love history, students, and missions, and I've done a lot of reading and research in these three areas. I've concluded that the last 250-plus years of Protestant missions from the West have been spearheaded and sustained primarily by college students. They have provided most of the impetus and manpower to fulfill the Great Commission from the eighteenth through the twenty-first century. Though not all were college students, this sampling of mostly college-aged revolutionaries from both sides of the Atlantic will stir your heart:

1. Ludwig Von Zinzendorf

The 1700s produced many students who were world-changers, and Count Ludwig Von Zinzendorf was head of the class. Born in Germany in 1700, he grew up and attended the University of Wittenburg to study law. At age nineteen he was looking at a painting of Christ in agony on the cross and an inscription that read, "All this I did for you, what are you going to do for Me?" From that moment on he knew he could not do anything but commit

"I know of only one passion . . . and it is He."

Count Ludwig Von Zinzendorf

the fuel and the flame ♦

himself to spreading the gospel throughout the world. He started a twenty-four hour prayer vigil focused on world intercession that continued unbroken for a hundred years! As a result his mission society, the Moravians, sent out more missionaries in the next twenty years than all the Protestants or Anglicans had sent out in the previous two hundred years! He had a passion to mobilize and send workers to the farthest places on earth.

2. John Wesley

Born in England in 1703, John Wesley was the son of a minister, but was not yet converted when he started at Oxford University in 1720. Religiously brilliant but still unsaved, he became the leader of a small, dedicated group called The Holy Club. Their spiritual disciplines and "methods" formed the basis for the Methodist denomination. Wesley came to the States in 1735 to be a missionary to the Indians in Georgia, but he made many mistakes and returned to England very discouraged. While on the voyage back, he met a Moravian missionary whose life and words impacted him. Not long after arriving back in England, Wesley gained assurance of his salvation and began preaching the gospel message everywhere— sometimes 10,000 to 30,000 people would wait patiently for hours to hear him. During his lifetime of itinerant ministry, he traveled 250,000 miles, preached 40,000 sermons, and gave away over 90 percent of his income.

3. William Carey

The legacy of Zinzendorf and Wesley created whirlwinds of global impact for the Savior that did not end at their death. In fact, the person who is hailed as "The Father of the Modern Missionary Movement" was greatly influenced by their examples. William Carey was a self-educated, college-aged young man when he caught a vision for the world. He would stand at his shoe cobbler table as he worked, and pray over a crude copper-plated world map he had crafted and hung on the wall. When he repeatedly tried to convince a group of ministers to take the Great Commission seriously, they scolded him by saying, "Young man, sit down. When God chooses to win the heathen, He will do it without your help or ours!"

In response, he wrote a small book that analyzed the need for world evangelization, and he convinced a few of his friends to form a tiny missions agency that sent him to India in 1793. Carey and his book ignited a bonfire of evangelistic activity that led many mission agencies to form over the next twenty-five years. Carey himself spent his entire life in India preaching the gospel, planting churches, and translating the Scriptures into forty different languages and dialects.

"Expect great things from God. Attempt great things for God."

William Carey

4. Samuel Mills and the "Haystack Five"

While Carey's bravado was making waves in England, his little book had made its way across the Atlantic and into the hands of five students at Williams College in Massachusetts. On a rainy August afternoon in 1806, Samuel Mills, an awkward freshman with a squeaky voice, and four other college students gathered to pray. In all there were three freshmen and two sophomores. They had been reading Carey's book and wanted to spend some time interceding for the world. As the rain subsided and after they finished prayer, Mills turned to his friends and exhorted them, "We can do this if we will!" These five young collegians not only initiated the first nationwide student movement, they began the first six mission agencies in North America. Although at the time there were just twenty-five colleges in America (averaging about hundred students each), the "Haystack Five" helped launch small world-mission study and prayer clusters called "Society of the Brethren" on a number of them. These five students supplied the fuel, and God made sure the flame grew bright.

5. Hudson Taylor

God was passing the baton from student to student, placing in them a vision and passion for reaching the world. This leg of the race was to be spearheaded by a sickly medical student in England by the name of Hudson Taylor. Even though he battled depression, he committed himself to go to a coastal city in China as a missionary. After some time there, he yearned to go into the interior where the bulk of the masses lived and died without ever hearing about the Savior. His radical ways of asking *only* God for financial help and living with and dressing like the Chinese caused the other missionaries to ostracize him. Amid much opposition he broke away in 1865, formed the China Inland Mission (CIM), and started to recruit students from England and other countries to help him reach the Chinese.

> *"If I had 1,000 lives I would give them all to China."*
>
> **Hudson Taylor**

Taylor had a divine wind behind him, and he asked God for great things, believing he could move men to give and to go by prayer alone. Before the missionaries were kicked out by the communists in 1949, CIM had sent almost 6,000 missionaries into China's interior. Taylor, "The Father of Faith Missions," was the first of the approximately 70 percent of today's full-time Christian workers in the world who, by faith, live on monthly support rather than a guaranteed salary.

6. Lottie Moon

Born and raised in a wealthy Virginia family before the Civil War, Lottie Moon was a well-educated and cultured woman that measured all of four feet three inches. Rebelling against her mother's deep-seated Baptist faith, Lottie ran off to college where she ended up mocking Christians. Eventually she returned to her roots, admitting, "I went to a campus revival to scoff and returned to my room to pray all night." Sailing for China as a single twenty-three-year-old female missionary was unusual but par for the course for this diminutive, yet bold pioneer. She passed up a marriage proposal from a prominent seminary professor, which was difficult, but she justified it by proclaiming, "God had first claim on my life, and since the two conflicted, there could be no question about the result!" At first her ministry was confined to teaching at a girls' school, but she finally struck out on her own to do evangelistic work in north China. Despite tremendous opposition, nationals did come to Christ, a church was established, and thousands were baptized over the years.

Lottie is most known for her vigorous recruiting of volunteers and money for missions. She mobilized thousands of women in the States to pray, volunteer, and enlist others to give to foreign missions work. Severe drought broke out after China's Boxer Rebellion in 1911, and Lottie gave away *all* her money and food to help the starving. Other missionaries tried to rescue Lottie in time to save her life, loading her frail and famished body onto a ship headed for America, but she died on board late one December night in 1912—Christmas Eve. How appropriate that the Southern Baptist world-missions funding effort, which has raised hundreds of millions of dollars over the years, is named for Lottie Moon and takes place at the same time each year—Christmas.

7. C.T. Studd and the "Cambridge Seven"

In the early 1880s, God used a group of young college students in England, called the "Cambridge Seven," to ignite the most effective mobilization effort of all time: the Student Volunteer Movement (SVM). These seven young aristocrats—two of them famous athletes and two military officers—helped catapult the little-known China Inland Mission Agency from obscurity into what one newspaper called an "almost embarrassing prominence," inspiring hundreds of recruits for the CIM and other mission societies. After a year-long tour of the British Isles speaking to packed-out audiences, the "sporting hearties" (what another newspaper had dubbed them) set sail for China in February of

1885. Their written story about giving up fame and fortune for a missionary call, *The Evangelization of the World*, was distributed to every YMCA and YWCA throughout the British Empire and United States.

The impact was amazing, and by the time the Seven arrived in China, CIM had already signed up 163 missionaries. The number doubled by 1890 and reached 800 by the year 1900; these numbers represented one-third of the entire Protestant missionary force. The willingness of these popular, athletic, and wealthy young men to forsake all the comforts of England to spend their lives in China's back country was a story the press could not pass up. It was also a story God could not pass up, as He used it to spread a wildfire of interest and decisions across the universities of the Western world.

> *"I'd rather run a rescue shop within a foot of hell than live within the sound of a chapel bell. If Jesus Christ be God and died for me, nothing I sacrifice is too great for Him."*
>
> **C. T. Studd**

8. Luther Wishard

In America in the late nineteenth century, there was a recent college graduate named Luther Wishard who was appointed to be a representative for the England-based YMCA and to travel around to different U.S. colleges chartering these Christian growth clubs. In 1878, after hearing the story of the "Haystack Prayer Meeting" at Williams College seventy years earlier, this unlikely revolutionary realized that world missions was the missing ingredient in his life and message, so he

> *"The movement spread from Princeton College to two hundred other colleges, from America to Ceylon. It will continue to spread until the students at the colleges in the Orient and the Dark Continent are united with the students of America in one world-wide movement of Christ for the students of the world and the students of the world for Christ."*
>
> **Luther Wishard**

journeyed to Williams to do business with God. Kneeling in the snow next to a campus monument in memory of Samuel Mills and the "Haystack Five," he poured out his heart before the Lord, praying, "I am willing to go anywhere at any time to do anything for Jesus. Where water once flowed, let it flow again."

That day he made an unreserved surrender to carry on the legacy handed down from Mills' group. His newfound purpose stated: "Let the students in these closing years of the century consummate what our fellow students in the earlier part of the century attempted. . . .What they began is ours to complete. They had willed, but our wills must now be brought into the plan to consummate their daring purpose." He yearned to go overseas but was willing to stay to mobilize his generation of students to reach the world for Jesus Christ.

9. Robert Wilder and the "Mount Hermon 100"

In 1886, just months after the "Cambridge Seven" sailed to China, Luther Wishard contacted the same man who had led the Seven to Christ during one of his crusades in England—D.L. Moody. Wishard invited him to come that summer to speak for a month at the Mount Hermon Conference Center in Massachusetts to a group of 251 college men from eighty-nine U.S. universities. God used Moody, Wishard, and a Princeton senior, Robert Wilder, to ignite the crowd; and a hundred students gave themselves to a life of cross-cultural missions. Although the conference was supposedly just four weeks of Bible study, Wilder had brought with him a declaration that read: "We are willing and desirous, God permitting, to become foreign missionaries."

"We are willing and desirous, God permitting, to become foreign missionaries."

Declaration the "Mount Hermon 100" signed

By the end of the month a hundred men had signed the statement, and these "Mount Hermon 100" became the SVM's foundation upon which 100,000 students would be recruited to reach the world over the next forty years (20,000 actually went overseas, and 80,000 stayed behind to support and to form the Laymen's Missionary Movement). Some of the 100 became traveling mobilizers (Wilder was the first SVM traveling mobilizer), and others, zealous missionaries. These firebrands chose to add a phrase to the title of the book the "Cambridge Seven" had written a year earlier. Emblazoned in their hearts was the expanded motto: "The evangelization of the world . . . *in this generation!*"

10. Grace Wilder

Grace Wilder, Robert's older sister, was born in 1863, the daughter of an American missionary to India who was a recruit of Samuel Mills of "Haystack" fame. After thirty years in India, due to her father's ill health, Grace's family returned home to the Princeton area in 1876 where, a few years later, Grace enrolled at Mount Holyoke College. While there, Grace started a weekly Bible study for girls, where she challenged them to sign a declaration stating: "We hold ourselves willing and desirous to do the Lord's work wherever He may call us, even if it be in a foreign land." Thirty-four girls signed it. At the same time, her brother Robert started a weekly meeting in their home for Princeton men. Although Grace could not attend, she would hide in the next room and intercede for each of them.

Months before the Mount Hermon conference, Grace recruited Robert to begin praying that a nation-wide missionary movement would spring out of the July 1886 conference. They wrote a declaration and their prayer was that 100 men would sign it. Once the conference ended, Grace immediately went to work as the unofficial SVM women's rep to recruit girls to the movement. She asked, "Can we not enlist every one of the 600 schools where young women are educated, so that united we may undertake our work, that of carrying the gospel into every nation?" At age twenty-six, she sailed for India with her widowed mother to continue the missionary work her father began. She died in 1911 at age fifty, having given her life to mobilizing college students and evangelizing the unreached.

11. Cameron Townsend

In 1917 Cameron Townsend, also a student volunteer, spent a few months in Guatemala passing out Spanish Bibles to mountain villagers. One day he came upon an unreached jungle tribe and handed a Bible to a native, but then he realized the man didn't speak Spanish. Through a translator, the native abruptly asked Townsend, "If your God is so smart, why doesn't He speak *my* language?" The young missionary was pierced to the heart and decided to drop out of college and spend the next ten years translating the Scriptures into this tribe's language. "Uncle Cam," as he would later be called, ended up starting the most respected linguistic organization in the world, the Wycliffe Bible Translators. They have brought the Scriptures to life in thousands of languages and for millions of people around the globe.

Many students were impacted by the SVM during these years—students like Samuel Zwemer, who became the "Father of the Modern Missions Movement to Muslims," and Donald McGavarn, a missionary to India who came back to begin the Fuller School of World Missions and help the Church understand who the "unreached people groups" are. In fact, one out of every thirty-seven U.S. students during that era signed SVM's missions declaration, and if you applied that same ratio to the number of college students we have in the United States today, we would see almost 400,000 young people signing up to be missionaries!

Modern Day Heroes

The last seventy years have seen un-precedented growth in the reaching of college students for Jesus Christ. People like Bill Bright with Campus Crusade, Dawson Trotman with the Navigators, Stacey Woods with InterVarsity, along with groups like Campus Outreach, Every Nation Campus Ministries, Coalition for Christian

> *"College students today are waiting to be challenged and led in the greatest revolution in history—the fulfillment of the Great Commission."*
>
> **Dr. Bill Bright**

Outreach, Great Commission Ministries, Student Mobilization, and the International Fellowship of Evangelical Students have started world-changing movements that touch millions of students for Christ. Outstanding denominational ministries like Chi Alpha, Baptist Collegiate Ministries, Wesleyan Centers, the Christian Church Campus Ministries, and Reformed University Fellowships have sprung up with strong vision and commitment to the Word of God, discipleship, and world evangelization.

Numerous local churches across the country have caught the vision for reaching students and have committed staff and program resources to capturing universities for Christ. Grace Bible Church in College Station, Texas, University Baptist Church in Fayetteville, Arkansas, and Seattle, Washington's First Presbyterian Church are all seeking to transform college campuses into seedbeds of spiritual awakening. There is a whole crop of organizations raised up to challenge and mobilize this generation of students

> *"Every spiritual awakening has been spread by university students."*
>
> **Dr. J. Edwin Orr, author**

into action: Louie Giglio's Passion Ministry, Greg Fritz's Caleb Project, Jeremy Story's Campus Renewal Ministries, Todd Ahrend's mission mobilization Traveling Teams, along with the Fellowship of Christian Athletes, International Students, Inc., and a host of others.

What Did These Student Firebrands for Christ Have in Common?

1. They were young and idealistic. They believed God could and would work mightily even though, at the time, they were viewed as arrogant, rebellious, and foolish.

2. *They had strong vision.* They knew exactly what God wanted them to accomplish and applied their faith. They were convinced of their calling.

3. *They usually had vocal opposition.* Their detractors were, many times, other believers or Christian institutions who were either stuck in tradition, jealous, or afraid to launch out.

4. *They enlisted others.* They didn't try to go it alone but were zealous in recruiting other young men and women to join them in their vision. Their dedication attracted many.

5. *They persevered over the long haul.* They never gave up even though they lost their spouses, children, health, and fortunes. They dedicated their entire lives for the sake of the gospel.

And, finally, the most important golden thread that ties together the other common characteristics is this: *They each had a deep foundation in their walk with God.*

Their journals were full of daily Bible study applications and heart felt intercessions as they sought the Lord through mountains and valleys. They spent years preparing their hearts, minds, and life message by saturating themselves with the Word of God. Many, like Jim Elliot and David Brainerd, would spend hours a day in worship and specific supplication for nations, workers, and spiritual fruit. Each paid a price to build a deep, lasting foundation. As a result, God had a strong base from which to build them into giant skyscrapers for Jesus Christ. The impact and legacy of their lives is carried on today.

What about you? Have you decided whether or not you want to follow in the footsteps of these world-changers? There's a tremendous cost, and yes, some of these pioneers lost their lives for the gospel. But today Jesus is asking you to do something much tougher than dying for Him. He is asking you to *live* for Him, and to

> *"What would happen if God arose and He enlisted and empowered this generation of students? What could God do in the years to come through this spiritually powerful percent?"*
>
> **Patricia Burgin**

make an unreserved commitment of all that you are to Christ and His purposes on earth. The place to begin is your foundation. Jesus spent three decades allowing the Father to prepare Him for three short years of ministry. If the Son of God needed that much time to build a foundation from which to launch His life's work, how much more do we mortal men and women need?

If you're still in college, I beg you to use this time to build a deep and abiding foundation that will serve you for a lifetime. It's not that you can't continue to build on this foundation after college; you can, and you must! But you will *never* have as much time and opportunity as you do right now. After graduation entanglements will come and seek to thwart your building process. *Now* is the time to focus. *Now* is the time to get as much spiritual training as possible. Before going on to the next chapter, stop and do some personal evaluation. Examine your roots. Look at your foundation and determine how much work it needs. ✦

Discussion and Application Questions

1. What can we learn from Eric's story?

2. What does it mean to have a "strong personal foundation?"

3. Read Luke 6:47–49. Based on this passage and your personal opinion, why is it important to lay a strong personal foundation?

4. Is there anything that is keeping you from laying this kind of foundation in your life?

5. Why do you think college students are so strategic?

6. Which student "world-changer" impressed you the most? Why?

7. Why do you think the Student Volunteer Movement had such great impact?

8. What do you believe will be required to see a second Student Volunteer Movement begin?

9. Are you able to pray the prayer that Luther Wishard did in 1879: "Lord, I am willing to go anywhere at any time to do anything for Jesus"? Why or why not?

10. What do you think Wishard meant by the second part of his prayer: "Lord, where water once flowed, let it flow again"?

11. During college, what kind of impact would you like to have for Jesus Christ? How about after college?

12. To have that kind of impact, what kind of personal foundation will it require?

13. List some things you can begin to do this year, this month, and this week to build a strong personal foundation that will last you a lifetime. Spend some time on your list, and get as specific as you can.

Read your applications and pray together that God would build a deep, strong, personal foundation to last throughout your lifetime.

chapter 2

develop your character

nna, a Christian student at Boston College, had been dating Chad happily for almost six months when the bomb hit. She found out he was secretly seeing Christy, one of her sorority sisters, who had been e-mailing him notes and pictures of herself. It hurt Anna badly to see her relationship with Chad vanish while he and Christy became inseparable, seeing each other almost every night. In her quiet time one morning, Anna came across Ephesians 4:31, "Get rid of all bitterness, rage and anger," followed by verse 32, "Be kind and compassionate to one another, forgiving each other, just as in Christ God forgave you" (NIV). At that moment she knew *exactly* what the Lord was telling her to do: release the anger and bitterness she held toward Chad and Christy.

As the tears flowed Anna felt the shackles fall off and the cleansing of Christ's forgiveness wash over her. With a new freedom and perspective, she set out to show kindness and compassion, especially to Christy, who she was pretty sure was not a Christian. A few weeks later, a devastated Christy came to Anna's room after Chad had dropped her and moved on. Christy was different though, asking for forgiveness and seeking solutions for her shattered life. Late that night, because of the unconditional love she felt from Anna, Christy bowed her head and invited Christ to come into her heart as Savior and Lord. They became best friends, growing together spiritually by leaps and bounds. These two girls experienced the supernatural love and forgiveness of Jesus Christ in the face of a cruel and undeserved betrayal, and their lives would *never* be the same. Yielding her will to God's, Anna allowed the character of Christ to flow through her and, in turn, draw Christy to the Savior.

Don't Get Spiritual Amnesia!

After Anna gave Jesus Christ His rightful place on the throne of her heart, she began to get her marching orders from His Word, tapping into the power of the Holy Spirit. She was then ready for. . . change! Yes, God promised us we would change *if* we are truly born again: "If anyone is in Christ, he is a new creation; the old has gone, the new has come" (2 Corinthians 5:17, NIV). About 400 A.D. the brilliant, but worldly, Augustine became a Christian, and he happened to pass his former mistress on the street one day. She turned to him, seeking to lure him back into her web of adultery, and purred: "Augustine . . . it is I." Without even stopping he shot back, "Yes—but it is not I!"

> *"Character is the key to world evangelization. Every worker has high purpose, but the weakest point is always character."*
>
> **Sherwood Eddy, author and missionary statesman**

When we turn from our sin and embrace the Sin-bearer, we become a Christian or "Christ one." We are now each a walking, talking mirror, continually reflecting more and more of the character of Jesus to those around us. One list of the qualities we are to exhibit is found in Galatians 5:22–23: "The fruit of the Spirit is love, joy, peace, patience, kindness, goodness, faithfulness, gentleness and self-control" (NIV). As you build your foundation in life, these are the kinds of materials you want to make up your character and personality. Not only will others be drawn to you because they see these fruits in you, but these traits are the very Christlike qualities you are to pass onto others. When a person squeezes an orange, orange juice comes out. When grapes are crushed, grape juice pours forth. How about when a Christian is squeezed or crushed? What comes out? Christ and the fruits of the Spirit, or our own carnal and worldly reactions?

> *Let no one look down on your youthfulness, but rather in speech, conduct, love, faith and purity, show yourself an example of those who believe.*
>
> **1 Timothy 4:12**

Most students are infected with a deadly strain of what I call the "Acquired Integrity Deficiency Syndrome." You may be struggling right now, feeling like you just don't measure up because you see so many areas of your life where you fall short. If you'll commit to view yourself like God views you, it will produce in you a healthy confidence and self-esteem. Most of us look at ourselves as sinners. Yet the Bible calls us *saints, holy ones,* or *righteous ones* 240 times, while at the same time it refers to unbelievers as *sinners* over 330 times. When we joined God's family we were completely forgiven of our sins, and we stand holy and blameless in God's sight because the Father only sees the righteous blood of Jesus when He looks at us. We are truly saints (who occasionally sin!) in His eyes, rather than sinners. Believe it, and if you ever forget your position in Christ, go to the appendix and meditate on the passages listed in The Cure for Spiritual Amnesia.

Four Qualities Every Christian Laborer Must Possess

As I study the New Testament, I see these four character qualities highlighted:

Quality #1: Love

We're going to talk a lot about the Great Commission in this book, but what's even *more* important is the Great Commandment. Jesus commanded us to "Love the Lord your God with all your heart, and with all your soul, and with all your mind" and then to "Love your neighbor as yourself" (Matthew 22:36–39, NIV). He told us that if we can keep these two commands, everything else will take care of itself. Love for God and love for others is not a feeling, it's a decision we make—each and every day. When you are on your death bed, you will be asking only two questions:

> Who did I love?
> Who loved me?

You won't be thinking about your GPA, MBA, IRA, or BMW. You will be overwhelmed by the depth (or lack of depth!) of relationships you formed during your brief stay on this planet. Paul affirmed this concept by saying, "But now abide faith, hope, love, abide these three; but the greatest of these is love" (1 Corinthians 13:13). You can possess all gifts of the Spirit, all Bible knowledge, all acts of service, but if you don't have love, "you have nothing," as Paul says at the beginning of 1 Corinthians 13—the love chapter. And according to my math, *nothing* is a very small number!

> *"A life that is wrapped up in itself makes a very small package."*
>
> **Dr. Howard Hendricks, author and seminary professor**

Question: Why are some students so unlovable? Answer: Probably because no one has ever *truly* loved them! When others attach worth to us, we, in turn, tend to attach more worth to ourselves. Everyone is searching for personal happiness, but it's found not in possessions, accomplishments, or pleasures, but as a byproduct of healthy relationships with those closest to us. Frank Minirth and Paul Meier, both authors and psychologists, give us an insightful definition of depression: "Lack of intimacy with God and/or others." They claim you could empty half the hospital beds in America if you dismissed or cured all the people suffering from depression.

Mother Teresa was often asked what she felt was the major problem in the world. Her answer? Loneliness. The students around you are secretly desperate for someone to love them unconditionally and to believe in them. They may not have received this affirmation from their moms or dads or youth leaders, and many will spend the rest of their years searching for that individual who will put his or her stamp of approval on their lives. College students are used to "fair weather friends"— relationships that come and go on a whim. One guy even bragged to a friend recently, "Oh, I still have a lot friends I haven't used yet!" Like Jesus, lay your life down for others and put others' needs ahead of your own. I used to think the number of memory verses and converts you had was the highest measure of Christian maturity and Christ-likeness. Now I believe the highest measure is a four-letter word: L-O-V-E.

Quality #2: Holiness

Picture this: You just made some of your favorite iced tea, you reach into the kitchen cabinet to get one of your beautiful, blue crystal goblets, and, all of a sudden, a big roach jumps out of the glass at you! What would you do? Pour in the tea and swig away? Not a chance! Any sane person would look around the cabinet and see what else is available—even if it's just a jar of peanut butter that you'd recently emptied and washed. The important thing is that it's *clean*!

> *"God doesn't want you to 'Christianize' your life, but to crucify your dreams, desires, ambitions . . . and to seek His."*
>
> **Todd Ahrend, international director, The Traveling Team**

In the same way, God is looking for clean vessels that He can work through. "In a large house there are articles not only of gold and silver, but also of wood and clay; some are for noble purposes and some for ignoble. If a man cleanses himself from the latter, he will be an instrument for noble purposes, made holy, useful to the Master and prepared to do any good work" (2 Timothy 2: 20–21, NIV). The Lord is not impressed by what we say, do, or look like on the outside. He puts a stethoscope on our heart, not trying to identify our ability but our availability. Bottom line: stay clean and God will use you, regardless of who you are.

Not to be confused for a suggestion, the Lord commands us to "Be holy, because I am holy" (1 Peter 1:16, NIV). We are to present ourselves as a living and *holy* sacrifice unto the Lord. That is simply our reasonable act of worship according to Paul in Romans 12:1. If there was ever a time in our nation's history (and in the lives of millions of college students around the world) for us as Christian workers to model holiness, now is that time! We are being bombarded daily with thousands of unholy messages from Satan, the world, and our own flesh, seeking to drag us off and devour us. We are only as spiritual as we choose to be; and unless we're regularly feasting our minds on the holiness of God through the Word and worship, we will not be victors in this Christian race.

Dr. A. W. Tozer was a twentieth-century pastor and author in Chicago who, as a young student, would go each morning to the lake and lay face down in the sand from four to six A.M. simply "thinking about God." If I were laying face down *anywhere* at those hours, I have a feeling it would include some very loud snoring! Tozer believed that the most significant thoughts anyone could ever think would be about who God is. His deep meditations on the nature of God prompted Him to write the classic *Knowledge of the Holy*—a small book with short chapters on twenty-two different attributes of God that Tozer picked out. As you go through it, you'll read a paragraph and get on your knees to worship this absolutely holy God who fashioned us. You'll then read another paragraph and fall on your face, broken over your own sin and lack of holiness. Needless to say, it takes a while to get through! Get it, read it, absorb it into your life, and give God permission to penetrate every fiber of your being with His holiness—a quality every Christian worker must possess.

Quality #3: Servanthood

Kanakuk Kamp in Branson, Missouri, has become one of the largest camps in the world, and I had the privilege of being their head counselor for the two summers following my graduation from college. Even though I had previously been a counselor there and knew all the ropes, coming back to lead their staff of strong varsity athletes from campuses around the country was quite intimidating. This small, pudgy, fair-skinned twenty-three year old (whose claim to fame was second place in intramural ping pong) was now called upon to be the visionary leader for huge linebackers, wrestlers, and tri-athletes. Instead of trying to "fake it 'til I make it," I chose a different route, modeled by the leaders of the Kamp, father and son Spike and Joe White.

> *A servant:*
> *"Someone who gets excited about making other people successful."*
>
> **Bill Gothard,**
> **author**

They called it servant leadership, where the organizational chart was turned upside down and the objective was to love and serve the people who report to them—instead of the other way around. I learned that the only way I could *ever* lead (i.e. influence) these superstar counselors was to lovingly pray for and serve them. Getting up at 5:20 every morning to intercede for the men prepared me to spend the day encouraging them, loving them, and looking for personal and spiritual needs to meet. At first I sensed some resistance toward me, but by midsummer the mutual respect, unity, and presence of the Lord was stronger than I'd ever felt. Because I chose to pray and serve versus acting like the big shot, their hearts melted toward my leadership.

A Leader Is a Servant

In a much greater way, Jesus came to earth not "to be served, but to serve" (Mark 10:45, NIV). If the Son of God humbled Himself to put others' needs ahead of His own, how much more should we?

He illustrated in living color that the path to greatness is not up, but down. I believe if Jesus were asked to give a one-word definition of a leader, He would simply say *servant*. Embracing the attitude of a humble servant will protect you against pride when God starts to ignite your campus for Christ. Jesus addressed this issue in Luke 17:10 (italics added), "So you too, when you do all the things which are commanded you, say, 'We are unworthy slaves; we have done *only* that which we *ought* to have done.'" Humble obedience. Nothing more. Nothing less.

> *"We make a living by what we get, but we make a life by what we give."*
>
> **Winston Churchill**

What if you made the decision now to spend your life serving others rather than being served? What if you began to define success by how well the people around you are doing rather than how you are doing? The question remains, Who would look out for number one if you were spending all your time trying to help number two, number three, and number four reach their goals?

As I write tonight, I look out my window and see one of the students who has lived with us the past two years and who models servanthood wherever he goes. Brian, a recent college graduate now participating in the Leadership Training Center in our home, is raking all the leaves in our backyard—without anyone asking or requiring him to! When Brian first moved in, his quiet and reserved personality got lost in the crowd of extroverts; but it didn't take long before all of us realized there was a servant among us, constantly putting others needs ahead of his own. Whether it's cleaning up after dinner, helping one of my kids with homework, or washing someone's clothes, Brian is the first to volunteer and the last to leave when there's a job to complete. Because everyone respects him so much, Brian now wields considerable influence (without even trying) with students, staff, and even my family. He's proof that the last shall be first and a true leader is simply a servant.

Quality #4: Faithfulness

We live in a day of short, "I want it now," attention spans. It's the age of the "flitters and the quitters," when we can't comprehend that the Christian life and ministry is actually a marathon, not a hundred-yard dash. But Jesus was looking for men who would stick with Him over the long haul. Paul also put a premium on faithfulness when he exhorted his young disciple, Timothy, to entrust himself only to "faithful men who will be able to teach others also" (2 Timothy 2:2). Actions speak louder than words according to Proverbs 20:6, "Many a man proclaims his own loyalty, But who can find a trustworthy man?"

You can test yourself to see what your FQ (Faithfulness Quotient) to God and others is:

A. Are you faithful in the small things?
   Jesus tells us we reap what we sow in Luke 16:10, "He who is faithful in a very little thing is faithful also in much." You want God or others to give you big responsibilities? Start with the ones you've got and complete them *all* with integrity and excellence.

B. Are you faithful in the tough times?
   King David challenges us to follow through on our commitments in Psalm 15:4 when he describes a godly man as someone who "swears to his own hurt and does not change." Keeping your word even when it costs you will prove just how reliable and credible you really are.

If you hope to develop *any* faithfulness in the students you wish to impact, you must be a pacesetter in this crucial area. Develop the conviction that you will *always* follow through in your commitment to the Lord and others. Final note: It's critical that you make the ministry team and leader whom you report to a *greater* priority than the team of men or women you lead and disciple. Why, you ask? Like a chain reaction that produces strong levels of leadership or weak ones, you will reap what you sow. The degree of faithfulness that your young disciples see you exhibit toward your leader is the same they will exhibit toward you. We cannot ask others to do something *we* are unable or unwilling to do.

Four Pitfalls Every Christian Laborer
Must Guard Against

On the flip side to the four qualities every Christian laborer must possess, here are four pitfalls that many have fallen into:

Pitfall #1: Fear

Not long ago, each of the living winners of the congressional medal of honor (the medal that says *VALOR* on it) was asked to give his or her definition of courage. You would think that this group would say courage is the *absence* of fear. To the contrary, the most common response was, "No, it isn't the absence of fear—it's *doing* what you're afraid to do." We all appear confident, but without realizing it, we live our lives dictated by our fears. Even though there are 300 "fear nots" in the Bible, we still sometimes choose that which is safe and comfortable and avoid those things that are difficult or intimidating to us.

> *"All of us have layers of fear around the 'real us'. They are defense mechanisms."*
>
> **Larry Crabb, author**

Prior to his execution, Paul left young, timid Timothy in big, bad Ephesus to develop the fledgling church there. Timothy was struggling and close to allowing the enemies from within and without to dominate him when Paul's letter arrived. In these tear-stained pages, the final letter Paul would ever write, he gave his frightened colaborer a jab: "For God has not given us a spirit of fear, but of power and of love and of a sound mind" (2 Timothy 1:7, NKJV). In verse 8, though, he delivers the knock-out punch, getting right in the face of his long-time disciple, ordering him not to be ashamed of:

A. The Lord—"Do not be ashamed of the testimony of our Lord"
B. Paul—"Nor of me, His prisoner"
C. The gospel—"Share with me in the sufferings for the gospel according to the power of God"

If God has given us His power, love, and discipline, what are we doing relying on our own resources, or even worse, pathetically backing down from a little worldly opposition? The real issue is not how to escape our fears, but how to handle them.

These 2 Timothy verses became real to me when I started to hang out with Vic, the main individual who discipled me in college. He was a senior ROTC student who doubled as a resident assistant in a men's dorm, but from all appearances his primary goal in life was to show *me* how ashamed I was of the gospel! One night as I was coming over to his dorm for our weekly small group, Vic hopped on the elevator right as the door closed. Instead of greeting me though, he leaned up against the side of the crowded elevator and, acting like he didn't know me, said, "Hey, buddy. What's that in your hand?" Of course, everyone had their eyes glued to the lit floor numbers above, pretending they weren't listening to *every single word* exchanged between Vic and me. I paused to catch my breath and sheepishly responded in a low voice, "It's a Bible, Vic." "A Bible!" Vic shouted, "That's not that stuff that talks about Jesus Christ being the *Son of God*, is it?!" After turning eighteen shades of red, I finally lowered my head and whispered, "Yeah, Vic. That's what it says." The elevator door finally opened as Vic was finishing me off with a riveting, "You don't really believe that stuff, do you?"

Even though at the time I wanted to vanish from the face of the earth, I was later very grateful to Vic, who exposed my unwillingness to *totally* identify with:

A. Jesus Christ (who is to be the only One I'm seeking to please)

B. Vic (who was like the apostle Paul on our campus)
C. The gospel (which is contained in the Bible I was carrying)

Like a modern-day Dr. Jekyl and Mr. Hyde, I wanted to be cool and accepted by my fraternity brothers and appear spiritually radical to the other Christians on campus. I can remember the exact day and place I was walking in front of the library when I made the *once and for all* decision that I would be one person, not two! I'd been playing both sides of the fence and was determined not to allow others' opinions to control me any longer. God will light the flame of revival on your campus, but you'll need to provide the fuel. You need not read any further, though, if you're going to allow fear to paralyze you. Decide now to walk *toward* your fears, forsaking your "esteemed reputation" in favor of suffering for the gospel. Why? Because your heart burns with a passion to see *every student* on your campus come to faith in Jesus Christ. But don't fool yourself. It will cost you big time.

Pitfall #2: Sexual Immorality

Matt Kaufman, a writer for Focus on the Family's college webzine, *Boundless*, speaks plainly about how sexually immoral choices have impacted students' lives: "College students know all too well the pain of rampant divorce and families with no fathers. They know the pain of sexually transmitted diseases, and worse, of hearts ripped apart by sexual encounters devoid of true commitment. They know the pain that follows abortions—the sense of a loss so deep and soul-felt they can't begin to describe it. Whether they've felt the pain themselves or they've seen it in friends who've cried on their shoulders, they've learned the hard way that sex isn't all it's cracked up to be. Moreover, they

> *"No soldier in active service entangles himself in the affairs of everyday life, so that he may please the one who enlisted him as a soldier."*
>
> **2 Timothy 2:4**

the fuel and the flame ♦

sense that life simply *must* have more meaning than they've been told—that the cynicism and self-service they see around them simply *can't* be all there is."

Billy Graham believes sexual sins leave the biggest scars in people's lives. Proverbs 6:32 supports his thesis: "The one who commits adultery with a woman is lacking sense; He who would destroy himself does it." We can be forgiven of this and any sin, but for some reason it's almost impossible to forget these "sins of the flesh" because they seem to be seared in our minds for many years to come. Whether it's premarital sex or the cheap substitutes we find in a lot of TV, movies, and romance novels, they rob of us of our innocence, purity, self-esteem, and, worst of all, fellowship with the Lord.

It's especially hard for guys to bring "every thought captive to the obedience of Christ," because we are *so* stimulated by what we see. Most collegians have computers, and almost 100 percent of the dorms have Internet access piped right into the students' rooms. In one survey, 95 percent of professed Christian college students agreed that looking at internet pornography is sinful, can hurt relationships, and can be addictive. Still 41 percent of the women and 68 percent of the men admitted, *intentionally* viewing sexually explicit sites. Check your PQ (Purity Quotient) as you evaluate yourself in light of these three principles for victory:

A. Guard your eyes and heart
   Job made a pledge to himself in Job 31:1 when he stated, "I have made a covenant with my eyes; Why then should I look upon a young woman" (NKJV).
B. Watch what you touch
   Paul exhorts us to exercise incredible self control in 1 Corinthians 7:1, "It is good for a man not to touch a woman."
C. Be engaged in ongoing evangelism
   John remembered the key to the apostle's victory over Satan in Revelation 12:11, "And they overcame him

because of the blood of the Lamb and because of the word of their testimony, and they did not love their life, even when faced with death."

The great Episcopalian minister Samuel Shoemaker believed that if a Christian leader was not involved in personal witnessing, it was just a matter of time until he or she fell into sexual sin. There were times late at night when Shoemaker was studying in the church office that sexual temptations would invade his mind. When that happened, he would lay down his books, put on his coat, go down to the street, and witness to the very first person he came across. He said that the devil would go running! It's true that if we're not engaged in the spiritual battle, our energies often end up channeled toward personally destructive thoughts and behavior.

Pitfall #3: Pride

As a cocky young freshman, I was walking along one cold day with the senior who was discipling me. Impressed by how many students I was influencing, I subtly boasted, "I'm really struggling with pride." He stopped, looked at me, and said, "What do *you* have to be proud about?" Having my arrogance totally exposed, I stuttered and stammered, "I guess nothing." Some people say pride is the opposite of humility, but I believe being humble is *not* thinking less of yourself, it's not thinking of yourself at all! Focusing on giving God glory, rather than trying to steal it for ourselves, is the key according to Isaiah 42:8, "I am the LORD, that is my name! I will not give my glory to another" (NIV).

> *Pride:*
> *"Man is the only animal that when you pat him on the head, his head swells up."*
>
> **Dr. Chuck Swindoll, author and pastor**

South American missionary C. I. Scofield taught that most Christian leaders go through these three stages:

A. Obscurity—This is the phase where he is a nobody. He is simply taking baby steps as a believer, trudging along trying to figure out how to live the Christian life. He may give up in this stage because no one has really affirmed him for all the spiritual efforts he has expended.

B. Popularity—In this stage the believer has moved from being a nobody to a somebody, and others recognize her as a person with wisdom and biblical knowledge. People praise her for her zeal and reward her by coming, asking questions to her, and sitting at her feet. Feeling like "Mrs. Big," she may bomb out here if she swells up with pride.

C. Suffering—If a Christian makes it through the second stage, he may not endure the third. Unlike Job, when trials and affliction come along, he may blame God or others. His vision and joy may be drained and his personal growth and ministry may shrivel up. If this happens he will make his pact with the world and quietly slip away to a life of quiet hopelessness.

Many aspire, but few attain; and we would do well to implore God to maintain the right mix of encouragement and testing in our lives to keep us dependent on Him. The Lord can't use us if we are seeking to accomplish great things for ourselves. When I first started college, I observed that several upperclassmen in our ministry had started "action groups"—weekly Bible studies where the leader was discipling each member. I, too, wanted to have my own "action group." I enthusiastically recruited four fraternity brothers to join my little flock, but it disintegrated within a matter of weeks.

Those guys could see right through me and discerned that this group's purpose was really to make *me* look good in the eyes of others. I was forced to come face to face with 1 Peter 5:5, which says, "God

> *"God never uses anyone greatly until He tests them deeply."*
>
> **Dr. A. W. Tozer,
> author and pastor**

opposes the proud but gives grace to the humble" (NIV). There have been times in my life when I've sensed the God who I was *supposedly* serving was actually thwarting my well-laid plans in order to humble me. Now that's sobering!

Pride—We Are Always the Last to Know!

The marks of pride are usually evident to everyone—except ourselves! It raises its ugly head in the forms of defensiveness, prayerlessness, comparison, and unteachability. We need to ask ourselves this question: Can I follow well? Most Christians are part of the "Loners for Christ" club and are against leadership unless, of course, they can be the leader! You might say, "Oh, I really don't need any spiritual leadership over me. I'm being discipled by God." Really? The reason Jesus was the greatest leader of all time was because He was the greatest follower of all time and "only did the things He saw and heard from the Father." If the Son of God felt the need to humble Himself to spiritual authority, how much more should we?

You'll never become a great leader until you learn how to be a great follower. If you don't have someone discipling you, it's probably because you don't want anyone discipling you! If that's true of you, why don't you stop right now, turn to the Lord, and let Him search your heart for any

> *"A coach is someone that makes you do what you don't want to do, so you can be what you want to be."*
>
> **Tom Landry, former coach of the Dallas Cowboys**

pride or independence. Pray about which individual you could ask to encourage, to disciple, and, yes, even to rebuke you when necessary. Become a humble, teachable disciple and someday God will honor you with young disciples who will seek you out in the same way. Rarely have I met anyone who was discipling others who hadn't themselves *first* been discipled.

Pitfall #4: Bitterness

Landlords in college towns are notorious for taking advantage of student tenants. I experienced this firsthand after graduation when I moved out of a duplex near the campus where I was ministering. Even though my roommates and I left the place in much better shape than we found it, the owner presented us with a list of damages and their estimated costs. What a coincidence that the total just happened to equal what our deposit had been! After I picked my jaw up off the ground, I politely but firmly protested and provided proof that the penalties were unjustified. As the weeks went by, she ignored my phone calls and letters, and my frustration grew into a deep-seated bitterness. I had been wronged, and my resentment was starting to permeate every hour of my day, every conversation I had, and every relationship in my world.

It was obvious to the man discipling me that an all-pervasive anger was controlling me. He showed me Hebrews 12:15, where in plain terms we are commanded, "See to it that no one comes short of the grace of God; that no root of bitterness springing up causes trouble, and by it many be defiled." Instead of turning over my initial frustration to the Lord, I had allowed it to grow deep roots into my soul, which were choking the lifeblood out of my once-vibrant faith. Not only was I unable to extend any grace to my offender (much less anyone else), but I was also poisoning all of my healthy friendships by making people listen to my one-man smear campaign. This landlord's petty offense had grown to gargantuan proportions, and I was truly guilty of "defiling many," as the writer of Hebrews warns us against.

How I Got Rid of My Bitterness

My discipler suggested that the only way to rid myself of the bitterness was to apply the "extra mile" principle in Matthew 5:39–41 and go to the landlord, apologize, and then offer to give her *more* money on top of what she had already stolen. Although shocked, I knew he was right, and I set about to do surgery on the vast root system that had engulfed me. I drove over to her neighborhood, but had to circle the block *ten* times before I had the courage to knock on the door. When she answered I was shaking so badly that I barely got the apology out of my mouth and the twenty-dollar bill out of my pocket! Even though she scoffed at both, I had accomplished something that, for me, was monumental. In the face of overwhelming injustice, I had absorbed the pain she had inflicted and was able to offer her grace in return. In that moment, the Lord ripped the roots of bitterness from my heart and replaced them with the profound emotion that I was experiencing—"the fellowship of sharing in his sufferings" that Paul describes in Philippians 3:10 (NIV). I was free at last!

I think Christians give up on their ministry (or at least are rendered ineffective) because of this sin more than any other. It may not be a confiscated security deposit that rattles your cage, but it could be that some ministry leader doesn't follow through on their discipleship commitment, and you take it personally. We have to understand that many students don't see the importance of keeping their word, keeping their appointments, or keeping their mouths shut when they said they would! When you get bitter over another person's unfaithfulness, betrayal, or slander, the person it most destroys is staring you in the mirror each morning. Take a long look, and determine to extend the same grace to others that the Lord lavishly poured out upon you. ✦

Discussion and Application Questions

1. What can we learn from Anna and Christy's story?

2. What is character?

3. Why is developing character important?

4. What is "spiritual amnesia"? What is the cure?

5. Which of the four qualities every Christian laborer must possess is your strongest? Why?

6. Which of the four qualities is your weakest? Why?

7. List a specific application or two that you could work on this week and month to build up this area.

8. Read 2 Timothy 2:2 together. With so many other important qualities, why do you think Paul told Timothy to look for "faithful" or "reliable" men to disciple?

9. Have you ever fallen into one of the four pitfalls Christian laborers must guard against? Tell us about it.

10. Which pitfall do you think you are most susceptible to? Why?

11. If this is your most susceptible pitfall, what are some specific steps you can take this semester to safeguard against it?

Read your applications and pray together that God would develop deep character in each of you, now and throughout your life.

chapter 3

build your convictions

althrough Katherine came from a fairly moral and religious home, she had secretly decided to become a sorority party girl when she hit college. Sure enough, she was able to accomplish that goal and much more, as she spent her weekends in drunken stupors and in the beds of accommodating upperclassmen. By Christmas, though, life had become empty and boring, and she began searching for more. Soon after, one of her friends invited her to a worship and share time a local church was sponsoring on campus. She had never seen people so real, so vulnerable, and so accepting. That night she bowed her head to ask the Lord to come in and save her, a sinner.

The change was immediate and everyone saw it. Her vast network of friendships now presented opportunities for bold witness. Some turned her off, but many responded to her testimony of a transformed life. Different Christian groups on campus recruited her to give her testimony at their meetings, and the church asked her to be one of the soloists in the choir. Katherine was on a spiritual high when a group of her sorority sisters asked her, a freshman and new Christian, to lead a house Bible study for them. However, trouble was on the horizon for this girl who sprang up quickly but had no real roots to draw from. In place of laying a deep personal foundation, she instead became very prideful about the newfound celebrity status she received from the Christians on campus.

A turning point took place one Monday morning in late April. After a glorious time of Bible study and praise the evening before, she woke up and felt nothing—no joy, no sense of God's presence, no desire to pray or witness. Absolutely nothing. Had she lost her salvation? Had God left her? Was she really a Christian, or was this all an act? Thoughts of doubt and betrayal flooded her mind. She didn't have a spiritual leader she could go to and she was embarrassed to admit this to her girlfriends, so she decided to go it alone. One day of no fellowship with the Lord turned into two, three, a week and then two weeks.

Belief:
Something you'll argue for.

Conviction:
Something you'll die for.

Three weeks later she snuck out to a party of one of her old boyfriends, looking to find some kind of high to replace the one she had lost that Monday morning. Not only did her testimony fall apart in the ensuing weeks, but her life began to unravel as well. By July she had married one of her old bedmates, moved into a trailer home, denied any Christian commitment she once had, and decided not to return to college. A tragic story of a girl who had incredible potential but whose spiritual life was a mile wide and an inch deep. She knew the right thing to do and had all the right answers, but she lacked any lasting convictions.

Honesty Is Always the Best Policy!

Talk is cheap. I can fool you, and you can fool me. I can tell you that I believe Bible study and prayer are important. I can say, "Amen, brother," when you speak of personal holiness and servanthood. However, the proof of my Christian maturity is whether my beliefs have trickled down from my mind and mouth and into my spiritual bloodstream to become a reality in my life. One definition of character is *what we do when no one else is around.* The same is true of convictions. What we are in private is . . . what we are! God has a twenty-four hours a day, seven days a week video camera that not only sees our actions but our motives too. "And there is no creature hidden from His sight, but all things are open and laid bare to the eyes of Him with whom we have to do" (Hebrews 4:13).

> *"In my opinion, eight out of ten Christian leaders do not walk with God."*
>
> **Dr. Howard Hendricks**

Let's not do a repeat of Adam and Eve, thinking we can hide from God so He won't know what we have done. Let's be honest and admit that we are in desperate need of His grace, His mercy, and His power. The Christian life He has called us to live is not difficult, it's impossible! Apart from a moment by moment empowering by the Holy Spirit, we will live defeated, frustrated lives with little or no fruit. The concept of total dependence on God needs to be stuck in your frontal lobe as you begin to build this foundation that needs to last you clear into eternity.

When designing a building, as in life, you'll not only need a detailed plan but also a checklist of quality resources. First, though, search your heart to determine what rocks and roots need to be ripped out before you sink deep the steel girders and building blocks. Paul referred to himself as a wise master builder and exhorted the Corinthians to use the right materials in their spiritual foundation. He wrote in 1 Corinthians 3:11–13: "For no man can lay a foundation other than the one which is laid, which is Jesus Christ. Now if any man builds on the foundation with gold, silver, precious stones, wood, hay, straw, each man's work will become evident; for the day will show it because it is to be revealed with fire, and the fire itself will test the quality of each man's work."

Paul is telling us that the foundation is Christ Himself. We must be careful how we build upon that base, using precious and enduring materials, rather than worthless ones that will quickly perish. Ultimately, we will come before God and be rewarded according to the quality (it doesn't say quantity) of our building. God's aim in this passage is to show us the difference between what is eternal and what is temporal. The building blocks in our foundation must be values and convictions that are from God's quarry, not man's.

What Are You Exchanging Your Life For?

What are your convictions? The main way to find out is to look at what you're exchanging your life for right now. Are those things eternal or temporal? For example, whatever you exchange your time and money for is what you value. Let me take a look at your checkbook or your schedule, and I'll tell you exactly what's important to you. You might say, "I don't have a schedule." No, everyone has a schedule. It may not be a good one, but everybody has one!

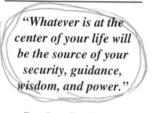

"Whatever is at the center of your life will be the source of your security, guidance, wisdom, and power."

Stephen R. Covey, author

Not long ago, my family and I spent almost a year in the Ukraine, helping develop our campus ministry there and learning more about what is involved in reaching students in other cultures. In each city we visited there were currency exchange booths everywhere—little metal huts with a tiny window and a person peering out. Outside on a sign would be that day's exchange rate for the U.S. dollar, Russian ruble, and sometimes German deutsche mark. With only a handful of Americans in that country, I wondered why there were thousands of these exchange huts—I soon learned why. The Ukrainian people would work day and night, slaving at jobs you can't

Mother Teresa died at age eighty-seven with no money, belongings, family, or net worth on earth. What did she exchange her life for? A big account in heaven!

the fuel and the flame ♦

imagine. Old women would stand out in sub-zero degree weather from 7 A.M. to 10 P.M., selling small cups of beans or seeds for almost nothing. I saw one man who would stand all day long holding two hangers of women's underwear, hoping for a buyer. There were beggars everywhere.

These desperate people were exchanging their time, their health, their very lives to earn a few *grevna* (Ukrainian currency) a day. They would work and save for weeks, sometimes months, before they could rush down to the currency exchange booth and trade in their giant stack of ever-inflating grevna for a single, crisp piece of paper with Ben Franklin's likeness on it—a U.S. $100 bill, their symbol of stability. It was "all about the Benjamins," as they would raise it to the sun, making sure it wasn't a counterfeit, then race home to stash it under the bed for safekeeping. They dared not put it in a bank or entrust it to one of the varied "investment opportunity" schemes. Their total security was based on how many of those $100 bills they had hidden away.

All of us are exchanging our lives for something, aren't we? We exchange our lives for what we *believe* is valuable. Jesus understood this principle very well when He said, "For whoever wishes to save his life will lose it; but whoever loses his life for My sake will find it. For what will it profit a man if he gains the whole world and forfeits his soul?" (Matthew 16:25–26). Life is like a card game. We only have one hand, and we've got to push all our chips to the middle of the table and lay our cards down, believing we have a winner. If we are pinning those hopes on anything but the eternal person and work of Jesus Christ, we will forfeit our lives—yes, our very souls.

What's in Your Treasure Chest?

Jesus said the answer to this dilemma is found in what we put in our treasure chest. Whatever we count as valuable we will treasure. We will hide, protect, and nourish it, just like those Ukrainians with their stash of $100 bills. Here are the instructions from our Heavenly Banker: "Do not lay up for yourselves treasures on earth, where moth and rust destroy and where thieves break in and steal; but lay up for yourselves treasures in heaven, where neither moth nor rust destroys and where

thieves do not break in and steal. For where your treasure is, there your heart will be also" (Matthew 6:19–21, NKJV).

I'd like to challenge you to pray about what you treasure and write them down, those things or beliefs that you are going to hide in your heart—your treasure chest. For whatever you esteem, whatever you exchange your time and money for, whatever you truly treasure, your heart will naturally follow. The implementation of those values is what I call convictions. I would like to recommend seven convictions for your consideration as possible foundational building blocks for your life and ministry. I believe these are seven essentials that you need to give yourself to with absolute dedication. If you will plummet to the depths of these seven convictions, you will be laying up some fantastic treasures in heaven. You will be trading your life for that which is priceless and everlasting. These are the crown jewels of the Christian life and ministry. To ignite your life and campus for Jesus Christ, you must passionately embrace them.

Seven Building Blocks for Your Life and Ministry

Building Block #1: Devotion to Jesus Christ

I'm not asking you here about your devotional life (although I will later!). Our devotional *life* is simply an outgrowth of our devotion *to* Jesus Christ. One definition of devotion is "an unswerving adherence to something." Do you have an unswerving adherence to the person of Jesus Christ? Is He the Lord of every area of your life? Campus Crusade's *The Four Spiritual Laws* booklet is an excellent tool, because it asks people to choose which of two circles

"If Jesus is not Lord of all . . . He is not Lord at all!"

Dr. A. W. Tozer

represents their life. One has "self" on the throne of the person's life, and the other has "Christ" on the throne. There can only be one person on the throne. One King. One Master. All the other areas of life are subservient to *who* is occupying that throne.

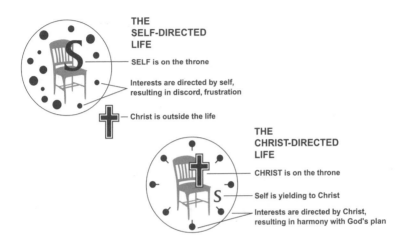

THE
SELF-DIRECTED
LIFE

SELF is on the throne

Interests are directed by self,
resulting in discord, frustration

Christ is outside the life

THE
CHRIST-DIRECTED
LIFE

CHRIST is on the throne

Self is yielding to Christ

Interests are directed by Christ,
resulting in harmony with God's plan

Christian business executive Bob Buford, in his excellent book *Half Time,* describes a crossroads in his life, when he hired a high-powered consultant to help get his stressful life, business empire, and ministry interests figured out. As they closed the door and sat down at a conference table, the consultant drew a box on a pad of paper and asked one question, "Bob, what's in the box?" Buford was confused, and so the consultant explained: "There can only be one thing in the box; one priority that is the most important one in your life; the obsession that controls and dominates everything else; the preeminent thing around which everything else will flow from. What is it, Bob? What's in the box?"

If you do not choose one thing to be at the center, the inertia of life will choose it for you.

Buford had to take a day or two to wrestle with this. Should he put business, money, family, or ministry in the box? He knew this was a decisive moment in his life. After much prayer and thought, he knew he could put only one thing in the box, and all his relationships and pursuits would revolve around it—for the rest of his life. He came back the next day and took the pad from this non-Christian consultant and wrote two words: Jesus Christ. From that point on, everything was different in his life. He now ran every decision through this grid: How does this opportunity or activity exalt and enhance the person and work of Jesus Christ?

When I was a freshman in college, I slept on the top bunk in my fraternity room. On the ceiling I taped one verse that I would look at each morning and night. It was Luke 6:46, where Jesus cried out, "Why do you call me 'Lord, Lord' and do not do what I say?" (NIV). A translation might be, "Don't insult me with your phony flattery. Don't say you're a sold out follower unless you're going to obey me in *all* things!" Meditating on that verse kept my mind on Christ and His purposes as I daily did battle with the enemy of my soul. Each day I stepped out of that room, there were fifty guys watching and waiting for me to trip and fall. I could either fully obey my Lord Jesus, or fade right into the woodwork of mediocrity and compromise.

> *"There is only one road. The road is a journey into the depths of God."*
>
> **Dr. Rodney Wood, pastor and conference speaker**

John Piper, an author and pastor in Minneapolis, shares this concept of the Christian life when he says, "God is most glorified in us when we are most satisfied in Him." What is it that satisfies you? If you could spend time with anyone or do anything, who or what would it be? Make the anchor of your life extended daily time fellowshiping, worshiping, and interceding with the Lord Jesus. Your love for Him will grow as you exchange parts of your day to commune with the living God. Value Him above all others and all else. This has to be the bedrock conviction that guides your life. It's the *only* thing that is in your box. It only takes a spark to get the fire going, and this is where the spark originates.

Building Block #2: Saturation with the Word of God

Marcus was an angry, black teenager who escaped the violence of inner-city Canton, Ohio, to attend the University of Akron. He immersed himself in the college party life, and after one night of heavy drinking, a friend turned to Marcus and said, "You need to read the Bible." Although Marcus hadn't given any credence to the Scriptures, he began to read passages each night before doing homework. He found that his eyes were opened to the truth. He dug deeper and started studying the Word, sitting for

> *The Bible was given to us not to increase our knowledge but to change our life.*

hours "reading, believing, doubting, crying, smiling, and all the while being convicted of sin." The repentance was so thorough that he yearned to expose others to the truth God had revealed to him, so he began small group Bible studies through the ministry of Coalition for Christian Outreach. Today, as a staff member for CCO, Marcus continues to saturate himself with the Word and to help hundreds of students do the same.

You, too, have a decision to make regarding this book. Do you believe the Bible is from God? Is He powerful and sovereign enough to give us a book that is without error and that accurately gives us the mind of Christ? To doubt the authority of the Scriptures is to doubt God Himself. Settle in your heart today that the Lord has given us an infallible book that is to be read, studied, taught, and applied to all areas of our lives. We talk to God through prayer, and the Word is His means of talking to us. There are groups that will try to add, subtract, or change the Scriptures. They may even be a part of a "higher criticism" group that evaluates whether sections are genuine or not. The fact is, they are claiming that the Bible is inspired in spots, and they're inspired to pick out the spots! It is the height of arrogance.

You get to know what God is like through what He reveals to us about Himself in the Bible. You have no substantive message to give to students apart from the Scriptures. Collegians are hungry for truth—genuine, authentic truth. Go to almost any campus in America and do a little research project: find the student ministries that have a strong view of the Scriptures and the ones with a weak view. Almost without exception, the groups that believe the Bible is the complete and authoritative Word of God will have many more students involved than the ones with a lesser view. You can't fool most students. They know the real thing when they see it. Life begets life. Vision begets vision. Hope begets hope. Only God's Word gives us life, vision, and hope!

The Navigators have the "Hand Illustration," which shows the importance of utilizing these five methods to get a grip on God's Word in your life. The four fingers represent hearing the Bible taught, reading it, studying it, and memorizing it. Lastly, meditating on (or continually thinking about) the Scriptures is the thumb. Ask God to build these disciplines into your life and to give you a friend who can work with you daily to saturate your mind and heart with the Scriptures. As you fill your life with the Word, it will start to work its way into your values, your habits, and, yes, your convictions! You will start to "bring every thought captive to the obedience to Christ."

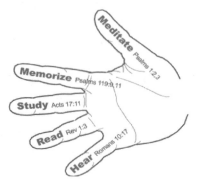

Consistency in these basics will give you victory over sin. One person put it well: "Either the Bible will keep you from sin, or sin will keep you from the Bible." Absorb God's book into your life and you will be a different person. This unconditional commitment to the Word will serve as the unbending standard of truth in your personal life and ministry. If you are going to ignite others on your campus for Christ, it must be your daily instruction and training manual!

Building Block #3: Empowered by the Holy Spirit

Everybody wants power. Nations, corporations, politicians, military officers, athletes, celebrities, and even some Christian leaders desperately seek authority and influence. Many students fall into this trap too by working hard to impress and dominate others through joining social clubs, fighting for top grades, having the best-looking date, or showing off their bodies. For some reason we think that popularity or wealth or strength or position will give us the power we thirst for. But Psalm 62:11 reveals to us where real power resides: "Once God has spoken; Twice I have heard this: That power belongs to God." If we want authentic supernatural energy, we had better plug into the power source—God Himself through the person of the Holy Spirit.

> "The world has yet to see what God can do with a man that is fully consecrated to Him. With God's help I aim to be that man."
>
> D. L. Moody, nineteenth century evangelist

God the Spirit is alive and real with a purpose on earth defined by God the Son in John 16:14, "He will bring glory to me by taking from what is mine and making it known to You" (NIV). The Holy Spirit's job is not to turn the spotlight on Himself, but onto Jesus Christ, so that all mankind can honor and glorify Him. He illuminates the person and work of Christ so that saints and sinners around the world can see Jesus for who He really is: Savior and

King. When we receive Jesus Christ into our life, the Holy Spirit comes and takes up permanent residence in us; and our task then simply becomes to *allow* Him to control and empower us for godly living and service. We can attempt to be a follower of Christ in our own power, but it will result in a crushed and pointless existence with nothing to show for all our labors. As for me, when I come to the end of my rope, I humble myself, surrender, and pray, "Lord, I can't—but then you *never* said I could. Lord, you can—but then you *always* said You would!" That prayer, from Major Ian Thomas, founder of the Torchbearers ministry, helps me to quickly put Christ back on the throne of my heart.

To this day I still utilize Bill Bright's simple but profound concept of spiritual breathing when I sin. In order to keep short accounts with God, I try to immediately identify the anger or lust or jealousy that I've allowed to enter my mind and heart, then specifically confess it to God. Like our physical breathing, this is exhaling the bad air followed by inhaling a big dose of the fresh, clean air. I do this by thanking Him for forgiving and cleansing me with the purifying blood Jesus shed on the cross for my sins. Then I pray, "Now fill me with Your Spirit. Control me. Help me abide in Christ. Work in me and through me today that I can walk in faith and obedience." I may or may not feel forgiven or filled, but that is beside the point. Jesus promised that "If we confess our sins, he is faithful and just and will forgive us our sins and purify us from all unrighteousness" (1 John 1:9, NIV). Below is Campus Crusade's diagram called the "Fact, Faith, Feeling Train," which sheds some light on the necessity of believing what God has to say about us, rather than believing our feelings.

The engine is supposed to pull this train, not the caboose. Each day we have a decision to make as to whether we are going to pour our faith into God and His Word or into how we might happen to feel that day. The train can run with or without the caboose, but when we are faithful to depend wholly on the Lord, God will sometimes bring along feelings of peace, joy, and love.

FACT   FAITH   FEELING

| God and His Word | Our trust in God and His Word | The result of our faith and obedience |

Building Block #4: Bonding with Other Committed Believers

I was incredibly blessed to have both a great local church *and* campus ministry to participate in while in college. I didn't try to choose between the two, but instead sought to plug in and serve in both arenas. The church and parachurch ministry can have a beautiful partnership if they choose not to compete but complement one another. My philosophy is that every Christian student ought to have a contribution strategy when the saints are gathered and a conquering strategy when the saints are scattered.

    A. Saints gathered

"And let us consider how to stimulate one another to love and good deeds, not forsaking our own assembling together, as is the habit of some, but encouraging one another; and all the more as you see the day drawing near." This is what Hebrews 10:24–25 teaches, commanding us to come together regularly to edify one another in our Christian lives. When a good local church creates an environment where the Scriptures are taught as the Word of God, there's godly leadership, genuine worship, and a caring congregation. When you find a church like that, plug into it, find

> *Young people are searching for a cause to give purpose to their lives. They need to be re-introduced to the church and introduced to Christ.*

a place of service, and bring other students along with you. Find ways to contribute your time, talent, and treasures to that body of believers.

Every Sunday morning in Fayetteville, Arkansas, we would see how many of University Baptist Church's front rows we could pack with eager, hungry college students. Week after week, Pastor H. D. McCarty filled our minds and hearts with the wonder of knowing and following Jesus Christ. He's easily one of the five men who have most influenced my life, but I'm sure there are thousands of others who could say the same. Not only was he solidifying *my* walk with Christ and evangelistic zeal each service, he was also reinforcing all the convictions I was trying to instill in the men I was discipling.

I came and brought guys to the church retreats, prayer meetings, and early morning men's breakfasts. I helped with Sunday school and the youth ministry. When guys needed baptizing, I brought them to the pastor. Even though I was also involved in a parachurch campus ministry, I could clearly see how absolutely essential it was to honor, serve, build up, and give to my local church. Besides, once students get through college and move on, usually the only *real* options for spiritual nurturing in most communities are local churches. College is the time to learn how to pick a good church and become a strength to its leaders and members.

B. Saints scattered

Once you have a church home that you can make a significant *contribution* to, you have a decision to make about how to implement your *conquering* strategy. Although I was on staff with a church that focused on reaching students, most churches don't have an aggressive "on-campus" presence and, instead, usually support the many excellent parachurch collegiate ministries in the area. Whether it is to your church and/or campus ministry, find a group of believers who have a strong plan for witnessing and discipling students and who truly seek to plant the flag of Jesus Christ at the center of your school.

Don't try to conquer the campus on your own—even the Lone Ranger had Tonto! King Solomon shared his concept of teamwork in Ecclesiastes 4:9–10: "Two are better than one because they have a good return for their labor. For if either of them falls, the one will lift up his companion. But woe to the one who falls when there is not another to lift him up." Just as Jesus sent His disciples out two by two, you need to team up with a partner who shares your heart to reach out to other students with the love of Christ. Choose a strategic place on campus to live where you can have maximum contact with the students you want to minister to. Have a blast as you and your friend band together to see God first light the fire *in* you, and then spread it *through* you!

Building Block #5: Evangelizing the World

The "E" word is a scary one for a lot of people—Christians and non-Christians alike. We'd much rather use a softer, less threatening word like *share*. I have nothing against terms like this, unless we are using them to relieve us of our responsibility to win people to Christ. *Webster's* definition of *evangelize* is "to preach the gospel to; to convert to Christianity." Is it wrong to have as your goal to win someone to Christ? I have had people accuse me before, saying, "You don't really care about that guy, you're inviting him over for dinner and basketball *just* so you can lead him to Christ!" My answer? "Exactly!" And for the charge of not caring, I beg to differ. If love is meeting other people's needs and the essential need everyone has is to establish a personal relationship with their Maker and Savior, then the greatest act of love I could *ever* show anyone is to give them an opportunity to start that relationship.

The great need is not for more believers who will "say a word about Jesus" or to simply "let your life do the talking." You and I would not be part of God's family today unless Jesus, Paul, and others had chosen to boldly *speak* the gospel along with living it out. The Lord is trying to implant a sense of urgency into us in John 4:35, which says, "Do you not say, 'There are yet four months, and then comes the harvest'? Behold, I say to you, lift up your eyes and look on the fields, that they are white for harvest." Jesus is not only saying that many, many people are ready *right now* to convert, but He also may be taking a subtle swipe at some people's brand of "friendship evangelism," where there's a whole lot of friendship, but not much evangelism!

I've been guilty of allowing fear to dominate me into procrastinating sharing the gospel with someone I have befriended. I have either said to myself that the timing is not quite right or that I needed to win their trust a little more. The problem with that thinking? Three, six, twelve months later it gets harder and harder to break the news that for months now we have chatted about every imaginable part and interest in our lives—except the most important one! We would never think about not telling a friend about our family, our education, work, hobbies, or concerns, and yet we purposely leave out the most important person in our lives, yes, the most important person in the universe!

We need not waste our time on any of this discussion concerning reaching a lost world if, in fact, they're not really lost. There's only one word more politically incorrect than the "E" word, and that's the "H" word. Yes, to say that there is a literal place called hell and that non-believers are going to spend eternity there could be your ticket to a mandatory "sensitivity training session" at your campus! Many professors seem to have a personal agenda to stamp out such archaic concepts as absolute truth. One day, as one of my teachers was ranting and raving that there was no such thing as absolutes, I got into trouble after I slipped my hand up and asked, "Are you *absolutely* sure about that?"

> *"And there is salvation in no one else; for there is no other name under heaven that has been given among men by which we must be saved."*
>
> **Acts 4:12**

Some of our more "caring" and "enlightened" profs present the so-very-seductive line of reasoning that there are many roads up the mountain and all who are sincere will make it to the top. Like eating birthday cake with poison in it, that bit of heresy is a little hard to digest, especially knowing that twenty-three people died in the last ten seconds and an estimated nineteen of those into a *Christless* eternity. Friend, if there was ever a time to decide if Jesus was shooting straight with us about heaven and hell, now is that time. Unless you have an unequivocal conviction that *Jesus* is the way, the truth, and the life, and that *no one* comes to the Father except through Him, you need not read any further.

Building Block #6: Multiplying Your Life

The first command the Lord gave mankind is listed in Genesis 1:28: "Be fruitful and multiply, and fill the earth, and subdue it." Lest you think God was simply talking about physical reproduction and not spiritual, I refer you to Jesus' expansion of the concept in John 15:16, "You did not choose Me but I chose you, and appointed you that you would go and bear fruit, and that your fruit would remain."

Jesus chose us for a reason: all Christians everywhere are to bear fruit that *remains*. Most of us, though, judge the fruitfulness of ministries by the quantity produced, not the quality. What impresses us is, How many were at the meeting? How many decisions were made? How big is the sanctuary? What is the ministry budget? These are all questions asked by a person who is consumed with addition, not multiplication. Our nation's era of handcrafting "one at a time" products for people has long since been replaced by mass production. And so it is with our ministries, and many of them gain esteem because of the numbers they draw.

> *In order to make a disciple, you must first be a disciple!*

If Billy Graham were to win 10,000 people a day to Christ,

we would all be amazed and full of praise to God (and Billy!). Even though we might stand on the sidelines and cheer him on, it would still take him twelve hundred years to win the world to Christ, at today's population! But suppose I were to lead you to the Savior and then spend a year building deep into your life, and then we both turn around and do the same for someone else the following year. Now that there are four of us, we would begin this third year of ministry by each of us finding another person to win and disciple. If the chain remained unbroken the enormous power of multiplication would kick in, and the world would be won to Christ in an incredibly short thirty-two years!

> *"Activity is no substitute for production and production is no substitute for reproduction."*
>
> **Dawson Trotman**

Are you patient enough to focus on a few and build deep into their lives? Can you resist the temptation not to compare yourself with those around you who seem to be "blowing and going" with large group meetings that bring the leadership adoration from the masses? Jesus touched many, yes, but He trained a few. Let's take our cues from the Son of God, who spent three years primarily investing Himself into twelve men. Don't get me wrong, I hope and pray your ministry attracts large numbers of students to your activities, but *never* forget that the Great Commission is to "make disciples," not just gather crowds. Becoming fixated with multiplying your life into others is a key to bearing fruit that *truly* remains.

Leadership Is a Process, Not an Event

Dr. Tim Elmore, President of Growing Leaders, has worked with students for years and understands the keys for building leaders that last. He has a firm belief that leadership development is primarily a process, into which events can fit. He shares, "If all we do is offer big events, we may inspire students, but we'll never get beyond the excitement and emotion of the event." In the church, we often place too much emphasis on "events" and too little emphasis on the "process." Remember, the purpose of events is simply to strengthen the process. Below is one of Dr. Elmore's charts showing the contrast between events and process.

EVENTS	PROCESS
1. Encourage decisions	1. Encourages development
2. Motivate people	2. Matures people
3. A calendar issue	3. A consistency issue
4. Usually is about a big group	4. Usually is about a small group
5. Challenge people	5. Changes people
6. Becomes a catalyst	6. Becomes a culture
7. Is easy	7. Is difficult

Building Block #7: Perseverance over the Long Haul

Spencer, one of my best friends, used to be a marathon runner who went to school in a different state. I'd promised him for years that I would run a marathon with him (correction: *start* a marathon with him!). So, 1,500 of us "runners" descended on Fort Worth, Texas, on a cold and rainy Saturday in late February to flaunt our testosterone. Even though I had made the commitment to run with Spencer months earlier, I had failed to include one minor detail in my schedule—training! You see, I was an indestructible, twenty-four-year-old Neanderthal who could climb any mountain, swim any ocean, and I certainly wasn't going to break a sweat over a puny, little 26.2-mile marathon! With my *vast* knowledge of long distance running, I figured it best to keep a light stomach before the race, thus the donut and coffee I had prior to the start.

Even though there was a torrential downpour, I was fine until the 22-mile mark, when I must have hit the proverbial "wall." I know this because during the final four miles of the race, three different medics bicycling against the flow looking for runners in dire need, each stopped, got off their bikes, grabbed me by the shoulders, and asked if I was okay! Exhaustion and thirst were attacking me, but the real killer was my own body—it was screaming out for food! I hadn't "carbed up" like real runners do, and my muscles had used every ounce of protein they'd ever possessed. The two things that kept me going was the fact that a girl I knew had passed *me*, Joe Athlete, and the knowledge that there was hot stew waiting for us at the finish line!

Early in the marathon, I foolishly sprinted out like an eager beaver, fantasizing that I was going to be one of the top finishers. I didn't last ten minutes before reality set in, and I began to pace myself, finally admitting it was going to be a *long* haul. Spencer, the true athlete among us, only had two hours and thirty-seven minutes to contemplate his life that day. I had a whole three hours and fifty-nine minutes to mull over the similarities between our Christian walk and a marathon. The main lessons I learned?

> *"Send us some of your campus workers, trained in success as well as failure . . . so that we may know that they will endure!"*
>
> **From India, 1886**

A. We need training if we're going to succeed in the "marathon of life."

B. We should have a steady diet of spiritual food and drink to sustain us long term.

C. There will be tremendous trials and stress in the Christian life.

D. Never, ever give up!

E. How we finish our Christian life says more about us than how we start.

The Christian life and ministry is like a marathon, and in some ways, the measure of a laborer is what it takes to stop you. Is it a discouraging semester, a broken relationship, the loss of financial support, a heavy-handed discipler, or losing that "lovin' feeling" for the Lord? If you terminate your all-out pursuit to fulfill the Great Commission because of one of these reasons (or a thousand others), you have sold out really cheaply. The enemy will provide many easy, even attractive, exit ramps for you throughout your lifetime. Instead, hang on for dear life to your *first love* and the mission He has given you on earth. This is the way Proverbs 23:23 puts it: "Buy truth, and do not sell it."

As we join God in building these essential convictions into our life, we need to remember this structure has to last a lifetime. It isn't a hundred yard dash, it's a marathon! The deeper and stronger these "girders of conviction" are sunk, the taller and stronger our skyscraper will be. Go back over this list of seven with your spiritual leader or partner and evaluate each area, ranking them from the strongest down to the weakest. Pray together and map out a plan to work on these critical areas of life. ♦

Discussion and Application Questions

1. What can we learn from Katherine's story?

2. In *your* opinion, how does a conviction differ from a belief?

3. Based on your definition of what a conviction is, name a few convictions that you hold right now. How do you *know* they are convictions?

4. Read Matthew 16:25–26. What is Jesus trying to teach us here? At this stage in your life, what do you think you are exchanging your life for? Why?

5. Which building block for your life and ministry is your strongest one? Why?

6. Which building block is your weakest one? Why?

7. List some specific ways you could strengthen this building block in the next three months.

8. In your opinion, which of the building blocks do you think is the most important? Why?

9. Is there a building block that you would add to the seven listed? What is it?

10. What can you do now to help insure you'll be walking with Christ and impacting others twenty years from now? Make a specific application to your life.

Read your applications and pray together that God would build deep convictions into each of you, now and throughout your lifetime.

chapter 4

prepare for impact

Peter was a freshman involved with InterVarsity Christian Fellowship at the University of Wisconsin-Madison when he and some of his Christian buddies decided to get serious about reaching others for Christ. Rick Richardson, author of *Evangelism Outside the Box* and IVCF staffer in Madison at the time, was diligently praying that Peter and other believers would take personal ownership of the ministry there. God answered his petitions, and Peter and six other freshmen began meeting every Tuesday at 5:30 P.M. to pray, confess their sins, and intercede for the campus and other students. The Lord began to burden them for their lost friends, and Peter, without knowing any better, invited one of them to join the group for prayer. This wasn't just any non-believer, according to Richardson, he was a "cosmic consciousness, pot-smoking, drug-and-alcohol-using student, who had sampled Marxist and New Age thinking, and decided to embrace atheism."

Although everyone was a little uncomfortable with the new addition to the group, they proceeded as usual with the worship, confession, and intercession. But as the meeting concluded, and the students began exiting, Dick, the non-Christian, raced over to confront Peter with a question.

"What was that?!" Dick demanded.

"What was what?!" Peter responded nervously.

"I don't even *believe* in God, but God was in *that* room. What happened?"

Overhearing the conversation, Richardson asked Peter if he could join the two of them for a coke and some conversation. After Dick spent three hours hearing Richardson explain the gospel, this outspoken atheist bowed in prayer to begin a personal relationship with Jesus. What convinced this hardened scoffer? Richardson says it was simply a group of "struggling, authentic, accepting freshmen, who had learned how to be people of the Presence."

Dick had encountered the presence of God in an authentic, Spirit-filled community and would never be the same. When the story of his radical conversion got back to the other six freshmen in the prayer group, they immediately began inviting *their* non-Christian friends to the meetings! Richardson reports that over twenty-five students found the Savior that year through the IVCF freshmen prayer gathering. Looking back, it is obvious that Peter was anxious for God to use him to impact other students on campus, but he wisely chose to prepare by constantly pouring his heart out at the feet of Jesus. He and his friends were determined to seek God's face until He showed up in very tangible ways. And show up He did!

It Only Takes One

When I was a student, I attended a conference where the speaker told us to stand up, grab a piece of chalk, and scatter ourselves across the cement floor of the gymnasium we were meeting in. After instructing each of us to draw a circle on the floor around ourselves, the speaker calmly announced, "Okay, now *don't* leave that circle until revival breaks out." First I paused, then after glaring at him I glanced around at the other foolish-looking people in their little circles, and then finally peered down at my own tightly drawn circle, which now had a very confining feel to it!

Silently stranded there, I wondered what was I supposed to do. Fortunately, the speaker went on to tell us that revival wasn't an annual church meeting with a promotional banner, but it comes when a group experiences heartfelt repentance and renewal. And then he added the kicker that gave all of us a queasy, uncomfortable feeling—he said it always starts with just *one* person. Needless to say, I had some soul searching to do.

On every campus, the Lord hunts for at least one guy or gal who will take His marching orders seriously. Yet in numerous places God grieves the lack of response, as He did with Israel: "I searched for a man among them who would build up the wall and stand in the gap before Me . . . but I found *no one*" (Ezekiel 22:30, italics added). It has been said that there are three kinds of people in this world: those who *make* things happen, those who *watch* things happen, and, lastly, those who *don't know* what's happening! If revival is going to break out at your school, it will be because you (or someone else, if you let it pass by) have volunteered to *be* the fuel the Lord uses to detonate a raging spiritual inferno across your campus.

Why Are You at College?

Walt Henrichsen, the author of the classic, *Disciples Are Made Not Born*, made this shocking statement: "If you are at college for *any* other reason than to be a missionary for Jesus Christ, you are there for selfish, sinful reasons." Whoa! I'm glad he said it and not me! Did this former pastor and Navigator representative go *too* far in his challenge to students, or had he found an open nerve that desperately needed to be uncovered and dealt with? If you're currently a student, have some fun with me as we take a road trip through the crevices of your soul:

"So, why *did* you come to college?" I ask in a laid back casual manner.

"Well," you say proudly, "I'm here because I want to get a *good* education."

Sitting up in my chair, I respond, "Okay . . . but *why* do you want to get a good education?"

"Mmmm," you ponder. "Well . . . because I want to get a *good* job."

Now I lean toward you and say, "A good job, huh? Why is it that you want to get a *good* job?"

"Wait a minute," you shoot back. "I see where you're going with this! Okay, I admit it. I want a good job so I can get a better salary."

"Well, *why* would you want a better salary?" I slyly inquire.

By this time you've probably decided the discussion is over, and I'm just hoping our friendship is not! The final destination of this interrogative joy ride reveals that if you and I are *really* honest, a big part of going to college is to get a good job, in order to make a better salary, so that we can . . . so that we can—*What? Say it!*—support the kind of comfortable lifestyle we have dreamed about! Maybe this is the exact motive your well-intentioned parents have drummed into your brain, but can you see why Henrichsen makes the statement he does? Ninety-nine percent of students, even "committed" Christians, are at college with a conscious (or possibly sub-conscious) personal agenda that is selfish, yes, even sinful!

Five Questions That Must Be Answered

Now that we've had our greedy little hearts torn open and exposed, let's try to deal honestly with five questions that must be answered if we're going to trade our agenda in for God's. Fasten your seat belt, and prepare for impact!

Question #1: What Is the Great Commission?

The large room was deathly quiet. While there were over 250 students wide-eyed and listening, no one dared glance away or take a breath. Every eye was fixed upon the speaker, Rip Roaring (pseudonym), as he paced back and forth like a trial lawyer grilling the witness. I was the college pastor, and Rip was the keynote speaker I'd invited to our weekend retreat. It wasn't until the terrifying conclusion to his nerve-racking talk that I understood I was getting much more than I bargained for! He raised his voice, zeroed in on some poor girl, pointed his long finger at her and bellowed, "*Whose* responsibility is the Great Commission?" Shriveling in his presence, she didn't know how to respond. So he went on to several more petrified students, asking each the same exact question.

Finally a brave young man on the front row boldly proclaimed, "It's *our* responsibility!" Oops. Wrong answer! Insert foot in mouth. He became the weakest link, and Rip turned his battle guns on him, snickered, and said, "Have you got a frog in your pocket or something?" We would have laughed if he had given us *any* indication he was making a joke, but he went on to explain that as long as we think the Great Commission is *everyone's* responsibility, it ends up being *no one's* responsibility. He finally, mercifully, ended our session by requiring us all to repeat in unison, "The Great Commission is *my* responsibility!"

Needless to say, I haven't invited Rip back again, but let me tell you the moral of the story. Yes, Rip's methods were rather intimidating, but the truth of his message burned in our hearts as he attempted to impress upon us that it was *each* of our jobs to "make disciples of all the nations."

How can I tell if you've taken personal responsibility for the Great Commission? Simple. You have a plan to pull it off. I'm sure you've taken personal responsibility for your studies, your finances, your exercise, your future, and, for sure, your love life. The way I know? You have goals and a plan for each of these areas, and you're working diligently to accomplish them. For most Christians, the

Great Commission is really the Great *Omission,* because they walk around in a heavenly daze with no visible, tangible strategy to fulfill this mandate the Lord has given *every* believer.

As you know, the Great Commission is found in Matthew 28:18–20 (italics added):

> [18]And Jesus came up and spoke to them, saying, "*All* authority has been given to Me in heaven and on earth. [19]Go therefore and make disciples of *all* the nations, baptizing them in the name of the Father and the Son and the Holy Spirit, [20]teaching them to observe *all* that I commanded you; and lo, I am with you *always*, even to the end of the age."

He Entrusted His Kingdom to a Ragtag Band of Jewish Nomads!

Speaking to His disciples between His resurrection and ascension, Jesus wanted to remind them, one last time, what the heart and soul of their life's work should be. It's unbelievable but true, but He entrusted the future of the church to a ragtag band of Jewish nomads. It was an all-encompassing imperative He issued that day, evidenced by His use of the word *all* four times. *All* authority, *all* nations, *all* that He commanded, and He finished by reminding us that He would be with us *al*ways. I get the feeling He was trying to make a point!

> *"The Great Commission is not an option to be considered, it is a command to be obeyed."*
>
> **Hudson Taylor**

Imagine this passage like a sandwich you're making for yourself. Verse 18 is the upper slice of bread, representing Christ's complete authority, or *power* that He provides you. Verse 20 is the lower slice of bread, symbolizing His *presence* that He promises you through the end of the age. In between these layers of His power and presence is the main course—the meat of the passage, which is the command to "make disciples of all the nations."

Have you ever wondered what it would be like if He'd given us this overwhelming assignment without the assurance of His power and presence backing us? Even *with* His promised resources always with me and in me, sometimes I'm *still* scared to death to face the cold, cruel, lost and dying world with this directive. Maybe you've experienced similar feelings, wondering , How can I possibly make a difference? as you look at the masses of students crisscrossing your campus without hope or direction. Take to heart the counsel that Paul gave young Timothy about managing his fears: "You then, my son, be strong in the grace that is in Christ Jesus" (2 Timothy 2:1, NIV). Our strength is *never* to be in ourselves but only in the unconditional love and power that Christ lavishes upon us.

Lastly, the main verb in this passage is "to make" disciples. The other actions of "going," "baptizing," and "teaching" are all participles that hang their full weight on the hub of the mandate to make disciples. A paraphrase of this text might read: "I've provided you all of My power. So wherever you go, you are always to be creating for Me new followers from every group on earth. First have them publicly identify with Me, and then show them how to apply all the truths that I handed to you. And be assured, My presence will be with you forever."

Question #2: What Is Your Life Objective?

Most students would say their whole lives are wrapped up in getting through college, but where in the Bible does it even say to go to college? George Washington, Abraham Lincoln, Harry S. Truman, Ernest Hemingway, Rudyard Kipling, George Bernard Shaw, and John D. Rockefeller never went to college. And where in the Scriptures are we commanded to make good grades? Some people (or parents) say, "Well, if God has called you to be in school, that means you need to do your very best," and they might go so far as to say that making A's is your "ministry calling" right now. If that's true, why shouldn't this concept apply to your job *after* college, where you will work *all the time*, possibly doing whatever it takes to climb the ladder at the expense of your devotional life, family, and personal ministry? The question is, When does the kingdom work take priority over school or vocation? Matthew 6:33 gives us some insight here: "But seek first His kingdom and His righteousness, and all these things will be added to you."

Many college students are notorious for seeking everything *but* the kingdom of God. In fact, they seem to major in the three S's: studies, sports, and social life. There are even groups on each campus that specialize in one of these three. Honors groups (studies), athletes (sports), and Greeks (social) sometimes seem to be single-minded in their focus. The only problem with giving your time and energies to these three S's is that God is silent about these things in the Scriptures. As valuable as they appear to be, nowhere does He tell us that we ought to make our studies, our sports involvement, or our social life a priority.

In contrast, I will list three areas that God clearly says that we should give ourselves to. These three W's consist of worship, the Word, and our witness to others. The ironic thing is that we spend almost all of our time on the things He is silent on and neglect (or downright ignore!) those disciplines He clearly commands for us to regularly engage. Amazing!

Here's how the "6:33 Principle" might work itself out in our schedules. Student One seeks other things first by locking into her daily routine priorities like studies, sports, and social outings.

STUDIES

SPORTS

SOCIAL

STUDENT ONE:
Seeks Other Things First

WORSHIP

WORD

WITNESS

STUDENT TWO:
Seeks God's Kingdom First

For instance, Rachel is a Christian, but she tries to squeeze in a quiet time or share her faith with a friend as long as it doesn't conflict with a date or studying for a test. Dave, on the other hand, seeks God first and has blocked out major chunks of his schedule to focus on those things the Lord has been clear about. He then uses wisdom about how to use his discretionary time. He studies (and makes pretty good grades!), plays intramurals, and goes out with his guy and gal friends, but even those pursuits he engages for the glory of God and the opportunity to share Christ.

Years ago, I stepped into a collegiate pastor position where all the students were caught up in a "making A's in school is my calling" philosophy. As we explored what the Scriptures taught about this, one of the premed students who was set free from this self-imposed legalism created the doctrine of "good 'nuf." He wanted to do well in his studies but not at the expense of not obeying God in his life and ministry. Whatever amount of preparation he could do before tests was just going to have to be "good 'nuf!" At the heavenly gates, the Lord is not going to check your GPA. Even here on earth, where I've earned my bachelor's, master's, and doctorate, I've never been asked my GPA. Whew!

My hope is that you'll consider connecting your life's purpose to this charge that our Commander in Chief has issued. It *is* a command, not a suggestion, and certainly not one of many ministry options that He *might* be calling us to. For me, though, the "want to" is much more motivating than the "ought to," and so I view the commission as an *opportunity* of a lifetime—an incredible privilege to colabor with Him in bringing the nations to the foot of the cross and, someday, to the foot of the throne!

If you don't pick a direction for your life, someone will pick it for you, and you probably won't like the end result! Without a thought-through, prayed-through, written-down objective for life, you'll take *any* road. Our earthly existence is a little like standing in front of a huge conveyer with all kinds of choices, options, opportunities, and directions on the rapidly moving belt, each one yelling out to us, "Pick me!" "No, pick me!" "Over here! Hey, I'm the best; look at me!" How in the world are we to discern what we *are* to do and what we are *not* to do? Most end up allowing the tyranny of the urgent to dictate their priorities and schedule.

Maybe you've been to a talk or workshop on "Discerning the Will of God," where you get tips on unlocking the secret plans God has for your future. I believe the Word of God *is* the will of God, and my contention is you can cast aside this Christian fortunetelling if you have a biblical life objective. It can be your "North Star," helping you determine what directions and decisions you ought to make. I'm not saying don't listen to the Lord or be sensitive to His leading, but if He has already given us His marching orders in black and white, why are we waiting for an emotional experience to *really* tell us what He wants us to do? The truth is, most of us spend time waiting on God when, in fact, He is waiting on us!

I've observed that there are three kinds of Christians:

A. Busy: This describes someone who has filled up his calendar with all kinds of activities, even spiritual ones. For him maturity equals "Christian busyness," that is, heading to a bible study now, then a concert, afterward a fellowship, over to the soup kitchen next, etc.. As great as these things might be, many times they are packed into people's schedules out of boredom, insecurity, not being able to say no, or because they have no life objective they're committed to.

B. Effective: This person can say no to many glorious opportunities, but she's not really sure what to say yes to. She's narrowed down her priorities to a *few* important things that relate to evangelism and discipleship, but she has no specific Great Commission plan. Using a shot gun, rather than a rifle, she sees God using her in the lives of a number of people, but deep down she knows she isn't making disciples.

C. Strategic: We have a lot of *busy* Christians, some *effective* ones, but precious few who are truly *strategic*. This student looks at his campus from God's perspective and has singled out the group he will reach and disciple for the Lord. Others may view him as too intense or no fun, but, in reality, he is finding tremendous pleasure in knowing he is doing one thing—and doing it well! This person will leave a *lasting* legacy behind.

One night, after a grand performance, a reporter interviewed the featured violinist, saying, "Ms., you *undoubtedly* are the world's greatest concert violinist! *How* did you become the world's greatest concert violinist?"

"Planned neglect!" she quickly answered.

"Planned neglect? *What* do you mean?" he pressed.

"I mean that throughout my entire life, I have planned to neglect *everything* that didn't help me become the world's greatest concert violinist."

You are going to have to neglect some things—good things—in order to find the time and energy to craft a worthy life objective statement and then, even more important, carry through with it. So, pick a day to get away in a cabin, park, or even back bedroom, away from people, music, and television. Grab your Bible and notepad, and spend hours looking up and praying over passages that deal with your walk with God and your burden to reach others for Christ. Here are three examples of biblically based, well-worded life objective statements for you to look at:

A. This objective pulled from the Westminster Shorter Catechism touches on a great theme: "Man's chief end is to glorify God and enjoy Him forever."

B. One that's not original but I've used for years is "To glorify God through knowing Christ and making Him known."

C. Mark Lewis, with the Navigators, came up with "To glorify God by raising up spiritual generations of student leaders flowing from the campus to the U.S. and the nations."

"A life-purpose and vision statement should be biblical and comprehensive, yet simple enough to remember and to provide clear direction."

Max Barnett, former director of BCM at University of Oklahoma

Wow, mine seems a little weak compared to Mark's, but, hey, we all have room to grow, right? And once the Lord and you come up with your life objective, you can then confidently stroll up to the conveyer belt of life, pray over the myriad of options whizzing past you, and make a very wise choice. You'll say, "No. No. No," and then finally, "Aha! Yes! *This* one helps me fulfill my life objective!" Without second guessing, you pick it up, put it in your pocket and into your life. You are on your way to becoming a man or a woman on a mission from God.

Question #3: What Is Vision, and How Do You Get One?

This third question forces us to look at the Great Commission, your life objective, your school, and even the vast spiritual needs and opportunities surrounding you. Allow your imagination to take a Spirit-led road trip. Step back from your life and campus for a moment and ponder two questions:

A. If God were to have His total way in my life, what would it look like?
B. If God were to have His total way at my college or university, what would it look like?

Now to him who is able to do immeasurably more than all we ask or imagine, according to his power that is at work within us. (Ephesians 3:20, NIV)

Vision comes from you and God having an "asking and imagining" consultation. You may want to include other student leaders, staff, and volunteers in the process, but make sure you get some one-on-one time with the "Vision Giver" to allow *Him* to expand *your* heart. The more you pray and ask, the more you imagine. The more you stretch out your faith, the more God will show you what He has in store. He promised He would in Jeremiah 33:3, saying, "Call to Me and I will answer you, and I will tell you great and mighty things, which you do not know."

Henry and Richard Blackaby have enlightened believers through their *Experiencing God* series, challenging us to discover what *God* is doing and to join Him. We don't just want a fellowship or activity, we want to colabor with the Lord of the universe and flow into *His* stream, not demand that He flow into ours! *If* we're going to be in step with the eternal purposes of God, we better understand what He values. The Bible teaches there are *only* three things that last forever: God Himself, the Word of God, and the souls of people. As you and the Lord start dreaming together, you may have to keep a pen and notepad near your bed. On numerous nights God is brewing so many ideas and visions in my head, I *have* to record them before there's *any* way I can sleep.

> *"The greatest tragedy to befall a person is to have sight, but lack vision."*
>
> **Helen Keller**

Do You Want to Be a World-Changer?

After extended time in the Word and prayer, God may have given you a passage that forms the foundation for your vision. You may be clinging to it as a promise from the Lord that He *will* do great and mighty things through you. Check out Tom Yeakley's (with the Navigators) booklet *Claiming Promises* to give you solid guidance on how to prayerfully and carefully transform a passage into a promise for your life and ministry.

Finally, I hope your vision extends beyond the borders of your campus. John R. Mott, a nineteenth century student mobilizer exhorts us, "Let us be satisfied with nothing less than leaving the deepest mark on our generation." You and I are sitting on a powder keg, ready to be lit, ready to explode, ready to impact millions of students and people around the world. We cannot be responsible for the last generation nor the next, but we can give our lives to the present generation. If you've dreamed of being a world-changer, now is a great time to be alive! Why has He put you and me here for "such a time as this"? I don't know, but it is an unprecedented opportunity if you want to help change history for Jesus Christ. Always include the world in your vision, and may *God* be with you!

Question #4: How Big Is Your God?

Your vision will never be bigger than your view of God. J. B. Phillip's tiny book with a huge message, *Your God Is Too Small*, proves that if we view our problems as large, it is because we have a small view of God. Phillip's hypothesis is that a small God equals big problems and a big God equals small problems. If reaching your campus for Christ seems like scaling Mount Everest on your hands, then you may need to take stock of just exactly who it is you serve. You may be feeling an incredible weight of responsibility at this juncture in your reading, but don't despair. Our responsibility is simply our response to *His* ability!

> "God is not in the business of solving our problems. He's in the business of developing people."
>
> **Dr. Howard Hendricks**

If you passed Bill Gates driving home one night and saw him

accidentally crash through some bridge railings into a swirling river below, I'm sure you'd attempt to save him before he drowned. As you pull him out, he gushes, "I was going under! I owe you my life! Let me reward you for your bravery." At this point, the world's richest man pulls out his checkbook, fills in your name, and says, "How much do you want me to write it for? *Any* amount! You name it!"

"Worship is a way of gladly reflecting back to God the radiance of His worth."

Dr. John Piper

You're a little embarrassed, so you kick the ground, rub your stomach, and respond, "Oh, I don't know . . . I hadn't had dinner yet. A Big Mac sure sounds good. How 'bout five bucks?" Gates looks at you incredulously, "Five bucks?" he repeats slowly. "That's *all* you want?" He feels stupid because he's never written a check that small, much less to someone who saved his life. He writes, you smile, wave, and drive off, leaving him there scratching his head.

In Mark 10:35–45, a similar situation arose as Jesus and His disciples were on the road to Jerusalem. Although he had trained them better, they were no doubt arguing again who would be the greatest in the kingdom, when James and John, affectionately known as the Sons of Thunder, swaggered up to Jesus and demanded, "Teacher, we want you to do *whatever* we ask of You!" The two men then took a step back, crossed their arms, and waited for the magic wand to appear.

Now, if you were Jesus Christ, the King of Kings and Lord of Lords, how would you have responded to these insolent little mortals, these microscopic specks that *You* had created out of dust? He may have

"You can have as little as you are satisfied with or as much as God wants to give you."

Dr. A. W. Tozer

been tempted to say, "Why you ungrateful, insignificant welfare cases. Who do you think you're talking to?" Instead of dressing them down for having cocky "you owe me" attitudes, He simply responded, "Okay, what do you want Me to do for you?"

Jesus *loved* to ask people this question; in fact, He asks a blind man the same thing just fifteen verses later! He yearned to find anyone who would boldly approach Him. He didn't take offense but quite the opposite. He received it as a compliment because it communicated that they believed Jesus *could* and *would* answer their request. How about you? Jesus has His check out with His name written at the bottom, yours at the top, asking, "What do you want Me to do for you?" I'm not talking about money here; I'm talking about what you're asking Jesus Christ to do in your life, on your campus, and in this world. Don't ask Him for molehills, ask Him for mountains. Compliment Him. Don't insult Him with puny, meager requests. How big is *your* God? I can tell how big you think He is by what you're asking Him to do for you!

Question #5: Are You Prepared for Spiritual Warfare?

Transport yourself back to 1863 for a moment, where you're a private in the Civil War. The word rings out that the enemy is lining up for a charge, so you and your fellow soldiers run to get in formation. You glance to your left, then right, seeing thousands of your comrades straight in a row. Peering ahead, you see the enemy arrayed the exact same way. The general gives the go-ahead, and everyone raises their guns, getting ready to fire their one shot. But, as you prepare to pull the trigger, you notice the enemy's lineup across from you is private, private, *colonel*, then another private.

I know you probably hate war as much as I do, but in this situation, *which* soldier would you point your gun at? In wartime, if a soldier ever kills or captures an officer, it's a much greater blow to the enemy than merely taking out a regular foot soldier. The spiritual battle is no different, and if you're fully engaged in "kingdom warfare," you're not only a strategic officer in God's army, but also a prime target of Satan, our enemy. Peter was fully aware of this in 1 Peter 5:8, "Be self-controlled and alert. Your enemy the devil prowls around like a roaring lion looking for someone to devour" (NIV).

At this very moment, is the devil prowling around your campus, your ministry, your dorm, or house searching for someone to distract? Discourage? No! To *devour!* He doesn't just want to sidetrack or trip you, his objective is to rip you limb from limb, grind you up, and eradicate you. Sorry for the graphic detail, but that is what the passage teaches.

If you're going to get serious about leading students to Christ, discipling them to maturity, equipping them for personal ministry, and launching them out to be world-changers, you are in a heap of trouble! You have moved up to public enemy #1 on Satan's hit-list, and don't be surprised if all hell breaks loose as you begin to take the Great Commission seriously. He doesn't waste his time on inward-focused, "bless *me* Lord" Christians, but if you really get down to business for God, Satan will work night and day, in order to pierce and purge you from the ranks of God's mighty men and women.

Besides the pitfalls of fear, immorality, pride, and bitterness that I addressed in chapter 2, the enemy has another very potent weapon in his arsenal: persecution. Paul warned Timothy about this in 2 Timothy 3:12, "Indeed, all who desire to live godly in Christ Jesus will be persecuted." This is a clear promise that if we're *not* being persecuted, then we must *not* desire to live godly in Christ Jesus. This is not a pleasant topic, and yet according to the Voice of the Martyrs ministry, there are more believers (over 165,000) being martyred for their faith each year than ever before in history. If we haven't found something in life worth dying for, then we really don't have anything worth living for, so bring it on!

> *"The university campus holds such a pivotal position in our world, it has become a battleground of immense proportions. Satan knows its strategic importance. The Church must not surrender this territory over to the enemy."*
>
> **Mike Armstrong, Christ on Campus, University of Arkansas**

I Was the Most Loved—and the Most Hated!

I faced tremendous opposition during my three years in the fraternity house. I prayed daily for each man's salvation, started small group Bible studies, and had a goal to share the gospel with every pledge every semester. I was the most loved guy in the house *and* the most hated! Besides the nasty notes and being shouted down in meetings, I was occasionally awakened with a senior's blazing eyes, bulging veins, and scowling face one inch away from mine, shrieking about killing me if I *ever* tried to cram my religion down one more pledge's throat.

The fun was just beginning though. The Christian movement in the house went from one member to twenty-five. One of the believers put up a calendar, showing what days Bible studies were held, which mornings were prayer breakfasts, etc.. But the opposition in the house, not to be outdone, *also* created a calendar, posting it right next to ours. "By coincidence" they would have a dope-smoking session planned during our Bible study, an early-morning orgy with a prostitute during our prayer breakfasts, and the mockery went on and on.

Each week one of us would stand up during dinner and announce where the College Life ministry meeting was going to be held. It wasn't even three seconds before the cackling began, a fork clanging against the glass got our attention, and the announcement, made that "Wild Life" would be meeting at Maxine's Tavern for binge drinking

> *"Christ knew His followers would be unpopular in many circles, and called them to press on nevertheless. Christians should be winsome whenever we can do so without compromising our faith. But we need to understand that being despised is part of our job description. If you love others enough to tell them the truth, you have to be ready to endure some hate in return."*
>
> **Matt Kaufman, writer, *Boundless* Webzine**

the *very* same night! Of course, we would all howl in laughter, fully understanding that how we respond to persecution is, for the non-believer, one of the most fascinating and attractive things about the Christian life.

When Nero, the Roman emperor, threw believers to hungry lions in the crowded arena, he and his leaders thought it would stamp out the Christian movement. Instead, believers *volunteered* to be eaten alive, to the amazement of the mob, who said to each other, "See how these Christians die!" The Christians' response to persecution paved the way for an explosion of faith in the Roman Empire and a spreading of the gospel to the West.

Enough history! Now, all you need to know is that you're no longer a weekend warrior but a full-blown, full-time combatant in this war of the worlds. In *this* clash of the titans, the stakes are high and your opponent is playing for keeps! And even though "greater is He who is in you than he who is in the world," you are *still* entering a battle zone, and it will be the greatest challenge against the greatest enemy you've ever faced, requiring you to be Christ-focused, Spirit-filled, self-controlled, alert, and prepared for impact. Ready? Be all you can be! ♦

Discussion and Application Questions

1. Why were Peter and his friends able to have such a great impact on the University of Wisconsin-Madison campus?

2. Think for a moment and then answer this question: Why are you in college?

3. Does your reason for being in college differ from God's reason for having you there? Explain your answer.

4. Read Matthew 28:18–20. Why is this called "The Great Commission," and what's so great about it?

5. Under the section "What Is Your Life Objective?" look at the two kinds of students. Which one are you? Why?

6. If God were to have His total way in your life, what would it look like?

7. Is there anything that you are holding back from God, keeping Him from having His total way in your life? If so, what is it?

8. If God were to have His total way at your college, what would it look like?

9. What will have to happen for God to have His total way at your college?

10. Read Mark 10:35–45. At this stage of your life and ministry, what is it you're asking Jesus to do for you? Does He want you to ask Him for even bigger things? If so, what?

11. List some prayer requests so big that *only* God could pull them off.

12. You *will* face spiritual warfare. How do you plan on winning the battle?

13. If you are going to have maximum impact for Jesus Christ on your campus, what specific changes or applications do you need to make this semester?

Read your applications and pray together that God would prepare each of you to dramatically and permanently impact your campus for Christ.

93

5½ = 18/148

chapter 5

plot out your strategy

ony grew up in Taiwan before coming to the United States to graduate from high school and attend college. Although he had gone to church as a boy, he purposed *not* to listen and deemed it "a waste of a Sunday morning." As an entering freshman at the University of Oklahoma, he chose to live off campus because he didn't want to room with someone he didn't know. Now away from family, Tony's newfound freedom allowed him to begin drinking excessively with older students. Although he felt miserable, he continued, and his habit became addictive. Late one night, his hands started shaking uncontrollably. As he was desperately looking for some alcohol to calm his nerves, the phone rang. It was Kevin, a Christian guy he had met, who was involved in the Baptist Collegiate Ministry (BCM), led by longtime director Max Barnett. The Lord used that phone call to get his attention, and that evening Tony admitted that God was all-powerful and all-loving and wanted to forgive Tony if only he would confess his sin and repent. Ending his session with the Lord, Tony prayed, "Please change me. Help me to live according to the Bible. Amen."

Tony stood up a changed man and determined to leave behind his drinking and worldly lifestyle. Kevin introduced Tony to Aaron, the leader of their weekly BCM floor Bible study. Aaron started meeting with Tony each week, memorizing Scripture, having quiet times, and learning what it means to live like Christ. Aaron also began taking Tony out witnessing, and, after realizing how inward and selfish he had been, Tony made a commitment to the Lord to share the gospel with one person per day. Tony says he prays daily for opportunities, and sometimes "God gives me three instead of just one to witness to!"

It is now Tony's third semester, and he has mapped out a plan to impact others for Christ. He saw how Aaron lived in the dorms in order to witness to students, so Tony moved onto a floor in one of the dorms where no other committed Christian lived. His prayer goal is to reach out to every student on the floor, and he proclaims that his semester began "the day the freshmen moved in." Along with building relationships and witnessing, he has started a small group Bible study on his floor. Even though there has been a lot of apathy and opposition to Tony, two freshmen, Cole and Tyler, have responded and are spiritually hungry to grow. Tony says he now meets one-on-one with each of them "just like Aaron does with me." Tony learned a strategy from Aaron that he is now passing on to Cole and Tyler, preparing them to someday take on a floor of their own to win and disciple. This sophomore from Taiwan wants to be a soldier for Jesus Christ and has adopted as his marching orders the Great Commission, found in Matthew 28:18–20 to "make disciples of all nations."

> *Plot: to chart, map, or make a plan secretly; to invent or devise a scheme.*

To understand the parallels between spiritual and physical warfare, we can look at how a combat soldier prepares (1) for the possible life-threatening force that will be waged against him in battle, and (2) for carrying out the mission in hopes of victory.

Both the defensive and offensive positions require hardship, training, and, yes, strategy.

> Suffer hardship with me, as a good soldier of Christ Jesus. No soldier in active service entangles himself in the affairs of everyday life, so that he may please the one who enlisted him as a soldier. (2 Timothy 2:3–4)

Paul understood that strategy is not just for the visible battles earthly armies fight but also for the supernatural invisible war that God has drafted us into. And even though our battle is not of flesh and blood, it is a more significant, more fierce struggle than *ever* took place in Vietnam or anywhere else. The word *soldier* in the Greek language is *strata logeos*, simply meaning "a word about strategy." Every soldier of Christ, then and now, must have a preplanned, predrilled strategy if he hopes to triumph.

The Desert Storm campaign in 1991 that the United States and her allies waged against Saddam Hussein was one of the greatest examples of military mobilization in all of history. Months and months were spent moving hundreds of thousands of soldiers, ships, planes, tanks, missiles, and supplies all for the purpose of quickly and decisively crushing the Iraqi invaders. What if, right before the attack, commanding officer General Norman Schwarzkopf pulled his horde of soldiers together on the Kuwaiti beach and instead of giving them a detailed strategy on how to attack the enemy, he impulsively

Strategy: a careful plan or method; the science and art of military command exercised to meet the enemy in combat under advantageous conditions.

grabbed his bullhorn and yelled, "Now, get out there and get 'em!"? I have a feeling our boys would *still* be out there wandering around the sand dunes, trying to figure out what he meant by "get 'em!"

In our ministries we *can* choose to discard strategy, saying that we are just "being led of the Lord." That may hide our laziness or fear of failure for a time, but it *will* catch up with us, like the championship intramural football games I quarterbacked in college where we possessed superior talent but were thrashed by teams who had perfected intricate plays. The reason? I deceived myself into thinking I could simply gather my guys in the huddle and brashly say, "Get open!" In ministry, vision is *what* you want to see accomplished, and strategy is *how* to implement it. As you plot out your strategy to plant the flag of Jesus Christ at the heart of your campus, there are six steps to follow.

Six Steps to Get to the Heart of Your Campus

Step #1: Always Begin with Prayer

I didn't say it, nineteenth-century Christian leader and author S. D. Gordon did. "Prayer is the *real* work of the ministry; service is just gathering in the results of prayer," he profoundly asserts in his potent little piece, *Quiet Thoughts on Prayer*. Why is it then that I can spend two hours with one of the guys I'm discipling and enjoy the heck out of it, but if you ask me to spend two minutes in prayer for him it's like pulling teeth? Here's a typical prayer:

> *"We must talk to God about men before we talk to men about God."*
>
> **Dr. Bill Bright**

> "Dear Lord, I, uh, pray for Matt right now, that you would, uh, bless him and, uh" (I look at my watch and it's only been ten seconds), "and Father, encourage him today and, uh, use him in someone's life today and, uh . . ." (I look again and only twenty seconds have passed!).

You get the picture. The enemy knows that walls are broken down and hearts are penetrated by specific, constant intercession for the souls of men and women. I have seen *so* many conversions and life changes that I *know* are a direct result of my petitions. What a fool I am then for neglecting, yes, forsaking *the* most important weapon you and I have, unleashing the power of God into someone's life through prayer. I can't say I understand why the Lord has chosen to move in others' hearts in response to our prayers, yet I am grateful and humbled by it. As Civil War chaplain E. M. Bounds shared generations ago, "To be little with God is to be little for God." We will be sorely disappointed if we think we can have a strong public ministry with students if we have a weak private life of intercession with the Lord.

> *"Prayer is a walkie-talkie for warfare, not a domestic intercom for increasing our conveniences."*
>
> **John Piper**

Dawson (Daws) Trotman, founder of the Navigators, came to Christ in his early twenties and immediately began to grow, memorize Scripture, witness, and pray. He challenged a friend to meet him for two hours of prayer every morning at 4:30 for six weeks. In the first few days they prayed for individuals in their church and city, but God expanded their vision, and, armed with a U.S. map, they began praying that God would use them in the lives of men in all fifty states. In the final weeks they were moved to pour their hearts out over a world map, realizing that the Lord wanted to use their prayers and their lives to touch nations for Himself. This foundation of intercession not only launched the Navigators ministry but galvanized Daws and his men as lifetime prayer warriors.

After reading *Daws*, an excellent biography on Trotman, I decided to ask five men to get up at 5:30 A.M. (we weren't quite as committed!) and pray together for two hours every day. We divided up the campus into every imaginable affinity group to pray for the students' salvation, that laborers would be raised up to go *to* them, and that laborers would be raised *from* them. We too would always end up in front of a world map, praying for the nations and giving special attention to the unreached millions in China. In the subsequent months and years we saw God do marvelous works in response to our petitions, and two from the early morning prayer group have since been ministering in China for about twenty years, along with many of their disciples who followed them there.

Pray in the morning. Pray late at night. Pray with other students. Pray by yourself. Pray without ceasing! The more you lift up your heart to the Lord, the more you position yourself in intercessory prayer between the Lord and others, the more you will sense Him going before you to touch and prepare the hearts of students. Hudson Taylor enjoyed proving God could and would respond to his prayers; thus his motto: "We want to see men moved by God—through prayer *alone*."

> *Every movement of God begins with prayer. Through prayer our hearts begin to beat with His heart. His passion becomes our passion. And we become effective instruments to speak and do His will in this world.*

Lastly, one of the most enjoyable things I do is to take prayer walks around the campus with a student for whom I desire to build a deeper burden for prayer and evangelism. Usually in the early morning or late night, and sometimes in multiple pairs, we will create a prayer circuit where each twosome stops in front of every dorm, Greek house, athletic facility, office, and classroom building to intercede for groups as well as individuals. Try it. You'll like it!

Step #2: Concentrate on Building Relationships

During my sophomore year in college, I befriended a young pledge from Louisiana named Mike. He was a handsome, wealthy, fun-loving partier, like a number of my fraternity brothers. On many star-filled nights, Mike and I spent hours on the roof of our chapter house talking about our lives, our dreams, and his soul. He knew he wasn't a Christian, but he came to understand *exactly* what he must do to become one. He even promised me one night that when he did come to Christ, I would be the first to know. Never in my life had I been more burdened by God to intercede for someone's salvation, spending over an hour in prayer many late nights just crying out to God on Mike's behalf, so absolutely sure the Lord was going to redeem his soul.

the fuel and the flame

One afternoon there arose a great commotion in the house, including one guy running through the hallways and screaming at the top of his lungs. I opened my door as he fled by yelling, "Mike has been killed in a car wreck out by the lake!" Horrified, I bolted out of my room and grabbed the first guy I found to verify if it was really true. When he shook his head yes, I staggered to my knees and sobbed. I could not believe it. No way could this have really happened! The Lord had promised me! In total denial, I couldn't speak, eat, or concentrate on anything for days. Instead of sleeping, I wandered around the campus in a daze for three straight nights, hurling deep, heartfelt accusations at God.

At the end of my rope one morning, I heard a knock, and a fraternity brother, who had never darkened my door, walked in. With a bowed head and tear-filled eyes, he gave me a side of the story that no one else had heard. He and Mike had been at the lake about to smoke marijuana when a local youth minister walked up and engaged them in a spiritual conversation. Mike became so convicted of his empty life and sordid heart that he prayed to receive Christ right there on the beach. Once he made his decision, he got up, threw his bag of dope in the water, and turned and said, "Let's get back to the house. I've got to tell Shad." As they were driving back up a steep mountain road, a speeding car rounded the curve in Mike's lane. He had an instantaneous decision whether to hit the car head on, and risk killing *everyone,* or sacrifice his own life by turning his vehicle to the right (and off the side of the cliff). He chose the latter and each one walked away—except Mike, who was crushed by the weight of his car.

The moment I heard him repeat Mike's words, "I've got to tell Shad," I *immediately* envisioned my friend in heaven with the Lord with a *huge* smile splashed across his face. He *was* saved! Mike *was* with Jesus and waiting for me to join him for an eternity spent in praise of the Savior. God *had* kept His promise to me, but waited three days to confirm it. From that point on, I determined never to give up on anyone, believing that God could answer our petitions, even in the latest possible moment.

If we love someone, we will pray for them, share the gospel with them, and lay our lives down for them. Our motive in ministry has to be genuine, authentic love for others, and the Great Commission should flow out of the Great Commandment. Surely our love for others comes from our love for God, as explained in 2 Corinthians 5:14: *"For the love of Christ controls us, having concluded this, that one died for all, therefore all died."* Because God put us on earth to build deep, abiding relationships, we love people more than things and more than tasks. In fact, the true measure of a person's success during this life is the quality of relationships developed with:

A. God
B. Family
C. God's family
D. Those who don't yet know Christ

Two Kinds of Disciplers

I had two different men disciple me in college. One took me through ministry materials each week during the "mandatory" one-on-one meeting we'd agreed on. At the end of my freshmen year, he graduated, we shook hands, and I've never heard from him since! Later in college, God gave me a second man to disciple me, Vic Underwood, who loved me in spite of myself. I'd never met someone who cared, served, prayed, and invested in my life like Vic did. He didn't do it to impress others or even out of obedience to God; he did it because he enjoyed being with me, the highest compliment you can pay anyone. Even though I was like a wild bucking bronco when it came to respecting or submitting to his spiritual leadership, he never gave up on me.

Vic and I lived together my senior year and I witnessed his servant's heart in the way he constantly made my bed and fixed the meals. I repaid his kindnesses by begrudgingly sitting in his early-morning Bible study with a blanket wrapped around my head to protest the ungodly hour. Once during a prayer walk we took together, in the middle of his very sincere petition, I glared at his bowed head and scoffed, "You're the biggest phony I've ever met!" If there was ever a time I deserved for someone to call me a slimy imbecile and whack me, it was then. Instead, he patiently smiled, put his hand on my shoulder, looked right into my eyes, and quietly uttered four unbelievable words, "I love you, Steve."

To be honest, I don't remember *any* pithy statements or deep doctrine that Vic gave me back in those days, only his unconditional love offered to an arrogant, rebellious college student. He saw potential in me and stayed in the saddle no matter how much I tried to buck him off. The investment he made has reaped eternal dividends, and almost twenty-five years later, he *still* cares, prays, and supports me!

If you want to see your campus ablaze for Christ, purpose-driven, love-filled relationships will have to permeate your life and ministry. Why? Because discipleship is a combination of direction *and* affection. My first discipler gave me all direction (i.e., going through materials) and almost no affection (i.e., building a friendship with me). Vic took us through some good stuff, yes, but the core of his discipleship was all about him pouring his life *into* me. The generation of students we're trying to reach are crying out not for slicker, more impressive materials, but for someone to believe in them enough to form a lasting bond—a relationship. It's *why* we're here!

Step #3: Plan for the Seasons of Ministry

Even when I'm an old man, I will probably still be dividing my year up the way students do: fall, spring, and summer. We all get a new lease on life and ministry, come mid-August. As the new school year begins, it's a prayerful time of planning out our work and then, hopefully, working out our plan! Just as the farmer performs a different function in each season, so, too, the campus worker must know what to do and when to do it! Read Isaiah 28:23–29 for some "back forty" wisdom from a farmer who understands that sowing, cultivating, reaping, and even preparing for the next season are essential procedures for successful annual crop yields. We're going to dig much deeper into these tasks in later chapters, but for now let's do a short overview on planning out a ministry year:

A. The fall

Whether it is just you starting out, or you have a team of workers colaboring with you, August is the key time to meet students and start the recruiting process. The goal for the first thirty days of school is to meet as many students as you can, recruit as many as possible to small-group studies, and invite every student to your large-group meeting (if you have one). The Greeks on your campus are probably rushing students to pledge their chapters, why can't you sponsor "rush parties" to recruit students to your ministry in the same way? This time of sowing can make or break you for the school year. Students come to campus with a fairly clean slate, but then they spend the first two to three weeks filling up their calendars with commitments and relationships that lock them in throughout the year. Make sure you get a slot in their whirlwind life before it's too late!

> *"Make no small plans. They will not move the hearts of men."*
>
> **Elton Trueblood, pastor and author**

The emphasis during September and October should be evangelism and recruiting. Each week, in your small groups and one-on-one, be looking for opportunities to share your testimony and a gospel presentation. Ask God to give you solid decisions as you ask students if they would like to invite Christ into their lives as Lord and Savior. Along with a consistent diet of witnessing, build relationships with new students through fun activities, and recruit them to any kind of fall conference or event you are planning.

As you continue to saturate your campus with prayer, you'll want to start following up with those students who come to Christ or really want to grow in Christ. Don't zero in on particular students too soon. Give them a chance to show their interest level and faithfulness. Loving and serving students individually and as a group will show them you really care. If you do have a large-group weekend event or a Christmas conference, use it to reinforce the vision and values you've been preaching in your one-on-ones, small groups, and any campus-wide meetings you've held. By the time mid-November rolls around, though, you ought to start to challenge each student to a higher level of commitment for the spring semester.

B. The spring

Students are usually eager to return to school after Christmas break. Those who attended a ministry event over the holidays are anxious to apply the truths they gained. If you presented each with a customized challenge to pray about over the break, they have had time to pray and decide if they want to take you up on the offer you made. Along with any investigative groups you might start (for non-Christians or young believers), you'll want to gather the faithful, growing students from the fall and incorporate them into a small group that will challenge them to take the next step in their maturity. Select the spiritually hungriest students and plan weekly time with them, developing them in quiet time, character, and witnessing.

As the semester wears on, begin to recruit students as a group and as individuals to any summer-growth or mission opportunities that you provide or know about. *Whatever* your students do during the summer, make sure you give each a good summer-growth plan to follow and a personalized challenge to become a ministry leader come fall. Always be planting seeds and planning ahead to the next cycle of ministry.

C. The summer

Some ministries gear down during the summer, but I have found it to be an incredible time to give focused training to the committed students. You have spent time sowing and cultivating; now is the time to reap. I have found that summer is a great season to consolidate the leaders and train them to colabor with you when August rolls around. If you don't have a summer training program in your ministry, why not start one yourself or plug them into one that another ministry has operating?

Our ministry started summer projects in 1981, and thousands have had their lives radically and permanently changed as a result. One of the highlights of the projects is the final "back to campus" week, where each student begins to pray and to plan for what kind of personal ministry they want to have when they get back into school. You might even want to have the student leaders come back to school a bit early for group prayer, planning sessions, and moving freshmen into their dorm rooms. The cycle begins again, except this time you have a whole new cadre of workers to assist you!

Step #4: Prepare for the Stages of Ministry

"If you don't know where you're going, any road will get you there" is an old saying that depicts many of today's ministries. Student leaders, staff workers, or volunteers may be very sincere in their efforts to minister to students; but unless they know where they're going and how to get there, it will be like they're taking a road trip but forgetting their map! Students will usually follow us, but we *have* to know where we are taking them! You can't be satisfied with just having a lot of students coming to

Fanatic:
A person who,
once he's lost
sight of his goals,
redoubles his efforts!

the fuel and the flame ◆

a weekly large group or involved in small-group Bible studies. Many church and parachurch collegiate ministries get stuck in the addition stage of ministry and are unable to multiply. You must have a plan if you're going to raise up student leaders who will minister in years to come.

The way to begin your ministry on campus is to invite students to "come and see," like Jesus did in John 1:39. Next, challenge students to "follow Me," just as the Lord did in Matthew 4:19. Finally, offer a partnership to the faithful collegians, in the same way Christ did in Mark 3:14 when He said, "Join Me." The Navigators call it moving from duck hunting to leading a duck hunt. The key to this kind of generational ministry is recruiting students to hunt ducks with them, and, once they get the hang of it, challenge them to lead a duck hunting expedition of their own. You're trying to shift the emphasis from students helping you with *your* ministry to you beginning to help them with *their* ministry. In other words, you can spend all of your time giving fish to hungry students, but why not start teaching them how to fish for themselves? Whether you're pursuing ducks, fish, or students, you're seeking to reproduce self-starters who can pass the vision and skills onto others! We will spend whole chapters on these topics in the second half of this book, but here is a brief overview of the three stages of ministry each year. Understand and follow these, and you'll be moving toward your goal of raising up lifelong laborers for Jesus Christ.

A. Investigation

During August and September of each year, you are the Sherlock Holmes of the campus. You will want to know the who, what, why, where, and how's of every corner of the school at every hour. What groups are gathering for early-morning study sessions? Which fraternities hang out in front of the library? How is the cafeteria divided into affinity groups? Which athletic teams are the most popular? What are the local hangouts where students congregate in the evenings? What dorms have freshmen or honor students in them? What values and perspectives are they embracing? Become the expert, and when students come onto "your campus," act as *their* host. I knew one campus worker who did such a good job of investigating his campus and getting to know every group that when he gave me a tour of the school in his Jeep, he looked at me with a big smile and said, "I *own* this campus!" He knew that he had gone right to the heart and soul of that school and its students and was well on his way to impacting it—from the inside out.

B. Penetration

This is all about meeting students, building relationships, and sharing the gospel. The campus can be a spiritually dark place to bring the Good News, and yet God wants to use you and me to take the light of truth to a multitude of students. In Kharkov, Ukraine, where I spent a year ministering to collegians, there were over eighty dorms in the city, with at least five hundred students in each. Sometimes as I entered one of the old unmarked buildings, I got the sense that I was the first Christian worker to *ever* come into this dorm. As I entered room after room and saw group after group of spiritually starved students hang on every word of the gospel, I learned firsthand what it means to bring light into darkness. This was Paul's mission in life, as expressed in Romans 15:20: "I aspired to preach the gospel, not where Christ was already named, so that I might not build on another man's foundation." Even as an old man, he never lost the cutting edge of penetration. Nor should we.

C. Concentration

Once a non-Christian comes to Christ or a dormant Christian is revived, next comes a time of follow up. The fruit has been born, now is the time to conserve it. With so much of a "love 'em and leave 'em" mentality in our evangelism efforts, the question I have is this: If we don't give the necessary attention and care to these newborn believers, why should we expect God to give us any more converts? Recruiting more and more students may make the weekly meetings look impressive, but the students' spiritual lives could end up being dangerously shallow. We should always be investigating and penetrating, but don't ever forsake building the basics of the Christian life into faithful believers who can someday be your colaborers in the harvest field.

Step #5: Decide Which Students to Target

Get out the most recent school annual, campus directory, and map of the college. Start to list all the different affinity groups at your college. Break down these different "people groups" by:

- Dorm floors
- Athletic teams
- Greek chapters
- Clubs and organizations
- International student groups
- Student government
- Off-campus groups
- Commuters

- Races
- Religions
- Majors
- Gender
- Faculty
- Other
- Classes
  (freshmen, senior, graduate, etc.)

Begin to pray over each group, and list individuals that you currently know. Some ministries also divide the student body into influential, interested, and isolated categories. In doing this, they are trying to target the students who have the broadest network of relationships in order to impact the maximum number of people on a campus. If you are interested in targeting the most influential students on a campus, appendixes 1 and 2 describe that more fully.

You will need to decide if you are going to focus your energies on penetrating one of the affinity groups you listed or simply on any individuals you meet on campus. If you choose to target groups, then you and your team members can pray, brainstorm, and match up with the affinity group that you most relate to, connect with, or feel led to reach out to. Maybe you were part of a sorority or you played high school sports or you traveled to different African countries at one time in your life. It makes sense to connect you with a corresponding group. If there is a large group of Chinese Malaysians, or a particular dorm that no one is targeting, that may be a signal from the Lord that He wants you there initiating ministry.

Focus on Freshmen

When I was head counselor at a camp, one of my jobs each May was to welcome and orient a fresh batch of college counselors, eager to learn, serve, and fit in. If I had told them we got up at 5 A.M. for calisthenics each morning, they would have all been there, ready to go. The veterans, though, were sometimes harder to motivate, because they had settled into a routine of doing things like they've always been done. The saying "it's hard to teach an old dog new tricks" can be true of camp counselors as well as college students! Whether it's someone trying to trick them into buying elevator tickets or you trying to recruit them to a floor Bible study, freshmen are much more open and receptive than upperclassmen.

As I write, I am looking out my office window at our back deck where tomorrow fifty of our campus ministry's leaders will gather for a cookout to have fun, to pray, and to plan how to reach out to the 2,500 freshmen moving onto our campus the next day. These leaders have arrived early to spend three days and nights helping freshmen move in to their rooms, building relationships, and inviting freshmen to *Happy Hour*, our weekly meeting. But most of all, they're just trying to make good first impressions.

The First Person I Ever Met

First impressions can be monumental events. I'll never forget the first person I met when I got to campus, the first person who helped me unload, the first person who showed me around when I felt like a lost puppy, and of course, the first person to invite me to a dorm Bible study. If you will commit to spending the first thirty days of each fall semester meeting, befriending, and recruiting freshmen, you will continually see your personal ministry being refreshed and reloaded with willing, hungry, and teachable young men and women who will follow you anywhere in repayment for your kindness toward them in their hour of need!

> *"Students are looking for a community to belong to before a message to believe in."*
>
> **Rick Richardson, InterVarsity Christian Fellowship**

My wife and I mainly focus on working with the fraternity and sorority students on our campus. I've been meeting this week with different guys, inviting them to be part of a Greek men's discipleship group I am starting this fall. I'm only inviting three guys from each of the top four fraternities to participate in this weekly time of studying the Bible, praying and reporting on our ministries. One of the requirements for each guy is to lead or colead a Bible study in their fraternity. I will be helping each of them spearhead a study or two among the most reachable and recruitable category of persons in their chapter. You guessed it—the freshmen pledges!

Not only are freshmen usually the most accessible, but if you can lead one to Christ, you have three to four more years to establish and equip them. Each spring and summer we train our campus leaders to come back in August and once again focus on the freshmen. It is a perpetual cycle that brings lifeblood into the movement each year and helps ensure a future generation of leaders. Freshmen—you gotta love 'em!

Step #6: Know What It Is You're Seeking to Produce

Before we actually implement our ministry, we first need to understand what our ultimate goal is. It's fine to know the seasons and stages of ministry, but what will the students look like when we are finished with them and pass them onto their next assignment in life? God is the one who is at work in them and through them, but He has chosen us to help shepherd them during this pliable phase of their life. To give us a little direction, we've included some profiles, which the Navigators and others have used in the past, to help the Christian worker understand the end result we are working toward. You might want to use these profiles to guide you in your ministry and also to evaluate where each of your students are and need to go. These profiles are not taken from any particular chapter of the Bible but are simply descriptions of some of the scriptural characteristics that ought to be present at each stage of a Christian's growth. Sprinkle them with grace, understanding that who and what we *are* is just as important (or more!) as what we *do* in the Christian life and ministry.

Profiles in the Discipleship Process

Profile of a True Convert

1. Change of attitude toward Jesus Christ—now favorable (John 8:42)
2. Change of attitude toward sin—now unfavorable (1 Corinthians 5:17)
3. Desire to grow spiritually (1 Peter 2:2)
4. Publicly professed commitment to Christ (Romans 10:9–10)

Profile of a Growing Christian

1. Meets the profile of a convert
2. Engaged in developing a relationship with God through the Word, prayer, etc. (Colossians 2:6–7)
3. Observable changes taking place in regard to attitude and actions as a result of application of the Word and/or conviction of the Holy Spirit (John 14:21)

Profile of a Disciple

1. Consistent and growing in the basics of the Christian life for at least six-months

2. Has developed a heart for God
3. Willing to make any sacrifice to grow, even change her schedule.

Explanations of Above
1. A disciple is a follower of Jesus Christ who is consistent and growing in:
    A. Lordship—Puts Christ first in the major areas of life and is taking steps to separate from sin (Luke 9:23; Romans 12:1)
    B. The Word—Continues in the Word through study, memorization, and application (John 8:31; James 1:22–25)
    C. Prayer—Has consistent daily devotional life and is developing prayer life (Ephesians 6:18; John 15:5–7)
    D. Fellowship—Demonstrates Christ's love by identifying with and serving other believers (John 13:34–35; Galatians 5:13)
    E. Witnessing—Is identifying with Jesus Christ in her environment and is actively sharing her faith (Matthew 5:15; Colossians 4:6)
    F. Has been growing in these five areas for at least six months
2. A disciple is manifesting a deepening intimacy with the Lord where love and gratitude for Jesus Christ is the motive for her attitude and actions (2 Corinthians 5:14)
3. A disciple is demonstrating a willingness to change priorities and time commitments in order to develop her relationship with God and to make herself available for training (2 Kings 2:1–6)

Profile of a Disciplemaker
1. Is continuing on as a disciple, but has now also made a disciple (i.e., has been the major influence in taking a

person from a new or growing Christian to a disciple)
(Matthew 28:18–20)
2. Has developed a heart for people (1 Thessalonians 2:8;
Philippians 2:17)
3. Is willing to make any sacrifice to help another grow,
even change her schedule (1 Corinthians 9:19–23)

Explanations of Above
1. Has provided the affection and direction for another
individual in becoming a disciple, utilizing the group
and/or one-to-one discipling method
2. Is willing to give up her rights and interests in order to
meet the needs of others and make disciples from a heart
motivated by love (1 Timothy 1:5)
3. Is starting to make life decisions (location, vocation,
mate, etc.) based upon how she can most effectively
fulfill the Great Commission

Profile of a Reproducer
1. Is continuing on as a disciplemaker
2. Has been the major influence in helping at least one
of her disciples to become a disciplemaker (i.e., has
produced a strong third generation)
3. Has the knowledge, skills, character, and vision to go
to another location to see this whole process begun and
repeated (Matthew 28:18–20; Acts 1:8)

Note: The characteristics of a disciple include having a heart
for *God* and being willing to make *any* sacrifice to grow. The
characteristics of a disciplemaker include having a heart for *people*
and being willing to make *any* sacrifice to help *another* grow.

A Disciple	A Disciplemaker
1. Has a heart for God	1. Has a heart for people
2. Makes *any* sacrifice to grow	2. Makes any sacrifice to help another grow

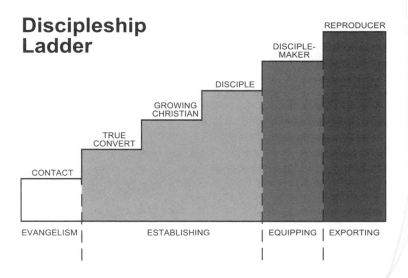

Discipleship Ladder

Beware of the Ditches!

Use these profiles as a way to measure how you and your students are doing in the overall discipleship growth process. These profiles can be utilized as something to shoot for in your lives and ministry, but don't take them to an extreme. One ditch is to take these profiles and make legalistic standards out of them, forcing everyone to conform to these in order to measure up to your brand of spirituality. Don't fall into this performance trap. Some, though, will swerve toward the other extreme, the free-spirit ditch. This is the lazy man's version of Christian ministry, where there's no need to plan, to organize, to develop materials, or even to pray specifically. Some of these folks live in an easy-come, easy-go fog that says, "We're just going to trust God, be available, encourage everyone to become like Jesus, and see what happens!" I'm certainly all for that, but God did give us a brain, a road map in the Scriptures, and ministry role models like Himself and Paul. So stay balanced. Stay on the road. Listen to the aged apostle as he tells us to have a strategy like a good soldier in Christ Jesus, to do the work of an evangelist, pour out our lives like a drink offering, and even suffer hardship, if need be.

Set Your Face Like a Flint

The year was 1517, and Hernando Cortez and his three ships of soldiers sailed from Spain to conquer and claim Mexico for his country. When they arrived in the Mexican bay, small boats ferried all the soldiers to the shore to prepare to march to the capital city of the Aztec empire and defeat King Montezuma. Once the soldiers were on shore, Cortez motioned for a few men to row back to the ships. As the soldiers watched, their curiosity turned into horror as the men lit torches and threw them onto the decks of the three ships. The soldiers stood speechless with eyes and mouths wide open as they realized they would never again see their home country or families. They had no choice but to turn, follow Cortez into the heat of the battle, crush the enemy, and win the war. There was no turning back.

Be assured that God wants to start and spread a raging fire across your campus. You're about to launch into the adventure of a lifetime as you see Him ignite a flame on your campus and in your world with some well-prepared fuel—you! Now is the time to burn your ships and set your face like a flint toward the campus. There can be no turning back. ✦

Discussion and Application Questions

1. What can we learn from Tony's story?

2. Read 2 Timothy 2:1–5. Before reading this book, did you feel like you had a clear-cut strategy for reaching your campus? If so, what was it?

3. What role should prayer play as you form and carry out your ministry strategy?

4. What was the difference in the two disciplers Steve had while in college? Do you have someone who disciples you? If not, why not? If so, describe the relationship you have with this person.

5. What kind of relationships do you want to develop with those you're trying to reach for Christ and/or disciple?

6. What are the seasons of ministry on your campus? What should you be trying to accomplish in each of the seasons?

7. Explain each of the stages of ministry. Why is each important?
      A. Investigation
      B. Penetration
      C. Concentration

8. List as many campus affinity groups as you can. Rank the top three groups you would be most burdened/motivated to reach out to. Explain your list and rankings to the group.

9. Where do you place yourself right now on the Discipleship Ladder? Why do you place yourself there?

10. Where would you like to be? Why?

11. Evaluate the discipleship profiles and write down a game plan to get you to the next step in the ladder.

12. This week, spend much time in prayer and planning, seeking to craft a ministry strategy to impact one or more of the campus groups you listed.

13. The first five chapters of this book deal with our personal preparation. The goal is to make us suitable fuel that God can ignite, using you to impact individual students as well as your entire campus. Are you ready and willing for God to use you? Why or why not?

Read your applications and pray together that God would use you and your strategies to dramatically and permanently impact your campus for Christ.

part 2

the flame

five keys to your ministry implementation

chapter 6

persist in dynamic evangelism

I got a call one day from Terry, a young college student whom I was discipling, who had just led Kirk, a high school football teammate, to faith in Christ. Sometimes we try to help a new convert like Kirk break with old habits by taking him to his non-Christian friends to give his testimony. After sharing his conversion story with these astonished pagans, the new Christian, out of sheer pride, is usually too embarrassed to smoke dope with them again. Terry had anticipated my challenge and had already set up a gospel appointment for Kirk to share his story with three former teammates.

I tagged along as a silent assistant so that Terry and Kirk could take the lead. It was all Kirk, though, as he dove right into *his* version of the gospel presentation that Terry had showed him the day before. Cringing and gagging at how Kirk was butchering the gospel to these fragile young souls, I barely contained myself. I resisted the temptation to jump in and save the day since Kirk was on a roll—I just wasn't sure where! Finishing his sermonette and with incredible intensity, Kirk turned to the first guy and asked, "Well, Sam, what do you say? Would you like to receive

Christ into your life?"

After a few awkward moments, Sam looked him right in the eye and said, "Yeah . . . I would."

Kirk then turned to the next fellow and said, "Lewis, do *you* want to take Christ as your Savior tonight?"

Another couple seconds of silence elapsed before he shot back, "Yep. Me too."

Without missing a beat, Kirk trained his eye on teammate number three to cross-examine him: "Tommy, you've heard these decisions, do *you* want to become a Christian also?"

Tommy nervously looked back and forth and finally said, "Sure."

Kirk then led them in a prayer of repentance and salvation, each of them repeating after him.

Bowing my head in prayer, I was in total disbelief. I was beholding the mother of all mess ups, yet these guys were giving their hearts to Christ, in spite of Kirk's assassination of the high and hallowed gospel message. "How can this be?" I asked myself, only to be riveted right to my core by the Holy Spirit, through Paul's declaration:

> When I came to you, brothers, I did not come with eloquence or superior wisdom as I proclaimed to you the testimony about God. For I resolved to know nothing while I was with you except Jesus Christ and him crucified. I came to you in weakness and fear, and with much trembling. My message and my preaching were not with wise and persuasive words, but with demonstration of the Spirit's power. (1 Corinthians 2:1–4, NIV)

Even though I feel strongly about knowing and presenting the gospel in a clear and concise manner, I'd forgotten that it is the *power of God* at work, not fancy words or memorized illustrations! That day I couldn't see the extraordinary boldness and initiative in Terry and Kirk because I was too busy critiquing their presentation technique. By the way, my cringing and gagging must not have discouraged them too much—both have been missionaries in a large, 1.2-billion-person communist country in Central Asia for almost twenty years now!

How Many World-Changers Are on Your Campus?

Let's speculate together. At this very moment, how many groups or individuals at your school do you think are preparing a battle plan to carry out a campus-wide, world-changing strategy of evangelism and discipleship? I would *like* to say you're one of many staying up late tonight plotting and praying to take over your campus for Christ, but we would be very naïve to think so.

Some would say the following estimates are very generous, but if you are on a campus of ten thousand, depending upon what part of the country you're in, there may be up to five thousand students who are members of a church or attended as a child. Out of the churched ones, there might be one thousand who are *truly* born-again Christians, who have received Christ into their lives as Lord and Savior, and who understand salvation is by grace through faith—alone. Of the 1,000 real believers, possibly 250 could actually be considered "growing Christians" and even fewer, maybe fifty, could be called "disciples" according to our profiles listed previously. Out of those fifty sold-out disciples, how many have *personally* led another student to Christ? Hopefully, twenty have. How many of the twenty have followed up with a new believer and begun to disciple them? Ten would be a liberal figure.

And finally, how many of those ten students could say they have been obedient to the Great Commission and have actually "made a disciple"? I would be amazed if there were five students on your campus right now who have taken another student through the whole discipleship process that Jesus laid out for us in the Scriptures. And, taking off my sandals in fear of treading on holy ground, I dare not even speak of the possibility of an undergraduate student on your campus becoming a "reproducer" (that is, equipping a disciple to become a disciplemaker, thus raising up a strong *third* generation!).

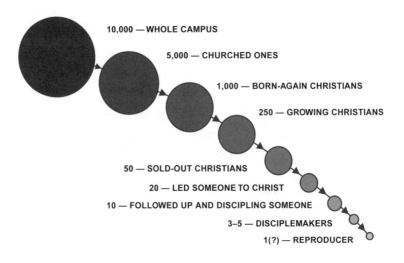

10,000 — WHOLE CAMPUS

5,000 — CHURCHED ONES

1,000 — BORN-AGAIN CHRISTIANS

250 — GROWING CHRISTIANS

50 — SOLD-OUT CHRISTIANS

20 — LED SOMEONE TO CHRIST

10 — FOLLOWED UP AND DISCIPLING SOMEONE

3–5 — DISCIPLEMAKERS

1(?) — REPRODUCER

When I meet a college student who has become a disciplemaker, and even more so, a reproducer, I cry out, "Unbelievable!" and get out my magnifying glass to study this specimen like a rare, nearly extinct animal. What makes him tick? Where did he get the vision, skills, and perseverance to do what maybe three, four, or five out of 10,000 students on campus are willing to do? If you *ever* find a student who has done this, stick to him like glue, don't let him go, adopt him as your mentor or at least your teammate. Bind your hearts together to raise up other disciples on your campus. If this person is unmarried and of the opposite sex, you might consider proposing on the spot, *before* others can! Some of my comments are facetious, of course, but winning students to Christ and helping them to become disciples and disciplers is a tall order! It is definitely a God thing, but He wants to use you to pull it off! And when you provide the fuel, God provides the flame.

If you've prepared properly, now is the time to implement your ministry plans. The next four chapters will outline the essential steps in fulfilling the Great Commission, called the four E's:

The winning, building, training, and launching of college students into the world to make an eternal difference for Jesus Christ is our objective. Buckle up and let's roll!

Begin with Evangelism

The year was 1944, and Hitler and his Nazi regime were threatening to take over all of Europe. The only hope to stop them appeared to be the American soldiers gathered in England, waiting for the go ahead to cross the English Channel for France the next morning. The British jails were full of AWOL Americans who had refused to fight or had attempted suicide. The reason? Everyone knew full well the Nazis had spent the previous two years fortifying the Normandy beaches with machine gun bunkers, mines and barbwire, and that there would be many casualties. At dawn when the American barges carrying soldiers got near the shore, the large loading ramps dropped open for our men to swim and run to the battle. Instead they were instantly mowed down by the Germans. For hours the American soldiers either lay dead or were paralyzed by fear, afraid to move into the line of constant Nazi gunfire. Some men lay in the fetal position, crying out for their mothers.

"Risk more than others think is safe. Care more than others think is wise. Dream more than others think is practical. Expect more than others think is possible."

a West Point cadet

Finally, one shell-shocked officer mustered the courage to rally his terrified men. Colonel George Taylor stood up in the blood-red water next to Normandy Beach and yelled to his ravaged unit, "Men, there are only two kinds of soldiers on this beach: those who are dead and those who will die. Now let's move into the beach!" His vision and resolve galvanized his men, and for the next five hours they made their way up the hill, climbing over dead bodies all the way, at last creating a breakthrough that the Allies could enter to win the battle and ultimately the war. It was a now-or-never decision: either they took the offensive or waited for their enemies to destroy them. Looking back, it may have been the most decisive hour in all of World War II.

This may seem overly dramatic, but just like those soldiers on that bloody June morning generations ago, we have a question to ask ourselves: "Am I going to stay in the water *or* advance to the beach where the battle is going on?" God grants us a brief window of opportunity to make our lives count. Will we waste it? Will we sit paralyzed? Will fear or distraction or apathy rob us of victory? Today may be the D-day of your life, as you wrestle with these questions that *must* be answered if we are going to go to the heart of the campus and implement an aggressive plan of reaching students for Christ.

It seems as if some Christians, though, would rather attack the Nazis with a squirt gun than do evangelism! The dreaded "E word" strikes fear into the hearts of many believers. The most exciting privilege the Lord Jesus has ever given us, to share our faith, can be the most terrifying for some believers. As scary as evangelism sounds, it is an essential beginning point for any person who wants to see students' lives transformed. Your goal is not simply to rearrange Christians but to bring non-believers into the kingdom as a result of presenting the gospel and asking them to respond.

Reaching the Lost or Reorganizing Christians?

During one of the consulting stints I do for different ministries around the country, I met with a large group of denominational leaders who wished to launch campus ministries similar to the ones we had started. Not asked to prepare anything in advance, I had barely walked into the room of twelve men, who were anxiously gathered around a conference table before the rapid-fire questioning began. Sensing where they were coming from, I interrupted and proposed, "What if we started out by me telling you the top ten mistakes I've made in starting college ministries?" As they took pen and pad in hand and waited in anticipation, I launched into number one: "The biggest mistake I've *ever* made in starting a campus ministry was trying to gather all the interested Christians together to launch the work, rather than starting from scratch and focusing on evangelism among non-Christians."

> *"Father, make of me a crisis man. Bring those I contact to decision. Let me not be milepost on a single road; make me a fork, that men must turn one way or another when they face Christ in me."*
>
> **Jim Elliot, missionary who was martyred by the Auca Indians in Ecuador, 1956**

I paused and glanced around, but no one wrote down a thing. Each man had a death stare fastened on me and dared not look at another. There were several seconds of awkward silence, and I knew exactly why. As cruel as it seemed, I had punctured the very plan they had carefully laid out during the hours before I arrived. I tried to explain to this group that the DNA of any ministry is determined by *how* the original core is created and that if the beginning group was not won to Christ through *their personal evangelism*, they would *never* be able to expand the ministry through evangelism.

For the most part, we do what's been modeled to us. The students in that campus ministry were simply going to go out and invite other Christians to their events, rather than penetrate into non-Christian circles with the gospel. Why? That's how they were "won." If those twelve leaders sitting around that table were not willing to focus a year or two in consistent evangelism to lay the foundation for their long-term work, they would end up like so many other groups—just reorganizing and recruiting Christians to various activities for fun and fellowship. Having not received any consulting requests from them since that time tells me I may not have told them what they wanted to hear!

Four Secrets for Winning Students to Christ

What does the chapter title "Persist in Dynamic Evangelism" mean? Checking *Webster's* for the definitions always helps:

persist to go on resolutely in spite of opposition; to remain unchanged; to stand firm

dynamic continuous activity that produces change

It means that evangelism needs to be the cutting edge of your ministry in *all* seasons. You don't *evangelize* for twelve weeks, then *establish* for twelve weeks, and finally *equip* for twelve weeks; but of these three, the engine that pulls your train always needs to be evangelism. As you launch out to share the Good News of Jesus Christ on your campus, try to discover and apply these four secrets:

Secret #1: Open Up the Funnel by Sowing Broadly

Amber was a little shy at first, but she really wanted to represent Christ in her dormitory. She had just returned from a summer training program her ministry had sponsored, and their "back to campus" emphasis helped give her the direction and boldness to plan her work, and then work her plan! She decided that she was going to try to meet every new freshman girl in her dorm as well as each student on her floor. Not only did she always keep her door open with a welcome sign on it, but she made it a point to introduce herself to anyone in the dorm she had not met. She arrived early to help girls move in, made posters for each of the girls' doors with their names on it, sponsored a popcorn and movie night the first weekend, and took three carloads of girls to her church that first Sunday.

Even though most of the other juniors had moved out of the dorm into their own apartments, Amber chose to stay put, and lay her life down for these young freshmen. It wasn't long until she was the ring leader of the entire dorm. Every girl liked and respected Amber, came to her with questions and problems, and wondered what it was that made her such a happy and sacrificial person. Amber started floating the idea of having a Bible study on each of the dorm's three floors. Girl after girl responded enthusiastically, even though Amber did not know where many of them stood spiritually. She identified the two most influential girls on each floor and asked them to host the study in one of their rooms and to help recruit the girls from their floor. Feeling honored to be chosen by Amber, the "dorm mama," they each went to work making posters, spreading the word, cooking up some munchies, and even starting competitions to see who could recruit the most girls to their floor study!

The Holy Spirit Was Penetrating Hearts

By late September, Amber had three full-blown, investigative Bible studies started, averaging eight to twelve girls in each one. Amber recruited Sara, a Christian friend from off campus, to help her round up the girls a few minutes before nine each night, bring in a load of New Testaments to pass out, and then launch everyone into a fascinating discussion on a chapter of John, each week trying to answer two questions: (1) Who is Jesus Christ? and (2) What does He want with me? Amber and Sara worked hard on preparing lead-in questions, involving each girl in the discussion, and pouring out their love and attention on one and all. As she and Sara interceded for each girl every morning, it was obvious the Holy Spirit was penetrating the hearts of many of them by using three powerful tools: (1) the truth of the Word, (2) the prayers of Amber and Sara, and (3) the girls observing the unconditional love Amber and Sara had for them and each other.

Three or four times a week Amber and Sara would treat a different girl whom they sensed God was working in to a cup of coffee, some chit chat, and a chance to hear and understand the gospel message. Over the course of the semester, the two leaders promised each girl the chance to get a customized presentation of how to have a personal relationship with God, and, miraculously, over thirty girls jumped at the opportunity. Amber had taken a step of faith, opened the funnel up very wide by meeting and serving over one hundred girls in her dorm, asked almost forty of them join small-group studies, shared the gospel with over thirty of them, and was now seeing girl after girl open up her heart to the Lord Jesus Christ. It was the most exciting, satisfying experience Amber and Sara had ever had in their entire lives. The Lord was on His way to transforming that campus because a shy little college student decided to put her trust in a big God, walk toward her fears, and pray, share, and love a bunch of young freshmen into the kingdom. Their work was just beginning.

You might be saying, "But Steve, you don't know me. I'm not a people person. I'd be uncomfortable doing what Amber and Sara did." Well, join the club, because we are all stretched when we have to go outside of our comfort zone and meet and love and share with people we don't know. I am still nervous and scared to this day. Is it a matter of gifting, or a decision to make? Read 1 Corinthians 9:19–23 and observe that Paul became *whatever* he needed to be in order to reach others. The question is, Will I be selfish with my life or selfless? There are two things we can learn from Amber:

A. Don't live in a holy huddle

It seems as if the longer people are Christians, the fewer non-believing friends they have. Christian students end up living with Christians; sitting with Christians in class, at meals, and at the library; and even praying for a job where there are all Christians! Their goal each day, after having a morning quiet time, is to attempt to scurry through the day, flying from one Christian friend and activity to the next, hoping to make it home that night *unscathed* by the world!

Amber's story prods you to ask yourself a very important question: Why do you live where you live? Was it a decision made from strategy or comfort? Many believers I know want to find a place where they can have their own bedroom, kitchen, stereo system, and entertainment center. They don't want any interruptions, curfew, or rules. When I see this, I can't help but think about Proverbs 18:1, which says, "He who separates himself seeks his own desire." Now before you get mad at me

> *"A ship in the harbor is safe, but that is not what ships are built for."*
>
> **William Shedd, missionary to Iran, 1915**

for meddling, let me say that if you are ministering on a commuter campus or your whole target group lives in a certain apartment, it may be best that you live at home or off campus. The point is if you and I really are Great Commission Christians, we're going to live in the *most* strategic place in order to impact students for Jesus Christ in the broadest and deepest way possible.

If I were trying to reach students in Austin, Texas, I wouldn't want to live in Denver, right? If I were trying to give my life and the gospel to a particular floor of guys or a fraternity house, why would I stick myself in some apartment miles from campus? I promise that you'll never again get a chance to live in this close proximity with such a large and receptive group of people. Take advantage of it! You'll be living in apartments and houses for the rest of your life; and if you can learn *now* how to walk with Christ and impact others for Him in the midst of a horde of other students, you will have the raw materials to do it anywhere, anyplace for the rest of your life!

I lived in my fraternity house during my college years. Once I finished with school, I moved into a house next to campus with several guys I was discipling. After seminary I came back to be the pastor of students at my college-town home church where we bought a nine-bedroom, four-bath house that backed up to fraternity row. We would have from four to seven guys and gals living and colaboring with us each year as we sought to reach the campus. We built a table that could seat sixteen comfortably and twenty-four if necessary, and it was *always* full. Jim Peterson of the Navigators says, "The most effective evangelism tool you'll ever have is your dining room table." I have seen that truth replayed thousands of times as we fed the body and then the soul with gospel sharing or Bible study sessions after almost every evening meal.

You would think I would mature out of the commune-living stage of my life; and yet now we live in a different college town, once again next to the Greek houses, but this time in a nine-bedroom, six-bath house that accommodates our family, seven college students, and a constant flow of guests! I don't share all this to say you must have a giant house and a bunch of students living with you (that's definitely not prescribed for most!) but simply to encourage you to live strategically. Whether you're single or married, a student or staff person, have a "kingdom reason" for living where you live. Do whatever you can to stand in the gap and insert your life into the group of students God has called you to reach. The supreme model is Jesus, who didn't just shout from heaven or visit us on weekends. God became a man and lived among us for thirty-three years.

B. Meet people and build relationships

The second thing we can learn from Amber is that every person is a divine appointment and it's important to take the first step in meeting other students and extending warmth and kindness to them. I like to use the acrostic "MIGS" (that's the name of the Russian military planes) to describe the process:

1. M-eet someone
    Introduce yourself, remember the person's name, and maintain good eye contact.

2. I-nitiate conversation
   Start with closed-ended questions (yes/no questions) and then move to open-ended. Pick up on any area of interest the person might have and begin to inquire.

3. G-uide the conversation
   As you get to know this person, move the conversation from superficial to deeper, more personal areas. Become a master at asking questions and listening with your eyes and heart.

4. S-tore and review information
   It's a challenge, but after meeting each person write down everything you can remember about each. Review the contacts weekly, and this becomes a prayer list. When you see these students on campus, you will be able to bond with them as you remember details of their lives. It helps you win the right to share the gospel.

Opening up the funnel means trying to meet as many students as you can in your target area(s) and going as deep as you can with each. As people build relationships, some ministries encourage their staff and students to keep a "Top 20" sheet that lists the closest twenty relationships they have with other students (Christian and non-Christian). Not a people person? Become one!

Secret #2: Get Creative as You Share the Gospel

Praying for people, meeting them, loving them, and sharing the Good News of Christ with them are the most fun things you'll ever do. Yes, it's sometimes a little shaky transitioning into a gospel presentation, but once you're discussing the greatest message in all of history, you will not want to be *anyplace* else, talking about *anything* else! Learn and practice a gospel presentation as well as a transition to introduce it. Role play it with Christian friends.

Then try it out on students whose standing you don't know and then on students who you're pretty sure do not know the Lord.

We live in one of the few cultures on the planet where we're uncomfortable talking about religion; and from what I can tell, it's the believers who are a lot more intimidated than the nonbelievers! If you're casual and relational about sharing your faith with others, it will put them at ease as well; but if you're uptight and awkward, it will frighten them away. You might smile warmly, look your friend in the eye, and ask a question like:

A. "Preston, if you could know God in a personal way, would you want to?"
B. "Ali, on a scale of 1 to 10, how sure are you that you're going to heaven?. . . Would you like to know for sure?"
C. "Clark, I've got a little presentation here that I'd love to show you that explains what the Bible says a real Christian is. Mind if I take a few minutes to share it with you?"
D. "Stephanie, I'm trying to learn how to share my faith. I'm wondering if you would allow me to share this little Christian booklet with you and get your response?"
E. "You know, Anna, I don't feel like I've been much of a friend to you. Over the last few weeks/months you've opened up and shared with me all kinds of things about yourself, yet I haven't even told you about the most important thing in my life. May I?"

Are You Able to Ask the Golden Question?

What is the most important question you could ever ask someone; the one they will never, ever forget; the one that could change their eternal destiny? This golden question I refer to is difficult to ask because our throats start to constrict, our tongues get dry, our eyes begin to dart, and our hearts pound faster. It takes

the fuel and the flame ♦

courage to explain the gospel to someone, answer his questions, gulp, and form these words, "Wes, . . . would you like to invite Jesus Christ into *your* life as your Lord and as your Savior . . . *right now*?" If there was ever a time to keep your eyes fixed on his, if there was ever a time to zip the lip and not try to rephrase or answer for him—now is that time! Yes, there might be three or four seconds of awkward silence that feel like eternity, but never again during his lifetime will the Spirit of God have a better opportunity to bring him face to face with a holy and loving Messiah who is asking him to make a decision.

> *"Behold, I stand at the door and knock; if anyone hears My voice and opens the door, I will come in."*
>
> **Revelation 3:20**

I believe the main reason many students have never received Christ into their lives is because no one has ever *individually* shared the gospel with them in a personal way, asked the golden question, and then had enough courage to *wait* for a response. In fact, nine out of ten students who I ask, "If you could know God in a personal way, would you want to?" always answer in the affirmative.

Don't just go after the student who "looks" interested or friendly. Sometimes the moral, good guy or girl is a lot further from the kingdom than the partier, because the good girl (even though she may have grown up in church) thinks deep down her works are somehow going to help her get into heaven. The partier, on the other hand, *knows* he's a lost sinner and is trying to drown his fears and insecurities in constant immoral activities. The successful athlete or Greek student may appear to have it all together, but deep down she needs a group, letters on her jacket, a sports car, a steady date, or a packed schedule to feel good about herself. I have beat my head against the wall trying to get the "good guy" to realize he's really lost so we can help him get saved, while a twenty-minute conversation with a campus hellion is sometimes all it takes for him to make a 180-degree turn around and become the new campus evangelist!

Fit the Approach to the Group

As you look at the characteristics of the people group you're trying to reach, pray for understanding and creativity as you customize a strategy to reach them. If the group is into movies, start an investigative group where you watch a popular film clip, then springboard into passages and discussion that relate to the scene. If you're trying to reach athletes, design a retreat where there is a lot of competition mixed in with serious talks. In order to reach internationals, who love to gather, eat, and discuss important topics, we created "FAN Night" (For All Nations), but it had to be on Friday nights, because that was the only time they were willing to participate in an activity that wasn't related to their studies.

> *"Our job is not to create interest as much as it is to discover it. Some people are exposed to the gospel, but not yet interested. Some are interested, but haven't been exposed yet."*
>
> **Mike Hearon,**
> **Campus Outreach**

Years ago, there was a very popular sorority on the SMU campus that was full of beautiful and very committed Christian girls. They made a pact with one another before the school year began to date *only* Christian men. Of course, they were being asked out right and left by all kinds of guys, but their standard response was always, "I'm sorry, but I can't go out with you because I have made a commitment to only date committed Christians." This not only created frustration in the minds of many an SMU male but also curiosity. So, many would ask, "Why not? What do you mean?" and the girls would then coordinate an appointment between the date-asker and one of her Christian guy friends who would share the gospel with the mystified student. Reports were this creative "bait and switch" strategy had profound results on the student body!

Secret #3: Gathering Groups for Evangelism Is Effective

Sowing broadly by sharing your faith in small and large groups can give you instant exposure to greater numbers of students as you seek to open up your funnel as wide as possible to see where God is working. Here are three ways to gather collegians for an initial input into their lives:

A. Team meetings

I use this phrase loosely, because it could apply to any affinity group you're able to gather for a short talk and an opportunity to respond. It may be an athletic team, pledge class, dorm floor, campus club, or other interest group. You've asked and been given permission to come to one of their meetings to either give a "salt talk," designed to make them thirsty for spiritual things, or an evangelistic message with a chance to receive Christ.

Recently, a student and I did a ten-minute salt talk during the weekly meeting of a fraternity on our campus. We introduced ourselves, gave a short address on what it means to be a balanced man (physically, socially, mentally, and spiritually), shared part of my testimony, explained the investigative Bible study we were starting for them, and then had them fill out cards that rated their interest level. The forty guys filled out the cards that asked them their name, phone number, e-mail, and classification. But they were also asked two other questions: "On a scale of one to ten (highest) how sure are you that you will go to heaven?" and second, "On a scale of one to ten how much do you want to be in this weekly small group-study?" We gathered all the cards to use as evangelistic contacts and conversation starters the rest of the semester.

We told the men we only had eight spots in the study, that the ones who wanted to be in it the most would probably get in, and that we would call them the next week. We chose the most influential guy in the chapter (because we knew he would help recruit the others) along with seven more men who wanted to be in the study the most but who also had marked between one and seven on the "How sure are you that you're going to heaven?" question (we wanted honest guys who were spiritually open). We called each of them personally, and all eight said yes, and showed up a few nights later for the investigative group study.

B. Investigative group

Call it whatever you want to, but create a tool that you can invite non-Christians (and students who you don't know where they stand) to come and join. Make it selective, fun, and full of truth.

1. Be selective

Those eight fraternity guys came to *each* investigative study because they felt special, chosen, and because they were asked individually to make a four-week commitment to *their* Bible study, not mine. We had developed in them a "privilege mentality," and they felt fortunate to be among the eight who were chosen out of the forty guys present at the large meeting. I can't tell you how many Bible studies we (and others) have tried to start that were for "everyone on the floor" or "everyone in the chapter" or "everyone on the team." Almost without exception they bombed, because if the study is for *everybody*, in some sense, it's for *nobody*. Even though flyers were put up and announcements were made, there was no individual commitment asked from anyone, no one felt special or selected, and the least little activity that the affinity group plans automatically cancels the study for that week. Promises made, promises broken on the part of well-intentioned participants can leave the leader discouraged, even bitter. Plus, the whole feel is that the participants are doing us, as the leaders, a favor by coming to *our* Bible study. It dissolves into a form of begging and badgering that, if we were really honest with ourselves, we knew was doomed from the start.

2. Have fun

If possible, pick a room to meet in that is right in the

heart of the affinity group you're targeting. Ask one of the more influential students who has a centrally located room to host the study and even help get everyone there on time. Don't ask this person to prepare for this study, only to come and contribute to the discussion. Greet them, enjoy them, build rapport, provide some refreshments, and let them know you like hanging out with them. Initially, you might want to choose a topic that meets a felt need (such as relationships, time management, how to be successful, etc), rather than some deep, theological issue. Make the duration of the study four to six weeks, and finish each session on time to allow time to catch up on the latest news. One dorm floor study I started took place in a packed out room of twelve to fifteen guys and resembled a day-time talk show where the host, guests, and audience are mixing it up so much you think a brawl is about to break out! I would drop by their rooms on the off nights and weekends to hang out, play some touch football, and discern where each man was spiritually. One by one, I would share the gospel with each man as I saw him responding to the Word or to me, always looking for the hungry, faithful ones that I could challenge to the next commitment level.

Jonathon, a senior corpsman at Texas A&M and involved with the Navigators, has done a great job of creatively sowing the gospel among sixteen freshmen in his corps unit. He prepares a big Sunday-evening meal at his apartment, where all the guys get away from the dorm, eat a home-cooked meal, and have an investigative Bible discussion. The Nav staff man adds, "Jonathon is tenacious in initiating new conversation with other students and has had a lasting impact with young cadets in his squad." He's seeking to truly be a good soldier in Christ Jesus!

3. Include the truth

My pastor always said that it is a sin to make the gospel boring. I agree! In this type of group, no one falls asleep, everyone gets to talk, and there are a ton of laughs that go along with serious periods of listening. In the midst of all this affection, though, you must have some good, solid direction too. Whether you're going through a chapter of John each week, using some end-times discussion materials you found, or are hitting on different moral issues, you must weave the Word of God into each session. The Holy Spirit promised He would use the Scriptures, not pithy stories or newspaper stats, to penetrate hearts. Hebrews 4:12–13 gives us all the ammunition we need:

> For the word of God is living and active. Sharper than any double-edged sword, it penetrates even to dividing soul and spirit, joints and marrow; it judges the thoughts and attitudes of the heart. Nothing in all creation is hidden from God's sight. Everything is uncovered and laid bare before the eyes of him to whom we must give account. (NIV)

As you and your group begin dissecting different passages, you may have skeptics who deny the truth or power of the Word. That's okay; don't try to prove the Bible is from God. Like a lion, turn it loose—it can take care of itself! A student can defiantly claim, "This passage can't really teach that Jesus is the only way!" And like the Hebrews verse just quoted, the double-edged sword is piercing her soul and spirit, thoughts and attitudes. She can deny the living and active Word all she wants, but each thrust of this powerful weapon is performing radical surgery—one life at a time, one verse at a time.

The key to a good Bible discussion? Well-prepared and well-asked questions by the leader. Work hard to bring thought-through, carefully-worded, open-ended questions that will really stimulate the group to talk about and apply the truth. "Did Jesus love His disciples?" will get a lot of blank, even embarrassed stares, because people feel stupid responding to such an obvious question. But "Tell us some ways that Jesus showed love to His disciples" is a much better conversation starter. Learning how to launch an excellent question, then guiding the discussion, and summarizing what you've discussed is an art form. This "launch, guide and summarize" method of Bible study discussion is found in the appendix. Read it, absorb it, use it, and have a blast as you see God use you and His Word to transform lives from the inside out!

C. Large group meeting

You may want to jump-start some ministry momentum by hosting a large campus-wide gathering like Kraig, a counselor at Kanakuk Kamp, did his junior year. At the end of the summer he went back to his campus, Texas Christian University, with a burden to impact the whole school for Jesus Christ. He contacted all the leaders of the ministries and campus churches to organize a huge evangelistic event called After Dark. He invited Joe White, president of Kanakuk Kamps, to give an evangelistic drama and message and invited a Christian artist to sing. Chris and the leaders prayed (a two-week, twenty-four-hour pray chain was set up!), recruited, and trusted God for big things. Over 1,100 students came that night (one sixth of the entire campus!), and as Joe gave the invitation, hundreds streamed down the aisles to make a decision and fill out information cards. Talk about follow up! Kraig and the other ministries divided up the cards, then spent the next several weeks praying for and meeting with the students, seeking to get them into small groups, plugged into local churches, and started in the growth process.

If you've got the necessary core of leadership to pull something like this off, it can be an incredible way to sow and harvest all at once. It takes a lot of planning and effort, but the real work begins once the event is finished and hundreds of students need someone to nurture, to guide, and to build into their lives. My belief is that God will not give us any *more* fruit until we take care of the fruit He's *already* given us! Kraig had a strategy and the vision and student leaders to make it a reality. He could see the incredible hunger in students' lives and was determined to leave behind a spiritual legacy. May his tribe increase!

Secret #4: Make the Message Simple and Transferable

Whether you read through a booklet with a student, draw out a gospel diagram, or use only the Bible going from verse to verse, come up with a plan and be able to share it clearly and simply. Don't add any pet doctrines, extra rules, or your version of American Christianity to the presentation. The power is in the message. Paul says in Romans 1:16, "I am not ashamed of the gospel, because *it is the power of God* for the salvation of everyone who believes: first for the Jew, then for the Gentile" (NIV). When I shifted my emphasis from trying to persuade people to simply trusting the power of God and the gospel to change hearts, I saw dramatic results.

Isn't it amazing that in the same amount of time it takes you to study for one, single test, you could learn to use a tool to share the gospel with others for the rest of your life? Most Christians, though, don't have a clear and confident method of presenting the gospel, and before you can learn two ways to share the gospel, you need to have one. A woman once criticized Bill Bright's method of approaching others and reading through the *Four Spiritual Laws* with them. After patiently listening to her tirade, he kindly asked what method she used. The woman got flustered and finally admitted she didn't really have one. Dr. Bright smiled, then said, "Well then, until you can give me a better method, I'll just stick with the one I've got!"

Don't Make Your Students Climb Mount Everest!

One of the gospel presentations I love to draw out for people is the bridge illustration, where Jesus Christ is shown to be the sole link between God and man. The only problem with this approach is that I use fifteen to sixteen different verses, plus a host of illustrations, questions, and stories. I might wow them with my knowledge and fancy transitions, but when I choose to witness like this, I may be adding but I'm not likely multiplying. Let me explain: whether it's the student I'm sharing with or the one I brought with me to observe, they both are thinking, "Man, I could never memorize and explain all this to someone! And how would I answer if someone asked me a question?"

The more complex the presentation we use in our witnessing and discipling efforts, the less we will be able to pass it on to others. Just because you may have years of experience and skills stored up doesn't mean you have to unload them all each time you have the chance! Think long term and mainly use simple and transferable concepts, methods, and materials that can be easily learned *and* reproduced by your young disciples. The keys for them getting started ministering personally are: seeing how it's done, believing they can do it, and then taking baby steps to apply it. Help them be successful by making the initial climb a gentle hill, rather than a sheer cliff up Mount Everest!

I just got a report on our ten-week Colorado Summer Training Project, where they trained the students to share the gospel at their jobs in a relational way and all day on Saturdays in a more intentional way. Each student was trained not only to share the gospel at least once each Saturday in the parks and streets of Summit County but also to ask for a decision after the presentation. The project decided to keep track of how many D.O.'s (Decision Opportunities) they gave folks during the summer. Out of 102 project students, almost 1,000 D.O.'s were given with 104 people praying to receive Christ. I don't know if every one of those decisions was genuine, but our folks did the best they could to follow up with them. The greatest effect may have been on *our* students, as they broke through the barrier of fear that paralyzes so much of Christian witnessing. This was the first time some of

> NOTE:
> There is a correlation between how many students you share the gospel with and how many become Christians!

them had ever shared the gospel, stirred up enough courage to ask the golden question, and then endured those few seconds of agonizing silence while the Holy Spirit went to work!

My Personal Testimony

You may call this kind of witnessing confrontational, and I grant you, it is by no means the most effective way to win to Christ students who will really stick with their commitment over the long haul. But even though this appears to be a "love 'em and leave 'em" style of evangelism, it can have a potent impact on the hearer as well as the teller. I actually became a Christian in an airport as Allen, a Campus Crusade staff member, took me out witnessing during my senior year in high school. As I read the *Four Spiritual Laws* tract to a teenage boy that Saturday morning, I realized I didn't even have Christ in my life! That afternoon I bowed my head and, for the first time, transferred the control of my life from me to Jesus Christ.

Almost every day over the next several weeks, Allen set up appointments for me to meet with many of the other athletes in our high school. As I presented the gospel just like it had been presented to me, a number of young men bowed their heads to receive Christ, and, despite my lack of follow up, are still walking with the Lord to this day. One young football player named Scott was the first guy I shared with—the day after I received Christ. I went through the booklet with him, and when I asked him if he wanted to receive Christ into *his* life, he paused, looked up at me, and said, "But, I'm Jewish!" I had not taken an apologetics course in seminary quite yet, so I shrugged my shoulders and replied, "That's okay!" I was thrilled as he gave his life to the Lord, and, to my knowledge, he is still growing today.

Besides keeping everything simple and transferable, it could be that one of the most fruitful ways you can bring converts into the kingdom is to go out witnessing with students in your ministry who *think* they are Christians and in the process get born again themselves! It's what got my attention! Even though it is great training, you might have a student who is averse to sharing his faith in a setting where you approach someone you don't know or set up an appointment with the purpose of explaining the gospel. Nine times out of ten, his unwillingness is not because of theological or philosophical reasons but because he's allowing fear to control him. I've never met a student who was unwilling to share the gospel during the *planned* times and then took the initiative to share during the *unplanned* times.

Modeling and maintaining a cutting edge of evangelism in your ministry is indispensable if the flame on your campus is going to grow and spread. But if you're not willing to keep pouring on more fuel, gather the "on fire" logs together, and keep fanning the flames, this blaze will smolder and die. If the evangelism spark requires courage, then establishing requires work—lots of hard work! ✦

Discussion and Application Questions

1. What are some things you can learn from the "Terry and Kirk" story?

2. Review the discipleship profiles in chapter 5, then go through the pyramid diagram at the beginning of this chapter and affix *your* estimates as it applies to *your* campus (i.e., how many on your campus, how many "churched ones," etc.). Share your results.

3. What does this exercise tell you about your campus? Where do you fit in the pyramid? Where would you like to be?

4. Review the four E's and the goal of each. Explain in your own words what each of these terms mean:
    A. A convert
    B. A disciple
    C. A disciplemaker
    D. A reproducer

5. Why is evangelism so scary for most Christians? Even though we're scared, how can we be obedient in evangelism?

6. What can we learn from Amber's story? Read 1 Corinthians 9:19–23 and talk about ways you can move from selfishness to selflessness in order to win others to the Lord.

7. Make a list of the top twenty closest relationships you have right now with other students. Make a note as to which campus group they most closely associate with (such as a certain Greek chapter, a dorm, an athletic team, a band, internationals, etc.). Now put a *C* next to the ones you're sure are Christians, an *NC* next to the ones you're pretty sure are non-Christians and a *?* by the ones you're not sure of one way or the other. Share the list with the group. Make some observations about each other's lists!

8. What does Steve say the golden question is? Have you ever asked someone the golden question? Share how it went.

9. Do you know how to share a clear gospel presentation, ask someone to make a decision, and lead them to Christ? If not, would you like to learn how?

10. What are some creative ways we can share the gospel (on a one-on-one basis) this semester with some of the people on our list?

11. What ideas do you have for sharing the gospel through gathering groups of students together?

12. Look at the list you created and determine if there is a campus group or two you want to pray for and to penetrate with the gospel.

13. With that same list, pray and think through which person you want to share the gospel with first, second, third, etc. Plan up to ten people. This will become your prayer/evangelism "Top Ten Most Wanted" list!

Read your lists and pray together that God would give you a love and a burden to obediently share the gospel with many different campus groups and individuals this semester.

103

chapter 7

invest yourself in establishing young believers

b rad was a big, strong, good-looking athlete, who had been one of the most popular and charismatic leaders of the campus ministry he plugged into. But this particular day he was reduced to tears as we huddled at a corner table in the student center. He was about to graduate from college and wanted to confess something to me before he crossed the stage for his diploma.

"Shad," he whispered, "I have led over a hundred guys to Christ since I started here as a freshman."

"That's fantastic!" I responded.

"No, that's *not* fantastic," he shot back. Then gazing off in the distance like he was searching for something he added, "You see, I don't know where a single one of them is."

"What do you mean?" I asked.

"I mean that I took them through the gospel, they prayed the prayer, I patted them on the back, never to be seen again. I have no idea where they are or how they're doing. I feel like I have nothing to show for all my efforts the last four years."

As much as I tried to console my friend, reality was staring him in the face. He had been desperate to develop a movement on the campus while he was there, but it was not to be. As he was nearing the end of his college career, he saw that there was no lasting legacy he was leaving behind. He was a great guy with great intentions, but he didn't have the training, direction, or perspective he needed to make a *permanent* impact during his college years. Leaving that appointment, I took a slow, thoughtful walk back to my fraternity house, determined that during my college years I would focus on building quality more than quantity in my personal life and ministry.

Delivering the Baby Is When the Work Begins

My wife and I have five children, four that were born in the same hospital room and a fifth that we adopted from an orphanage in Ukraine. During each pregnancy she ate all the right foods, we went to all the Lamaze breathing classes, and I even timed all the contractions on the big day. Even though she carried the biggest load (pun intended), it was definitely a team effort, with the help of the doctor and nurses, to endure the eighteen-hour delivery marathon. I remember when we brought our first child into the world and the mixture of joy and relief we experienced. How thrilling it was to snip the umbilical cord, see the nurse clean up little Marietta, and place her on my wife for the very first time.

> *"Neglected children usually become delinquent."*
>
> **Dr. Waylon Moore,**
> **author of**
> *New Testament*
> *Follow Up*

What if at that tender moment I were to turn to my wife and the beaming medical staff and exude, "Man, that was awesome! Good job, honey. Good job, everybody! That was quite an experience, but I'm sure glad it's over. Hop up, sweetheart, let's go. We've got a lot to do today, and we need to get out of here. Have a good life, little Marietta! Thanks for making this *so* special. See ya!"

As my wife and I would stroll out the door, waving goodbye to our newborn child left for someone else to care for, the speechless doctor and nurses would turn to one another and angrily spout, "How could *anyone* be so heartless and immature, so lacking in responsibility and foresight to not understand that bearing a child is just the *first* step; caring for and raising her over the next twenty (or more) years is the *next*?"

In the same way, the majority of Christian students I've known over the years were "birthed" in a one-on-one gospel presentation or group meeting during their growing up years but were then left at the hospital with no one to nurture them to spiritual maturity. Their spiritual father or mother put in the prayer and work to bring them into the kingdom but apparently did not invest any more of their time in this precious new life. This stage of a Christian's growth, between convert and disciple, is called "establishing." Here are five prerequisites to help you build into another believer the kind of foundation that God and others have built into you.

Five Prerequisites to Building Disciples

Prerequisite #1: Follow Up Is Essential

May I tell you why most Christians are spiritual orphans? It's because many of us want the glory and excitement of seeing a person come to faith, but we're not willing to pay the price of following up with them. Proverbs 14:4 spells out this same principle in farming terms: "Where there are no oxen, the manger is empty, but from the strength of an ox comes an abundant harvest" (NIV). If you want a harvest, you need to have strong oxen who will pull the plow so you can plant the crops. But if you have oxen, you'll need to give them a place to sleep and eat and . . . poop. Each day you'll have to come in behind

> *"Revival may be under way in your community, yet it may lose momentum, wither and die without effective follow up."*
>
> **Dawson Trotman**

those dirty, smelly animals with your "pooper scooper" and clean up behind them. It's a dirty job that must be done, and nobody wants to do it! Abundant Harvest = Strong Oxen = Messy Manger is the kind of mathematical principle you must understand if you are to produce the kind of deep and lasting spiritual fruit you yearn to see through your ministry.

Dr. Waylon Moore, in his excellent book, *New Testament Follow Up*, gives these estimates from his fifty years of ministry: 25 percent of Christians never pray, 25 percent never read their Bibles, 95 percent have never led someone to Christ, and 99 percent have never followed up with a new believer to establish him or her in faith! We want the glamour and praise of being able to tell others about how many decisions were made at last night's meeting, but we avoid the dirty, smelly work of coming in behind these baby Christians and cleaning up their messes! Some ministries with huge numbers at their meetings may *look* impressive, but if you examine them closely you might not find the depth they should have.

When a student bows her head and heart to take Jesus Christ as her Savior and Lord, she becomes a child of God. Born again, yes, but nevertheless a spiritual infant. Peter talks about these vulnerable, impressionable converts in 1 Peter 2:2: "Like newborn babies, long for the pure milk of the word, so that by it you may grow in respect to salvation." As the spiritual blinders fall off for the new Christian, she sees a whole new world full of exciting possibilities—and lurking dangers. Just as you wouldn't think about leaving a baby by herself in a car or grocery cart for even a minute, we should have the same sense of stewardship for our young converts. The reason Peter felt so strongly about following up with new believers is because Jesus, after His resurrection, pulled him aside and charged him three times, saying that if Peter *really* loved Him, he must "tend My sheep!" (John 21:15–17). We can *say* we trust God to work in new converts' lives and turn a blind eye to their needs, but how you pray *for* them and what you do *with* them will be critical in their initial development.

the fuel and the flame ♦

The First Twenty-Four Hours

The first twenty-four hours of a new Christian's life are critical. The Navigator booklet, *Beginning with Christ*, a tool I go over with new converts the very first day of their new life, lists the five things Satan will immediately begin whispering in their ear:

A. Regarding assurance of salvation: "You don't think you are saved and your sins are forgiven just by believing and receiving Christ? Surely that is not enough!"

B. Regarding answered prayer: "You don't think God is really personally interested in *you*! He's so far away and concerned about more important things. Surely you don't think he'll hear your prayers, much less answer them!"

C. Regarding victory over sin: "You have life alright, but you are a weakling and will not be able to stand against temptation!"

D. Regarding God's forgiveness: "Now, you've done it. Aren't you supposed to be a Christian? Christians don't do those things!"

E. Regarding God's guidance: "You don't really think God has a special plan for your life, do you? Why bother with Him? Make your own way!"

> *"The decision is 5 percent, following up the decision is 95 percent. Salvation is free, but discipleship costs everything we have."*
>
> **Billy Graham**

You can be sure that the enemy and even some of their non-Christian friends have been planting these questions and doubts in the fertile young mind of your new convert. Even though it was good seed that was scattered and planted in Matthew 13, only one of the soils actually survived and went on to be fruitful. I'm certain you'd like to have a better ratio than that!

Follow Up Essentials

Here are a few of the things I like to do with a new Christian as soon as I can after their salvation decision:

A. Present the gospel

What? you ask! You thought we had already done that. Correct! But, one of the best things you can do for a brand new Christian is to go back over, very slowly, point by point, verse by verse, the gospel message. You might even consider using a second illustration or tool this time (for example, if you used the bridge illustration the first time, use the *Four Laws* now to come at the gospel from a different angle). Make sure the new convert *fully* understands what they've done.

B. Memorize the assurances

Purchase the *Beginning with Christ* packet from the Navigators, or come up with your own verses. But get your new brother or sister in Christ to start hiding God's Word in his or her heart. The devil will go running if he or she has memorized verses on the assurance of salvation, answered prayer, victory over sin, assurance of God's forgiveness, and His guidance. For example, Billy Graham once said that he believed up to 95 percent of church leadership in America *does not* have an assurance of their salvation. If we are relying on feelings, experiences, or our good works to give us assurance, we will never obtain it. But if we study and believe the promises God makes in His Word, we can forever be sure we belong to Him.

C. Quiet time

If possible, try to have a quiet time with the new convert the very next morning. Show him how to read a chapter from the Bible, write down some thoughts, and make a daily application. Help him make a prayer list, making sure you slip in the final item on his sheet—praying for his roommate's salvation. Why not start now in helping him have an outward focus?

D. Invite them over for a meal

Bring the new convert into the fellowship of your family or friends as soon as possible. Let her see that she has a new set of folks she can hang with. Invite her over for dinner and bring her to your church. She's at a very vulnerable stage, trying now to determine which group she's going to identify with primarily.

E. Help them identify with Christ

The two biggest hurdles a young believer faces are being able to tell his non-believing buddies about his decision and breaking off the old sinful activities he engaged in. I'm not necessarily recommending this for everyone, but many times we have addressed this problem by asking a new Christian in front of his old buddies "Hey, why don't you tell these guys what happened to you Wednesday night?" As cruel as it may seem, popping that question to an unsuspecting new Christian did him a huge favor. Once he fully identified with Christ in front of his old friends he was much less likely to join them in old sinful habits—even if just out of sheer embarrassment!

Prerequisite #2: Each Individual Has Infinite Worth

Most of us, especially us boys, were pretty mischievous growing up. I could not resist walking by a newly poured sidewalk without looking both ways, pressing my hand in, and writing my initials in a corner. If one of the construction crew didn't catch it within the first two to three hours, it was there to stay! To this day, I still show my kids a signature I left thirty years ago!

In like fashion, new Christians are just like wet cement. Most don't have any idea what a real Christian is supposed to think and do and be, and as a result, they take their cues from the other believers around them. Whatever level of commitment and character they observe in the first three, six, or nine months is what they come to believe the Christian life is. That's why it is so important that you take the lead in helping form and shape their values and convictions—before the cement hardens! If you emphasize daily quiet time, they will. If evangelism is a daily way of life for you, they will adopt it also. If you spend a lot of time with TV or computer games, guess what? So will they! You truly reproduce after your own kind during this oh-so-impressionable stage.

A study done by Cornell University a few years back revealed that up to 80 percent of a child's beliefs, values, and self-esteem is formed by age six. If this is true, shouldn't we as parents want to be there during these early years as the primary influence in their lives? And yet, statistics show that most parents instead choose to work and put their children in day care, thus relegating the best part of their children's day to an hourly worker, who may be working there next month, or may not. Just as our young children are like wet cement, waiting to be formed, so are our young converts. Consistent, individual attention is key to helping them begin their new lives right and giving them a healthy long-term perspective of what a New Testament Christian *really* looks like.

Don't Rely on the "Discipleship Pipeline"

Don't just point new Christians to large meetings or retreats, hoping that somehow they'll find their way. The typical M.O. (mode of operation) for Christian ministries and churches is to create what I call the "Discipleship Pipeline," where, sitting at our desks, we formulate a master plan on how to make disciples through our ministry structure. We organize small and large groups, weekend retreats, and maybe even a Christmas conference or summer training program, all accompanied with training materials and promotional brochures. With all the programs and leaders in place, all we have to do is dump the new Christians and visitors into our neatly planned pipeline, confident the flow of activity and influence will carry them along and at the end of the year—presto!—a disciple pops out. We pat ourselves on the back for having found the formula to mass produce committed Christians from a distance, where we never really have to get our hands dirty by getting involved *personally*!

I know all about this, because I too have been guilty of creating this kind of well-oiled ministry machine, which can be a cheap, man-made substitute for the life-on-life investment that Paul exhorted Timothy to major in: "The things which you heard from me in the presence of many witnesses, entrust these to faithful men who will be able to teach others also" (2 Timothy 2:2). The word *entrust* here is a banking term that might better be translated as *deposit*. Paul's advice for Timothy was to find faithful individuals (who will teach others also) and dial the combination locks on the treasure vaults of their hearts, then deposit into these faithful ones the most precious things from Timothy's life and ministry.

The truth is, all of us are limited and have to be careful about who we choose to invest ourselves in. Some disciplers can personally give themselves to five, six, or even seven individuals. When one man told me he was discipling twenty students, I was tempted to enter him into the *Guinness Book of World Records*, since he far surpassed the Son of God, who discipled only twelve while He was on earth—and one of those bombed out! Don't feel bad if you only have the time, training, or gifts to disciple one or two, rather than six, twelve, or twenty! As one of my mentors in life, businessman Bill Smith, told me, "Steve, if you take care of the

> **Don't try to be a ministry machine!**
>
> *"If your output exceeds your input, your upkeep will be your downfall!"*
>
> **Leroy Eims, author of *The Lost Art of Disciplemaking***

depth of your life and ministry, God will take care of the breadth!" Good advice from one of my elders who's been building disciples for twenty-plus years.

The Potential of Just One Student

Are you able to look deeply into the eyes of a single student and see the world won to Christ? Is it people or programs you're focused on? It's intoxicating to have big crowds at your weekly meetings, but don't let that blind you to the real work of the ministry—pouring the life of Christ into one student at a time. What is the worth of just *one* individual? Would Jesus have died for you if you were the only human on earth? You're *so* valuable that He spilled His blood and gave His life in exchange for yours.

> "*Some men see things as they are and say, 'why?' I dream of things that never were and say, 'why not?'*"
>
> **Robert F. Kennedy**

To chain yourself each weekend to a few starry-eyed freshmen in your Bible study requires you to say no to your own agenda and rights, and adopt the conviction Jesus possessed as He chained Himself to hordes of sinful mortals for thirty-three years. If perspective asks, "What do I see?" then conviction asks, "What will I do?" Gaining the perspective of looking at each student not as a problem but as incredible potential will cultivate a conviction where we'll do *anything* to help another person grow in her relationship with Christ. As I write this, I am filled with excitement for those of you on the verge of taking *personal responsibility* for the Great Commission—to "make disciples of all the nations." Let's keep going!

Prerequisite #3: Major in Building the Basics

We started off this book by talking about laying a foundation in our own lives to be the kind of man or woman God can use to permanently impact others for Christ. Now is the time to take those same qualities, convictions, and disciplines and pass them on to others. As much as we would like to, we cannot give them something we do not possess ourselves. My church in college had an awesome circuit of guest speakers coming through on a regular basis, always bringing the latest and greatest "secret key" to the Christian life. I would walk out on a spiritual high after hearing each one, determined to apply the mystical principle I had learned. One month it was the exchanged life, and the next it was finding my spiritual gifts, and then it was fasting and praying for hours a day. I finally realized that the Christian life is not chasing after exotic doctrines or experiences but simply knowing Christ and making Him known in a deeper, more consistent way.

The Wheel Illustration

Here is one illustration that many laborers have used over the years as an evaluation tool and guide, called The Wheel. Shown below, it was originally introduced by the Navigators in order to

do a "Discipleship Diagnosis" on a believer, revealing strengths as well as areas of need. For millions of Christians, The Wheel has provided a clear-cut model of what it means to live a balanced, Christ-centered life.

A. Lordship of Christ (Galatians 2:20; 2 Corinthians 5:17)

The new convert may initially be enamored with you and your vision, but your job is to wean him off of you so that his affection is fixed on Jesus Christ alone. As a college student, Jim White of the Navigators put his hand on my shoulder one day and interceded: "Jesus, I pray that Steve would fall totally in love with you, from the top of his head to the bottom of his feet." Christ sitting on the throne of our heart every moment of every day forms the hub of our wheel, where all the power originates and connects to our lives. We don't live *for* Christ, rather "to live *is* Christ," which is what Paul's perspective was. Dave Dawson, author of *Equipping the Saints*, defines Lordship as, "Giving back to God the controls of my life so that He may use me to accomplish and fulfill His will through me." Pray every day that the young believers you're working with dethrone themselves, their own dreams and idols, and keep King Jesus in His rightful place.

B. Obedience to Christ (John 14:21; Romans 12:1)

If the hub of the wheel is Jesus Christ, then the rim represents us, the obedient Christians. Our job is simply to abide in Christ and let His love and power flow through us as we become more like Him. Obedience puts legs on our faith, and as we model this to those we are trying to help grow, they will understand that it is not only our obligation to obey, but our privilege. The warm, fuzzy feelings your young convert may have are great; but help them understand that according to God's math, love doesn't equal feelings, love equals obedience. Their daily willingness to say no to the world, the devil, and their own flesh will show and strengthen their love for Christ. Teach them, though, that no one can live this kind of life in his or her our own strength but *only* through the daily filling and empowerment of the Holy Spirit.

C. Word of God (2 Timothy 3:16–17; Joshua 1:8)

There are four spokes on this wheel that connect the person and power of the Lord Jesus Christ (the hub) to us (the rim). The two vertical spokes deal with our relationship with God, while the two horizontal ones deal with our relationships with others. The foundational spoke is the Word of God, the pillar that all the others are based upon. From day one each Christian needs to begin nourishing themselves from Scripture—reading, studying, memorizing, and meditating on its commands, promises, and principles. Bring new Christians to a Bible-preaching church as well as a weekly small-group study, where they prepare beforehand and discuss their findings and applications with other growing Christians. I have watched in awe as my wife has spent the last twenty years recruiting college girls to small-group studies and then trusting God to use His Word to radically transform them.

D. Prayer (John 15:7; Philippians 4:6–7)

If the Bible is how God talks to us, prayer is how we talk to Him. Start meeting with these young Christians in daily quiet times to build their intimacy and consistency with Christ, maybe using the excellent pamphlet, *Seven Minutes with God.* Teach them the CATS acrostic of (1) confession, (2) adoration, (3) thanksgiving, and (4) supplication as they develop organization and discipline in their secret times with the Lord. Teach them to pray for small things, for big things, for others, for the world, and to pray conversationally in groups. As you take prayer walks together around the campus, lifting up

> *"It takes six weeks to build a habit."*
>
> **Bill Smith, author of**
> *Quiet Time*

different groups and individuals, you will build a burden to see other students give their lives to Christ. If the young believer will start now to make prayer and the Word their daily anchor, they'll have a much better chance of surviving the storms of life and following through on these early commitments.

E. Fellowship (Ecclesiastes 4:9–10; Hebrews 10:24–25)

The key to success in our horizontal spokes is to make the vertical spokes the priority in our lives. God made us to be worshipers and workers, but in that order! It may only take a spark to get the fire going, but a burning log will die out if it is taken from the blaze and set aside. Ecclesiastes 4:9–10 teaches that "Two are better than one because they have a good return for their labor. For if either of them falls, the one will lift up his companion. But woe to the one who falls when there is not another to lift him up." Try to surround that young Christian with the type of believers you desire your friend to become like. As a young Christian, I attended two prayer groups: one that met weekly to casually pray for their grades and boyfriends or girlfriends and the other met each morning at 5:30 to weep over the lost souls in their dorms and for the internationals on campus. I'm sure you might be able to guess which group had a greater effect on me! There will be some devoted believers you'll want this growing Christian to rub shoulders with. But there may be some lethargic ones you'll want to steer your young disciple away from!

F. Evangelism (Romans 1:16; Matthew 4:19)

Unless you begin early and maintain a steady diet of planned and unplanned witnessing with the Christians you are trying to disciple, evangelism will probably never become part of their spiritual DNA. Some student leaders, staff people, or volunteers *talk* about the importance of witnessing, but exhortation without demonstration always causes frustration!

This is almost always the weakest spoke of the four, because many people say, "I'm just uncomfortable witnessing." Well, it wasn't very comfortable for Jesus to hang on that cross, and He certainly didn't do it to give us a salvation message that we would just keep to ourselves. Teach them how to give their personal testimonies and a simple gospel presentation, and then give them plenty of opportunities to share it in one-on-one and group settings. If you choose to start working with a student who has been a dormant Christian for a while, usually the only way to jackhammer the hardened cement in his life is to get him in different witnessing situations. Then and only then will he realize, "Maybe I'm not as mature as I thought. I want to be more teachable so I can learn how God can start *really* using me!"

> *"Most Christians think prayer and evangelism are electives for those wanting 'advanced placement courses.' They're not. They are core courses, required of every Christian."*
>
> **Ken Wilson, pastor, Fellowship Bible Church, Conway, Arkansas**

Consider using The Wheel during your prayer and planning times. Every week, evaluate each person you're trying to establish and create a specific action plan to strengthen the person's hub, rim, or one of the spokes. As this young believer grows deeper and more consistent in each aspect of the wheel, she will be moving closer and closer to being what Jesus calls "a disciple."

Prerequisite #4: Use Groups to Help Establish Believers

Never underestimate the power of peer influence in the lives of college students. Many times the only reasons they will go somewhere and do something is because of who else will be there or how much fun it will be. All of us are like that. We want to be part of a group that gives us direction and affection; a group that meets felt needs as well as real needs, and finally, a group we are proud to identify with and bring our friends to. As you seek to help establish young believers, try to get them to come to a regular large-group meeting of college students, a small-group Bible study, and a weekend conference or retreat.

A. Large groups

Of course the most critical large group you need to get young believers involved in is a good local church, and most college towns have several excellent ones to choose from. Introduce your friends to the church leadership, get them enrolled in a Sunday school class, find out what the procedure is for joining and getting publicly baptized, and find a place where you can give some of your time and funds. It won't be long before they start to benefit from the nurture and stability that a congregation provides. For years the staff at University Baptist Church in Fayetteville, Arkansas have been impacting students through their Sunday morning gatherings. They've even designed a worship service for the 800-plus students who come each week, complete with a praise band, testimonials, and excellent Bible teaching. Many of the parachurch campus ministries bring their students to UBC to be encouraged and ministered to.

Greg Matte and his successors have done the same thing through the Breakaway Ministry at Texas A&M where up to 3,500 students gather midweek to hear relevant topics creatively preached from the Bible. Leaders like these in church and parachurch ministries across the country know that students like to gather, socialize, genuinely worship, and discover meaning and direction through God's Word. Chi Alpha, Reformed University Fellowship, and Baptist Student Ministries are a sampling of denominational campus groups that do an awesome job of planning and pulling off high-impact weekly meetings where relationships are built and, more importantly, values are formed. Large-group meetings should not be a substitute for small group and one-on-one discipling but rather a supplement—a created environment that reinforces what they're wrestling with in their small groups. For a fuller explanation of the what, why, and how of starting a regular large-group meeting for your ministry, go to the appendix.

B. Small groups

Small groups are the backbone of your ministry. In some respects, the large-group meeting is a front for what's really going on behind the scenes. If your goal is ultimately to raise up disciples, disciplemakers, and reproducers, then the large-group meeting can be an introduction to your ministry funnel while the small group is a narrowing of it, continuing to raise the level of commitment to see who is interested. Much of Jesus' discipleship took place in the context of a small group. Whether you call it a growth group, vision group, discipleship group, action group, or just plain ol' Bible study, it needs to have a few essential characteristics:

1. A designated leader

Someone will have to take the initiative in planning, recruiting, and leading the small-group study. Don't think you need a seminary degree to do it; the essential ingredients are a love for the students and a love for the Word. Why not ask another laborer on your campus to assist you in your effort? It may be the first time they've ever had a chance to hop into the discipleship process with someone. Remember your goal is not as much to lead and direct as it is to serve and facilitate. Don't view yourself as a teacher but more as a recruiter, challenger, discussion leader, and, most of all, friend.

2. Designated participants

Pray by name for each of the contacts, new friends, new converts, and Bible study participants you spend time with. Determine which students have shown the most interest and have responded to you and/or the truth you've presented thus far. Don't make the small groups for just anybody, but create a set number of spots, usually between three and twelve, that you specifically invite certain students to fill. If possible, start small groups among people who know and like each other and have things in common (i.e., they live in the same dorm, are part of the same team, are all freshmen, are all internationals, are all off campus, are all education majors, etc.).

3. A predetermined purpose

Your goal is not just to have Bible studies, but to move new Christians along the growth process toward becoming disciples of Jesus Christ. If you want, give your group a creative name that will help everyone understand what direction you're headed in. Whether you choose relevant topics, fill-in-the-blank Bible study materials, or just take on a chapter a week from a book of the Bible, make sure your time each week is centered around the study and discussion of the Word. Don't teach or preach during these sessions, instead come prepared with thought-provoking questions that you and your assistant proudly open up one at a time, like beautifully wrapped Christmas presents, and watch with excitement as they devour each question, topic, and passage.

4. Standards

Now you're trying to "up the ante" at each level of commitment to find out who really wants to follow Christ and make a difference for Him. Evaluate each participant's spiritual hunger and faithfulness, and design a growth group with challenging but reachable standards. Three examples of standards might be (1) coming every week for an hour with no preparation, (2) preparing in advance for an hour and memorizing a verse, or (3) preparing three hours, memorizing two verses, and meeting for two hours. It won't take long to see who is going to be faithful to come, to prepare, to participate, and to apply what they are getting in the group. Progressively setting higher standards at each level not only challenges the students but gives you a way to select which ones you really want to invest in.

5. Beginning and ending point
    Always let the students know how many weeks or months the study will last and what time each week the study begins and ends. At this stage of development, I would encourage you to make the study no shorter than six weeks and no longer than a semester, no less than an hour a week and no more than two. Instead of exhausting the participants (and yourself!) with massive year-long commitments or open-ended studies that go past midnight every week, it's better to make the studies shorter, more dynamic, and more exciting each time, making them want to come back for more the next study.

6. Transition to the next level of commitment
    Always be planting what I call "vision seeds" in the minds of your participants. During the group discussion, casually say, "You'll need to know this when _you_ share the gospel," or, "This will be helpful when _you_ lead a study." This lets them know you believe (and expect!) that they will take what you're giving them and pass it on to others. As this study winds down, be thinking about what kind of a group you want to invite the faithful ones to. Give it a different name with higher standards and an always growing commitment to take personal responsibility for the Great Commission.

C. Conferences and retreats

Billy, a full-blooded Native American, enrolled at West Virginia University and immediately began to study all the other world religions to prove that Christianity could not be true. When Billy attended a weekend retreat with other Native Americans, many of whom were committed Christians, he finally admitted his desire to know God, his belief that Jesus was Lord, and his love for other students. His roommates were completely dumbfounded at the change. A couple of years later Billy attended a conference sponsored by Great Commission Campus Ministries, where God clearly spoke to his heart about pursuing full-time ministry. By the end of the event Billy concluded, "If this is my passion and desire, why not? Why wait? I don't want to miss out on the adventure God has for me!" Even though Billy had some lucrative job offers after college, God used these two events to confirm in Billy's heart the direction He had for him. Today, as a GCM staff person, he is influencing many campus leaders, always bringing them to retreats, knowing that the Lord will impact those students' lives just like He did in Billy's.

> *"Community is really important to today's college student. Conferences create a community where students can be motivated to take their faith seriously."*
>
> **Steve Sellers, director of global ministries, Campus Crusade**

This is the reason I try to recruit *every* student I can to these kinds of Christ-exalting events, because they serve as incredible spiritual milestones in young believers' lives! During the conferences and retreats I attended in college, I was exposed to speakers, topics, materials, and, most of all, other students whose radical commitment to Christ motivated me to go to the next level. If it is a prayed-through, well-planned, momentum-gathering event, it will not only take each student to a higher level in their Christian walks, but the whole campus will be impacted as well. As the students from your school come in contact with other students on your campus or other campuses, the melting, shaping, and sharpening begins. They will come back to school with all kinds of new visions, ideas, and plans for their own lives and ministries.

At the conference or retreat try to ask each student questions like: What are you learning? What questions do you have? How are you going to put it into practice? How can I help you apply this to your life or ministry? These kinds of questions can be asked individually or as a group and be accompanied by prayer and planning, seeking God's blessings as you all head back to campus with specific personal and ministry goals. As you know, events like this are notorious for lifting students to a spiritual high only to have them crash and burn back on campus. Don't forfeit all that God did in their lives by neglecting to capitalize on the momentum created. Stay focused the first ten days after the event, meeting with students and helping them to carry through with the specific applications and decisions they made.

Prerequisite #5: Disciples Are Made, Not Born

Disciples Are Made Not Born is the title of a classic book by Walt Henrichsen that I try to take all Christians through in the early stages of their growth. It emphasizes that there isn't a gift of being or making disciples; we are *all* commanded to be a disciple and to make disciples. Each of us will do it according to the level of commitment we have, the amount of time we're willing to give, the kind of training we have received, and flavored by the specific spiritual gifts God has given us. Some will be able to utilize groups of students to begin the process, while others choose to work with individuals. Regardless of our capacity or approach, we will be fulfilling the command to "Go, and make disciples" found in Matthew 28.

The way most Christian workers measure their own (and other's) maturity usually breaks down into three categories. Some of it has to do with personality types or gifting, some with the theology or the training you've received, but all of us tend to view maturity through one of these three lenses:

A. "I am mature based on what I know."

These people's motto, "If you want to grow, then you need to know!" describes their life and ministry. They are readers and thinkers who love to deal in theology, history, and original languages. Their libraries and tape players are full of sermons from noted Bible teachers that feed their belief that if they can just get enough information into their heads, they will somehow be more spiritual and, in turn, be able to emit spirituality to others. As a result, the "discipling" this person carries on involves studying books of the Bible, memorizing Scripture, and reading weighty books on doctrine and apologetics. Now I love all these things, but focusing on these alone in our ministry to others has the danger of creating in us (and our disciples) a legalistic, pharisaical gnosticism. This paralysis of analysis can give us a huge head, yes, but it leaves us with a shriveled heart and feet so small they can't carry us anywhere to apply all this knowledge.

B. "I am mature based on what I am."

These very godly Christians have depth of character in their walks with Christ that is evident to all. It's not their head that they operate from nearly as much as their heart. They put a premium on vulnerability and sharing feelings and struggles. "It is for me to be; it is for God to do" is their mantra. In their introspection, they may focus on solving their (and other's) problems, believing that discipling is really just a subset of counseling. To them, it's all about character and Christlikeness; not information, but transformation from the inside out. It's not gaining knowledge from the past or performing great works in the future that makes them feel that they're pleasing to God, it's about the present. After all,

the fuel and the flame ◆

we're not human *knowings* or human *doings*, we're human *beings*! As much as this kind of emphasis is entirely biblical and certainly needed, this person does run the risk of basing life simply on emotion and experience. This person has a huge and compassionate heart but such tiny feet and a little head that they can't think or walk; they just ooze all over people!

C. "I am mature based on what I do."

These go-getters of the twenty-first century are future-focused visionaries who measure everything by what and how much they do. With their goals and checklists, they think it's not the quality or depth of one's activity and performance that matters as much as the quantity and breadth of it. Theology and counseling are fine, but evangelism, discipleship, and missions are what life is really all about! Decisions are what they're pushing for, and when they do Bible study (if they have time!), observation and interpretation are stepping stones to get to the real objective: application! And it better be specific and measurable so they'll really know if they're growing! This activist may or may not know or feel much, but that's beside the point; because their motivation in the Christian life comes from the will. Secretly making fun of the "knowing" and "being" crowd, these self-appointed leaders may have a minute head and non-existent heart to go with their size-22 feet!

Having read the book to this point, you probably can tell which category I tend to fit in to! Don't be fooled into picking *one* of the three lenses to guide your personal growth or discipling, because the mixture of all three is essential for a healthy, vibrant life and ministry. If you've been so stuck in one of these three ditches that you can't even see out, don't despair. Pastor and author Chuck Swindoll tells us that God is a God of second chances when he shares, "It's never too late to start doing what is right!"

One Old Testament prophet found the right combination

between all three lenses: "For Ezra had set his heart to study the law of the LORD, and to practice it, and to teach His statutes and ordinances in Israel" (Ezra 7:10). I'm sure Ezra naturally had one of the "know, be, or do" bents to his life, but instead of hitting his one note, he chose to have a more balanced approach to his ministry with others. Here were the steps to his philosophy of ministry:

A. He *studied* the law of the LORD.
B. He *practiced* the law of the LORD.
C. He *taught* the law of the LORD.

Ezra is a model on how to use the Scriptures as our authority and message but not worship it or cut it off from personal experience. Instead, we should view it as a guide for becoming more like Jesus and as our marching orders to bring others into submission to Christ and His Word. As you are becoming a disciple and making disciples, work on *knowing* Christ, *being* like Christ, and *doing* what Christ did—laying His life down for the sake of others. Truly, disciples are made not born, and if you want to be used by God to establish new converts and young believers as disciples of Jesus Christ, you, too, will have to lay down your life.

Discussion and Application Questions

1. What can you learn from Brad's story?

2. What are the parallels between physically birthing a baby and spiritually birthing a new convert?

3. What does it mean to "follow up" a new Christian? Why is it so important?

4. Have you ever followed up a new Christian? Tell us what you did. Why have so few Christians ever followed up a new Christian?

5. If you had five follow up appointments with a new believer, what would you do first, second, third, etc. with them?

6. Why do most Christian workers focus on planning and leading large group meetings rather than trying to establish young believers in their faith individually?

7. Why is it so hard to invest a big part of your life to establish just one young Christian?

8. Explain The Wheel. How can The Wheel be used in your life? How can it be used when you are establishing another believer in his or her faith?

9. What is your strongest spoke? Why? What is your weakest spoke? Why?

10. In your opinion, what are the ingredients of a successful small group that could help establish young believers in their faith? Would you want to start one?

11. Do you measure Christian maturity primarily by:
    A. What a Christian knows
    B. What a Christian is
    C. What a Christian does

12. Read Ezra 7:10. How did Ezra combine all three of these points of maturity into his life and ministry? How can you become more balanced in your life and ministry?

13. Think back over the last twelve months. Is there someone you know who is a new or young Christian who could benefit from your spending time with them, seeking to establish them in their faith? Write down their name(s) and share them with the group. When and how will you contact each of these students in the next two weeks?

Read your applications and pray together that God would use you in establishing young believers through one-on-one relationships and small groups.

chapter 8

persevere in equipping the faithful to make disciples

ennifer grew up in a neat Christian family in south Georgia, but as she began her freshman year at Valdosta State University she asked God to give her someone who could help her understand her mission and calling in Christ. The ministry of Campus Outreach (CO) was engaging in their version of "rush week" (recruiting freshmen to get involved with their ministry), and Jennifer happened to meet up with Lisa, a CO staff member. As they got to know each other, Jennifer was drawn to Lisa's fun, personal way of talking with her and freely sharing her faith with others. Jennifer's spiritual hunger and faithfulness were very evident, so Lisa began to pour into her on a regular basis. They would study the Word together, go on evangelism and follow-up appointments, do contact work in the dorms, and start small groups among interested girls.

Jennifer was a woman of application, so everything that Lisa told her and showed her, Jennifer sought to implement into her own ministry. By her senior year, Jennifer had won over twenty women to Christ, had several discipleship groups, and met one on one with numerous girls, equipping them to start evangelizing and equipping also. Now Jennifer is a CO staff member at Georgia College, where over the last few years hundreds of women have come to Christ through Jennifer and the student leaders she has equipped. Through the 12 women she's been training, 121 female students attended their annual Christmas conference, and 50 of those were at their summer-long training program. Looking back, Lisa could have easily passed over Jennifer and focused on meetings and materials, but she chose instead to adopt Jennifer, bind their hearts together, and week after week not just *tell* her how to fulfill the Great Commission but *show* her!

Don't Just *Produce* . . . *Reproduce*!

If the process of bringing someone from a new convert or growing Christian to a disciple is called *establishing*, then the process of helping turn them reproduce that in someone else's life is called *equipping*. Lisa was not satisfied in just helping Jennifer grow in her faith or even learn to witness or lead Bible studies. Lisa wanted Jennifer to do what she was doing: win girls to Christ, establish them as disciples, and then equip *them* to evangelize and establish. By the time Jennifer graduated from college, there were several strong fourth generations in place (i.e., Lisa, Jennifer, Susan, Caroline).

We've talked about how important *investigation* is—finding out about the campus and all the different people groups. We've spent a lot of time discussing *penetration*—how prayer, relationships, and ongoing evangelism are essential to create a beachhead at the heart of your campus. Once God has given you new and growing Christians, *concentration*—helping them get established in their faith—becomes the top priority. In this chapter we move to the stage where you begin to multiply yourself, and *saturation* of the campus with laborers becomes the goal.

Continue to pray, think, and plan how to pursue an annual cycle of (1) investigation, (2) penetration, (3) concentration, and (4) saturation. Each fall you will come back with your fellow "saturators" and begin the process again. It may sound boring or repetitious, but it will be an exciting and life-changing endeavor as you continually provide fresh fuel for the flame.

The key words in the chapter title are persevere, equipping, and faithful:

persevere to persist in an undertaking in spite of severe counter influences, opposition, or discouragement

equipping to furnish for service or action; to make ready by appropriate provisioning

faithful steadfast in affection or allegiance; loyal; firm in unswerving adherence to promises or in observance of duty

It's one thing for you and me to become the fuel God uses to *light* a flame on our campus but quite another if He is going to multiply and spread it. He wants to raise up other students who will stand shoulder to shoulder with you to impact your school for Christ. To reproduce a student laborer who has the same conviction, perspective and "know how" you do is a monumental achievement that—apart from the power and blessings of God—is absolutely impossible!

Every bit of influence Satan has will be thrown at you to disrupt your efforts to *persevere* in this kind of ministry. The reason he will desperately seek to thwart you is that you are on the verge of doubling yourself. You are *equipping* a college student to think like you think, feel what you feel, and do what you do; and in so doing, you cut your job in half. At the beginning you may have felt all alone as you sought to win this world to Christ, but now God has raised up a new partner who will shoulder the responsibility with you. This will never happen, though, unless you recruit, select, and train a *faithful* student, who will be able to teach others also. Let's look at six strategies that will aid you to persevere in training faithful students to become laborers for Jesus Christ.

Six Strategies for Training Laborers

Strategy #1: Recruit to a Vision, Not an Organization

We must recruit to the vision of total dedication to the person and purposes of Jesus Christ, not to any human leader or ministry. The military recruits, colleges recruit, companies recruit, and countless other institutions, industries, and individuals recruit. Every single commercial or advertisement on TV, in magazines, and on billboards is designed to do one thing—recruit us. Whether it's new cars, beauty products, or lite beer, the commercial's objective is to make us think or feel that without a certain product, our lives will not be complete. These PR firms know how to hit our hot buttons, appealing to those deep dissatisfactions within and making us believe we deserve to have our every want and need pampered.

My question is, Everyone else recruits, why don't we? We Christians possess the only true solution to mankind's wants, needs, and dissatisfactions. If Jesus alone is our satisfaction, why aren't we constantly helping others to realize that? Most Christians demote themselves to a position of helplessness by admitting, "I wish I could help others, but only God can change hearts. I'll just pray and wait!" I contend that we can become *co-recruiters* with God in this effort to expose the real needs people have for Jesus Christ and the life He wants to give them.

The Holy Spirit Is a Recruiter

The primary role of the Holy Spirit is that of a recruiter. Many of His activities seem to center around:

A. Showing non-Christians their need to repent of their sin and receive Christ as Savior and Lord.

B. Showing Christians their need to repent of their sin and keep Christ as Lord.
C. Showing Christians their need to grow in Christ.
D. Showing Christians their need to win and build others for Christ.
E. Showing Christians their need to be equipped for service.

As you can tell, the common denominators are "showing" and "need." The Holy Spirit's constant objective is to show us our need. Why? So that we will do something about it! We humans are so self-satisfied that unless an outside force disrupts our comfortable little world, we will obliviously continue toward destruction. Years ago, Dave, a young student I was discipling, came up with this definition of recruiting: "Helping someone see their need to the point where they're willing to do something about it."

> *"And He, when He comes, will convict the world concerning sin and righteousness and judgment."*
>
> **Jesus, describing the role of the Holy Spirit in John 16:8**

By this time in your ministry you may have all kinds of students at different stages of interest and growth. How do you help each person take the next step in their spiritual journey, moving them up the discipleship ladder we presented earlier? Answer: You recruit them! Like an onion, you tenderly peel back layer after layer of pride, self-sufficiency, unteachableness, or ignorance until you finally help them see their need and they're anxious to do something about it.

Whether you are recruiting students to Christ, a small group, a discipling relationship with you, or just an upcoming conference, there are several things you can do as you allow the Holy Spirit to work through you:

A. Pray

Fervently ask God to open the hearts of students to see their need. In Ephesians 1:18, Paul prayed for others that the eyes of their hearts "may be enlightened." Prayer moves the hand of God, and our intercession can have direct impact on others as we shoot prayer arrows from our prayer closet directly to their hearts.

B. Love and serve

If there is any rebellion in the heart of your young recruit, loving and serving them has a way of melting it. Whether their lack of receptivity is due to you or the truth you're presenting, if they sense you really care and have their best interests at heart, ultimately they will listen.

C. Challenge

If, along with praying, loving, and serving, you are continually exposing students to the Word of God, then they are going to open up to your words of encouragement and exhortation. Yes, you need to be modeling what it is you're asking them to do, but it also helps for them to rub shoulders with other committed believers who can influence them.

D. Ask questions

Don't ever tell a student something that you can help them discover on their own simply by asking them questions. Well-worded, non-judgmental questions can be like a scalpel in the hands of a surgeon to cut right where the cancer grows. In the appendix, I have included a list of questions to make Christians hungry and a list of questions to make non-Christians hungry. Look at them, use them, and even come up with your own as you expose spiritual needs in others that you can help meet. Let's admit it, *only* God can reach down into the heart of a young college student and turn it, but many times He wants us, as His ambassadors for Christ, to be His tool.

In this chapter we are talking about equipping and training others to be laborers and, more specifically, disciplemakers. The problem is most of us *think* we are way ahead of where we really are. In two of our ministry's earliest summer training projects, I naively let students pick which project they thought they fit. Project one was for disciples, and project two was for disciplemakers. A large number chose project two, but by the end of the summer we realized that most students were just growing Christians trying to become disciples. In the process, we were able to gently show them they weren't quite as far along as they thought and needed a lot more training!

Soldiers in the Battle Want Training

If a person is not receiving training in her Christian life and ministry, it's probably because she doesn't want to. Plus, if one is not engaged in the spiritual battle, who needs spiritual training? Picture some soldiers at an army base in west Texas during peacetime, and an instructor comes into their class to teach them how to use an M-16 rifle. Chances are, he would have a very difficult time getting the details across to the bored, yawning privates. These soldiers are just in the military to do their stint and get out, and besides, who needs to know how to take apart and put together the rifle when none of them will ever use it in battle? Their teachability quotient (TQ) is very low because they don't see their need.

On the other hand, if the U.S. was suddenly thrust into a ground war in a foreign country and these men parachuted into enemy territory, they would have a completely different attitude. If they were in some hastily dug foxholes with a dwindling weapons supply and an army truck pulled up and a sergeant jumped out and started throwing M-16s into each soldier's hands with only three minutes to teach them how to load and shoot, do you think the men would be a bit more teachable? Of course! Because now they are in the thick of the battle, and their lives depend upon carefully listening to and immediately applying their training!

Strategy #2: Select Students Full of F-A-I-T-H

Thus far this school year, you may have met two hundred new students, had six team meetings, started four investigative groups, hosted two campus-wide evangelistic events, collected four hundred comment cards to follow-up, shared the gospel with seventy-five students, twenty-five of whom have prayed to receive Christ, and placed most of them in follow-up groups! That's all well and good, but what do you do now? How do you determine where, how, and with whom you spend your precious ministry hours each week? How do you narrow the funnel down to discern *which* students you should select to invest more of yourself in? I thought you would never ask!

It may sound exclusive to *select* anyone, because that automatically means you didn't select others. But what it really means is that students, ultimately, select themselves. I dream of working with students who really want to train to be a radical disciple of Jesus Christ. In fact, I was up late just last night with one of the young men leading our ministry, brainstorming about how to create a spiritual frenzy on our campus this school year. Our prayer is that this year the *central* issue on our campus will be Who is Jesus Christ, and what will you do with Him?

How did I pick this twenty-one-year-old fraternity guy to live with me and be one of my key men? I didn't. He picked me. I started two years ago with many guys that I shared with, had in small groups, challenged, recruited, and continued raising the commitment level for. One by one, most of the guys dropped out for one reason or another, but this young disciple hung tough. I picked him because he first picked me! In the final analysis, I am going to give my time and my life mainly to those students who *want* my time and life the most.

To be the best stewards of the gospel, we want to invest in people who will absorb the training we give them and take it as far as possible. The goal of selection is to train and invest in leaders who will be obedient to evangelize and make disciples. True laborers select themselves by consistently showing F-A-I-T-H, a five-letter acronym that will help you and I know what kind of a young man or woman we should be giving the best part of our ministry day to.

A. Faithful

You're looking for someone who will meet you at 2 P.M. in front of the student center, because that's what time the two of you agreed on; someone who will show up at each Bible study prepared, even if he has a big test the next day; a person who takes on the task of leaving the room you met in cleaner condition than he found it; a friend whom you share a personal struggle with and who won't share it with someone else. This student is faithful, reliable, and dependable. He simply will *do* what he says he will do. This was the kind of person that Paul told Timothy to look for in 2 Timothy 2:2 when he said "entrust these to faithful men."

B. Available

College students are notorious for filling up their schedules just so they can feel important and tell people their schedules are really packed out. Jesus told some fishermen to follow Him in Matthew 4:19–20, and they immediately dropped their nets and followed Him. That's availability! Look for students who are willing to be flexible, change their schedules, even give up things in order to meet with you or partake in a spiritual-growth or ministry opportunity. A student can have all the potential in the world, but if she's not prepared to make the time to become what God wants her to become, you will be beating your head against the wall trying to track her down. Let's face it; when someone says, "I don't have the time," what she's really saying is "I don't want to," because we all make time for those things we *really* want to do. Right?

C. Initiative

It's hard to steer a parked car, and that's exactly what some students are like. As much as you pray for them, challenge them, and bring them along as you do ministry, nothing seems to get *them* to take initiative in their own lives or ministries. Look for students who are doers, not just talkers, who will focus on accomplishing the task, rather than the possibility of failure. Look for students like David, the Old Testament teenage shepherd and giant killer. If you pour your life into someone who doesn't want to take what you've given them and pass it on, it's strictly addition, not multiplication, you've engaged in. God told us to be fruitful and *multiply*!

D. Teachable

Does the student you've selected want to spend time with you and even seek you out? Is this student open to you pointing out areas of his life that need work? Proverbs 9:8–9 says a wise person will love you for rebuking them; a fool will despise you. Care and correction are part of the discipling process; if a student is resistant to your input into his life, that may be a warning flag. If you sense this person is rebellious or unapproachable, then you might consider just praying for and loving him, and waiting for God to soften his heart.

E. Heart for God and People

Navigator staff leader Doug Nuenke believes that "some students can be faithful, available, and teachable initiators—but all for the wrong reasons!" So, to add to those qualities, he looks for students who genuinely seek God and love the lost. *People* are what ministry is all about, but the old joke "I love the ministry, it's just people I can't stand!" is more true than we'd

> *"Their joy in God overflows in love for others."*
>
> **John Piper**

like to admit. Some Christians love to strategize, organize, and lead because they're on a power trip. They try to make themselves feel important by controlling others, rather than having an authentic compassion and burden for them. Team up with students who really love God, like and enjoy others, have a network of friends, and are willing to sometimes push other priorities aside to help someone in need.

Jesus selected disciples. He wasn't playing favorites; it was the smartest, most strategic approach He could have taken. Luke 6:12–13 reveals He spent the whole night in prayer and then when morning came, "He called His disciples to Him and chose twelve of them, whom He also named as apostles." In similar fashion, Paul chose wisely and did not to waste his life by pouring into people who didn't want to make a difference for Christ. He challenged the young believers to prove themselves as lights in the world, "holding fast the word of life, so that in the day of Christ I will have reason to glory because I did not run in vain nor toil in vain" (Philippians 2:16). Pray diligently and be careful whom you choose. Don't select students before they've had enough time to prove to God, to you, and to themselves that they are full of F-A-I-T-H.

Strategy #3: Training That Lasts Is Taught *and* Caught

Have you ever been around a group of pastors when one turns to another and asks, "Hey Mac, where did you get your training?" What is he really asking? In reality, he wants to know where "Mac" went to seminary because most Christians think seminary is the place where you receive "training." Now, I've attended the largest denominational seminary in the world and the largest non-denominational seminary in the world and spent over eight years acquiring graduate degrees. It has been a great experience, and I have benefited greatly from the programs and people of these fine institutions, but let's call it *knowledge*, not *training*.

What Is Training?

In my opinion, training is knowledge, yes, but it is also skills, character, and vision. As much as the different seminaries I've attended have tried to give me and my colleagues some skills or build our characters or stir our hearts with vision, they are basically classrooms filling our minds with a lot of information. Don't get me wrong, knowledge is essential, and it forms the basis for the Christian life and ministry. But if the training stops there, we may not be any more than overeducated, modern-day Pharisees who are puffed up with pride. Skills, character, and vision are the applications of knowledge; and without these, excessive learning can be more harmful than helpful. Plus, if a person *thinks* she is trained because she has gained a lot of knowledge, she will not see the need for further training. And when she trains others, it will once again be a classroom-oriented, mind-to-mind, information-transfer exercise.

Soldiers, athletes, and even restaurant waiters submit themselves to training. Why shouldn't Christians?

So, as great as seminary is, don't think that you *must* go there to get training; and if you do go there, realize you're getting to first base—knowledge. There are three other bases you must touch to round out your training. As you *get* and *give* spiritual training to individuals and small groups that you've selected, make sure you pray, plan, and prepare diligently to emphasize all *four* components of spiritual training. The first two (knowledge and skills) can be *taught* over a relatively short period of time, but the second two (character and vision) must primarily be *caught* from a person close to you. Plus they usually take years to work their way down into our spiritual bloodstreams.

Each week spend time praying and thinking about each student you are meeting with on a regular basis. Don't just wing it, but come prepared, after asking these three questions each week: Where is my student at spiritually? What is his or her greatest need right now? What is the next step to meet it? Taking the time to discern their personal, spiritual, and ministry needs is difficult and wearisome, but if you don't do it, who will? Here are the four areas of training to focus on:

A. Knowledge
    Proverbs teaches that "as a man thinks, so he is." If you and your disciple can commit to filling your minds and hearts with the truth, the Holy Spirit can continue the transformation process. Jesus was full of truth, but He was also full of grace, because grace is the proper application of truth. I sit under the awesome Bible teaching of my pastor, but I also invite him to the Leadership Training Center we host in our home to give biblical and doctrinal overviews to the students living with us. As you think through a plan to train and equip your disciple, the Word of God should be the centerpiece. Paul exhorted Timothy to do the same with the men he was working with in 2 Timothy 3:16–17 (NIV):

> All Scripture is God-breathed and is useful for teaching, rebuking, correcting and training in righteousness, so that the man of God may be thoroughly equipped for every good work.

Start studying through books of the Bible with the students you disciple, agree on a Scripture memory plan, have a stash of expository sermons for them to listen to as they drive, take a major Bible doctrine each month and find out what the Word really teaches about it, or read through the Bible in a year and devour it. A week-by-week, month-by-month steady diet of the Word will help them develop core convictions and create a biblically-based filter with which to evaluate everything that passes through their minds. Besides, before we can "speak the truth in love" to the students on our campuses, we must first know the truth!

B. Skills

If the Word provides the what and the why, learning the skills is the how. How to study the Bible, how to have a quiet time, how to trust God with every detail, how to meet people and build relationships, how to present the gospel, how to follow up a new Christian, how to manage and delegate, how to, how to—the list is incredibly long. You must first tell them how to do it, then show them how to do it, observe them as they do it, give them feedback on how they did it, turn them loose to do it, and keep close so that you can encourage them to keep doing it! You'll move from teacher to partner to observer in each skill area. Each time you begin working on an area, whether it is personal or ministry related, you must think and pray through a simple, practical, and transferable plan to teach them the skill.

> *"Skills are not developed primarily from listening to messages, but through observation and personal practice. Teaching is the imparting of knowledge. Training is the acquisition of skills."*
>
> **Max Barnett**

It's critical that you model these skills to your young disciple, not just so they'll know how to use them, but so that they'll use them as a way of life. Timothy spent seventeen years watching Paul, and, at the very end, the aged apostle could confidently say to his partner in ministry, "You, however, know all about my teaching, my way of life, my purpose, faith, patience, love, endurance." One of my favorite "Timothys" was a student whom I met during his senior football season at the University of Arkansas. As Trey and I built a relationship, he chose to stay after graduation to get more training, and we spent time together every day studying the Word, praying over the campus, meeting students, and sharing the gospel. I have never met someone who was as much a "man of application" as Trey was.

He would watch me lead a Bible study and then immediately duplicate it with a group of swimmers he had recruited. He would watch me plan for a one-on-one discipling appointment with a student then do it himself. He wasn't satisfied in just knowing, it was the doing that wound his clock. He would watch and learn and apply all in one seamless step. Today, as a pastor of a church, he continues to be a man of application who has not only mastered a myriad of personal and ministry skills but has been passing them on to hundreds of others over the years.

C. Character

Different areas of knowledge and skill can be *taught* over a period of months. Permanent change in a person's character from the inside out has to be *caught*, usually over a period of years. This is such a foundational area, because if a student does not have basic character qualities like holiness, faithfulness, humility, and a strong work ethic, then no amount of knowledge, skills, or vision is going to salvage a life or ministry that is bound for shipwreck. Spend as much time as you can with your disciple in all kinds of different situations to see what areas of character are strong and which areas need work. Pray it into his life, model it for him, memorize passages, and create projects designed to help him develop a particular character area. It takes time. Don't expect a student who has been a "taker" all his life to become a "giver" after a twenty-minute Bible study on servanthood!

I Was Against Leadership, Unless I Could Be the Leader!

After reading chapter 5 you know that when I was in college I didn't think there was *anyone* who could really teach me anything. My conceit finally snapped the day my Bible study leader told me he loved me even though I had disdained his authority in my life. That was the final straw! All of my defenses broke down and my rebellious heart melted into surrender as I finally grasped how authentic his love for me was. Like Jesus, instead of striking back he absorbed my assault and extended kindness in return. After observing a real-life demonstration of what it meant to be longsuffering, I humbled myself and admitted that before I could expect anyone to receive my teaching, I must first be teachable. I was pretending to be a shepherd in our campus ministry, when in fact I was closer to being a self-proclaimed spiritual dictator!

> *"One living sermon is worth one hundred explanations."*
>
> **Robert Coleman,**
> **author of** *Master Plan of Evangelism*

In 2 Timothy 2:24–25 Paul exhorted Timothy to exercise Christlike leadership: "The Lord's bond-servant must not be quarrelsome, but be kind to all, able to teach, patient when wronged, with gentleness correcting those who are in opposition." I realized that I had been against leadership unless, of course, I could be the leader! The real phony was staring at me in the mirror, as I tried to hide my arrogance with a humility performance that could have won me an Oscar! In spite of all that, my discipler took the time to build into my life deep and abiding character, which is still with me today.

D. Vision

Shanti came from a broken home. She went to the University of Oregon at Portland on an academic scholarship. She had been raised in church but had never met any Christians with real vision for their lives until she got to college and met the Chi Alpha Campus Ministry students. She immediately sought out training from Curt Harlow and other Chi Alpha staff in order to develop her own ministry. She became an incredible "woman of application" as she took the ministry tools given her and started small groups in her dorm, all marked by serious study of the Word, prayer, intense relationships, and evangelism.

The staff also taught Shanti that she should only date and marry a man who had the same vision she possessed. She waited and prayed, and the Lord gave her a husband, Chad. Together they applied the Great Commission principles they learned in college to their church youth group. Now, after having raised up leaders to take their place in the church, they are preparing to go to North Africa to use his engineering degree and her teaching degree to minister in a closed country.

Vision Begets Vision

If you want your students to have a personal vision, a ministry vision, and a world vision, then your vision needs to be pumping through your veins. It can't just be a talk you give or a quote you read, vision has to be authentic in your life if it's truly going to be transferred to your disciples. Seek to give them an outward focus by praying *for* them and *with* them over campus and world maps. Always ask them about their personal goals, ministry strategy, and future plans. Consistently expose them to visionaries who can paint the broad strokes of bringing all of our hopes and dreams under the lordship of Christ and His worldwide enterprise.

> *"I only impart and pass on to others that which I possess."*
>
> **Mike Hearon, director, Campus Outreach of Augusta, Georgia**

Vision is the engine that pulls the train. Each believer needs to understand that all of life is about glorifying God by colaboring with Him to bring the nations in submission to His lordship. Having a clear-cut vision for your life and ministry brings meaning to all the efforts spent on gaining knowledge, skills, and character. Truly, without a vision the people perish! It will take an amazing amount of time to prepare to infuse your key students with knowledge, skills, character, and vision. But if you will persevere in equipping your disciples in these critical areas, it will produce an incredible multiplying effect in the long run!

Strategy #4: Ministry Teams Create Synergy

It may have taken you a year or two of very challenging grassroots ministry to get this far, and many people never do, but the formation of ministry teams can have an explosive effect in reaching your campus. The funnel continues to narrow as you take students through the investigative group stage, select the most responsive ones to form discipleship groups, and finally, invite the student leaders who have shown the most F-A-I-T-H to form a ministry team. Regardless of the names you give your small groups, these are the three basic stages:

A. Investigative group—strictly *inwardly* focused, trying to help each student make Jesus Savior and Lord
B. Discipleship group—combination of *inwardly and outwardly* focused, trying to help each student grow in Christ and begin laboring for Him
C. Ministry team—primarily *outwardly* focused, trying to help each student leader develop *his or her* personal evangelism and discipleship ministry

You want to select students to your ministry team very carefully. These can't just be the most influential, most involved, or even the ones who want in the most. These must be the 2 Timothy 2:2 student leaders who are faithful, yes, but who are "able to teach others" also. They need to be spiritually, socially, and emotionally able to create the funnel and go through the same process you just spent one to two years going through with them. You are inviting them to step up and stand shoulder-to-shoulder with you as you reach the campus and the world for Christ. You are asking them to become partners, and the shift has taken place where they are no longer part of *your* ministry, you are simply part of *theirs!*

My First Ministry Team

God granted me the privilege of putting together my first ever ministry team the year after I graduated from college. I decided to stick around a couple of years after I finished my bachelor's to get more training and to finish up the work I had started with these six men: John, Dennis, Ted, Lewis, Dave, and Terry. To finally get to these six men took two years and thousands of hours of prayer, relationship building, evangelism, one-on-one establishing appointments, Bible studies, conferences, and who knows what else! The initial funnel had included hundreds of men, but most took exit ramps as the months wore on and the commitment level rose. I still loved all of them, and they knew it; but I had literally poured myself out for these six, because they had endured and poured themselves out in return. Now, as the lone survivors, we were banding together to impact the campus for Christ. The best word I could find to describe it was

> **synergy:** the interaction of individuals such that the total effect is greater than the sum of the individual effects

I will never forget the first time we gathered in my one-room apartment near the campus to pray and make battle plans. As the hours rolled by that night, and with only a small lamp for light, we huddled in a circle, all leaning forward and listening. You could feel the power and sense of destiny in that tiny room, as each man knew the incredible price he had paid to be sitting there. I led four of the men to Christ through an investigative Bible study and one-on-one evangelism appointments. The other two I "adopted" because of their faithfulness to a Bible study I started and their passion to share the gospel with others. Since college, two of the men have spent their lives ministering in China, one in Germany, and two are lay leaders in their stateside churches. I do not believe the sixth man stuck with his spiritual commitment.

Think Big, Start Small, Go Deep

All six picked out a dorm or campus "people group" that they were going to pray for, get to know, share the gospel with, invite to small groups, and to see who rises to the top. My job was to pray for them, encourage them, gather them weekly for inductive Bible study, strategize with each one individually, and spend time in *their* target, helping them to establish *their* ministry. I was teaching each man how to start from scratch and, as Campus Outreach staff teach their student laborers, to "think big, start small, go deep."

When Dave or John or Terry met guys in their target area and built a friendship, we would say he had a "toehold" in that group. If one of those friendships blossomed into a discipling relationship, we would say he had a "foothold" in his target group. If one of the ministry team guys was able to equip a student who was now evangelizing and discipling in his own group, we would then tally it up as a "stronghold." Here's the progression:

A. Toehold—You have a friend in your target group.

B. Foothold—You are discipling someone in your target group.

C. Stronghold—You are equipping someone in your target group who is now taking responsibility to reach others in that group. You can start over in another target if you choose.

Our goal was to develop a stronghold in every affinity group on campus. By the time I left for seminary two years later, we had not reached our goal. But we did have a depth chart made up of 268 students who were all plugged in to small groups and were either discipling or being discipled by someone involved in our ministry. Our banding together radically impacted each of our lives, and the sum total of our joint efforts created a campus-wide movement of penetration, concentration, and a growing saturation of laborers being trained and placed in all kinds of groups.

One excellent strategy we implemented was the idea of a ministry house near the campus, where the leader would recruit several disciples to live with him for a year and focus on reaching a particular ministry target together. I have included an appendix item on how to begin and develop a ministry house. It's not for everyone, but it has worked for us the last twenty years!

Strategy #5: Reproduce Yourself through Key Students

You don't *have* to use groups to make disciples or raise up key students; you can do it through just one-on-one relationships if you choose to. However you do it, understand that you cannot produce disciples or disciplemakers in bulk. Samuel Shoemaker, the outstanding Episcopalian pastor, had it right when he said, "Men are not hewn out of the mediocre mass wholesale, but one by one." If you have used groups to narrow down the funnel and find the F-A-I-T-H students to focus in on, this diagram may provide another way to understand the process:

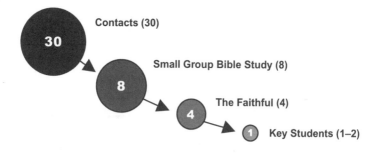

Contacts (30)

Small Group Bible Study (8)

The Faithful (4)

Key Students (1–2)

Let's say that in a particular target group or sphere of influence, you were able to meet thirty students and get to know each of them a bit. You prayed for them and loved them, and you were able to invite twenty to participate in a small group. Twelve say yes and eight show up. Through a series of increasingly challenging small groups and one-on-one interaction, there emerge four students whom you would describe as faithful. As you spend time with each of these four, you realize one or two are not just faithful, but men or women of F-A-I-T-H. These one or two students will be who you deposit your life into over the next months and years.

The apostle Paul had a ministry team consisting of Sopater, Aristarchus, Secundus, Gaius, Timothy, Tychicus, and Trophimus (Acts 20:4). Titus would certainly have to be included also, but as far as we can tell, Timothy (whom he spent seventeen years discipling) was his key man. The final letter we have from Paul is the tear-stained second letter to his protégé where, knowing the end was near, he expressed his desire to see him one last time:

> *"It's not how many men, but what kind of men."*
>
> **Dawson Trotman**

I thank God, whom I serve with a clear conscience the way my forefathers did, as I constantly remember you in my prayers night and day, longing to see you, even as I recall your tears, so that I may be filled with joy. (2 Timothy 1:3–4)

the fuel and the flame

Like parents who have great joy when their children grow up to embrace their values, Paul could depart this earth knowing he was leaving a legacy—someone to carry on his work the way he would. It is unlikely that Timothy made it to Rome before Paul was martyred, and yet the apostle could die a satisfied man, knowing that Timothy would perpetuate the message to "faithful men" who would "teach others also." The chain would not be broken.

If God blesses you with a key man or key woman to pour yourself into, you indeed are fortunate. Every moment is precious as you seek to pray, love, serve, and build into them the essential knowledge, skills, character, and vision needed to be a lifelong laborer for Jesus Christ. Now that you have a full-fledged partner in ministry, the equipping process continues as you lay out a game plan to empower this key student to be a laborer-leader who will do exactly what you do.

Strategy #6: Do Discipleship in the Context of Evangelism

Let me describe one of the biggest mistakes I've made in ministry. I would choose a guy to help spiritually and pull him aside every week in my basement or at Denny's to "disciple" him. Each session was packed with my latest nugget from the Word or keen illustration I could draw out on a napkin. And then after several months I would deem him ready to learn a gospel presentation, which took several more weeks to memorize and practice. The day finally came when we would go out and share it with a friend of his only to hurry back to our den of discipleship to debrief about the spiritual pilgrimage we just completed. Proud of my disciple's performance, I could then check off the box on my training-objectives sheet for him, marked "knows and shared gospel presentation."

What's wrong with this picture? When water flows into a pond and no water flows out, it is just a matter of time before the smell becomes unbearable. God made us to be conduits with water flowing in *and* out at the same time. We Christians are like manure: if you pile us up we really stink; but spread us around, and we can do a lot of good! Doing some *occasional* evangelism just to stay sharp in the context of ongoing discipleship can get really stale—really fast! Jesus was very clear in Matthew 4:19, "Follow Me, and I will make you fishers of men." I spent a few months of my quiet times one semester studying all the "I will" statements Jesus made in the gospels. Guess what I found? Every time Jesus said, "I will," He did! If that's true, then this verse must mean that if we're not fishing for men, we're not following Christ, because Jesus promised to make us fishers *if* we would only follow.

A 24/7 Walking, Talking Classroom

Study Luke 10 and Mark 1–3 to understand the Campus Outreach ministry's emphasis upon doing discipleship in the context of evangelism. Jesus called His disciples to be with Him as He traveled from town to town, crowd to crowd, teaching and ministering. Yes, occasionally He drew them away for some debriefing, prayer, or rest together, but for the most part He was always on the go, preaching and reaching the masses. His goal was to provide His men with a real, live, walking, talking twenty-four-hours-a-day classroom, full of object lessons for life and ministry. He was influencing many and, in the process, training a few, thus providing dynamic discipleship to His men in the context of aggressive, ongoing evangelism.

I will warn you, though, this kind of emphasis on evangelism has a way of attracting the right kind of students and repelling the wrong kind. Growing Christians who really want to be used by God to make a difference will immediately be drawn to you and your ministry as they observe the initiative you take. Others, though, who are just looking for a safe haven to hang their religious hat during their college years, will be frightened off by this radical and intrusive brand of Christianity. On their way out, as a defense mechanism, they might even attack you as being exclusive, insensitive, or unloving.

56

> *"My job is to bring people to Jesus. My job is also to bring people to other people who can bring them to Jesus."*

Mike Gaffney, college ministry director, University Presbyterian, Seattle, Washington

As you launch your ministry, it's fine if Christian students want to help you begin the work, as long as they're willing to join you in an ongoing outward focus of reaching the lost on your campus. While finding it difficult to motivate some of the mediocre "lifelong" Christians, you might discover the most fervent believers on your campus are those who came to Christ during their college years. Sometimes they'll take the same zeal and enthusiasm they had as a campus hellion and channel it into bold steps of faith and outreach. Bottom line: If you focus on reaching the lost, the hungry Christians will find you. ✦

Discussion and Application Questions

1. What can you learn from Jennifer's story?

2. What does it mean that we spiritually "reproduce after our own kind?" Why is this truth exciting *and* scary at the same time?

3. If someone were to ask you, "How do you make a disciple?" what would you tell them?

4. Have you ever made a disciple? If you have, how did you do it? If not, why haven't you?

5. How can we, along with the Holy Spirit, help students to see their need for spiritual training?

6. How do you know which student to start equipping? What are the signs that this is the "right one"? Read Luke 6:12–13.

7. List the four major areas of spiritual training and tell us how to utilize them to equip a student to be a disciplemaker.

    A. Knowledge (What areas of knowledge would you need to develop in a student discipler?)

    B. Skills (What personal or ministry skills would be essential to build into them?)

C. Character (What areas of personal character need to be developed in their lives?)

D. Vision (What aspects of the student's vision should be expanded?)

8. How can you use small groups to make disciples? To make disciple-makers?

9. How can you find a "Timothy"? If God gives you one, what will you do with him/her?

10. What does it mean to do discipleship in the context of ongoing evangelism?

11. What is meant by the phrase "Evangelism attracts the right kind of students and repels the wrong kind of students"?

12. You establish a believer to make a disciple. You then equip them to become a disciplemaker. What student are you equipping right now to develop their own personal ministry? How are you doing it? If you are not equipping someone, why not?

Read your applications and pray together that God would use you to equip your faithful students to begin evangelizing and establishing others.

chapter 9

mobilize your campus as a sending base by exporting laborers

Several years and ministry teams later, I had the opportunity to start from scratch on a different campus. It's a delicious experience not to build on another man's foundation but instead go where Christ has not been named (Romans 15:20). This time it was a small, liberal, liberal arts college that had a reputation for shunning any outside influence—especially the kind I wanted to inject! I started by just meeting students on campus, in the dorms, in the cafeteria, and even in my church and community. The investigative Bible studies I started whittled down to five guys, two of whom had just come to Christ and the other three made rededications. We kept upping the commitment level, studying the Word, having quiet times together, and praying for the salvation of the guys in their dorms. We were on our way.

Charlie, one of the five, had grown up in a Christian home but came to college to flirt and play. At first he was more or less humoring me, thinking it would be good to be able to tell Mom and Dad he was in a Bible study. During his freshman year, I invited him to the Christmas conference we were sponsoring, and you'd have thought I was asking him to pluck out his eyeballs from the look on his face! No one had ever required anything of him in his comfortable Christianity. As I took Charlie on evangelism appointments, God started to reveal to him that he had a lot of knowledge but almost no application. He became more serious about his faith and wanted to search the Word for answers, learn how to share the gospel, and even turn his dating life over to the Lord. (Some of that may have been because my wife led his girlfriend—and wife-to-be—to Christ and began to disciple her!)

Shifting from My Ministry to Charlie's Ministry

Miraculously, I got Charlie to one of our ten-week summer-training projects where he really flourished and came back wanting to colabor with me to reach the campus for Christ. I would spend hours with Charlie each week in prayer, ministry-strategy sessions, evangelism, follow-up, and, of course, the most spiritual activity of all—eating at our dinner table on a regular basis! I helped him start his own Bible study, and we worked on how to prepare questions to lead it. We started sponsoring campus-wide meetings and weekend retreats, and many times I would put Charlie in charge. I would give him these major responsibilities with only one condition: he was not allowed to do *anything* at the event. He would have to plan and delegate *every* detail in advance so that he would not lift one finger to make that event happen.

After a year of placing those cruel restrictions on Charlie, he became one of the most proficient planners, developers, and managers I have ever seen! Like me, he didn't view giving responsibilities to others as *dumping* it on them, nor did he see it as *delegating* to them. No, he and I saw giving away every task as an opportunity to *develop* someone's character and leadership ability.

By the end of his junior year, not only did Charlie have a whole dorm he was responsible for (with his key guys on each floor), but he was determined to join our staff and become the ministry's campus director at that college. I had been evangelizing, establishing, and equipping a number of students on that campus, but it was obvious to all that Charlie was my key man.

We spent his senior year preparing him to take over the leadership of that campus, get married, raise his support, and expand the work that had begun there. Charlie and Heidi stayed there for six years, raising up teams of laborers and finally replacing himself with one of his disciples, before heading off to seminary and then the pastorate. Today, Charlie and his family are living and ministering in a major U.S. city, using the knowledge, skills, character, and vision he gained while in college to reach laymen for Christ.

Please don't think that every skeptical freshman I've laid my hands on is now a prominent pastor in a huge church! The majority of the students I've worked with will not go in to vocational Christian ministry, but that doesn't mean they can't have an incredible worldwide impact as they consistently make kingdom-focused choices that further the gospel. It's not more spiritual to go into vocational ministry than the secular work force. God is not up there ringing His hands, worrying about what location or vocation we will choose. He is much more interested in whether we are obedient to the commands He has given us, which, of course, include the Great Commission. Regardless of who pays our salary or what employer's name is on our business card, the important thing is whether we are about the Father's business.

Seven Principles for Launching Reproducers

We've spent a lot of time looking at evangelism, establishing, and equipping. Let's add one more step to the process: exporting. I know this sounds like I'm shipping big wooden crates to overseas markets rather than helping graduating students find their most strategic place as they leave college, but I had to find a word that started with an "e"! Hang on and we will discover together how to launch (or export) Christian laborers into this lost and dying world. In order to come full circle and reproduce ourselves into students who will go and do likewise, we need to keep in mind seven important principles:

Principle #1: Mobilization Is the Key to World Evangelization

Early one morning in the fall of 1986, I was sitting in my little office having my morning prayer time when I experienced a dramatic revelation from the Lord. On the left wall was a map of the campus that I had divided into over thirty ministry targets, which I prayed over every morning and then spent the day trying to reach, alongside key student leaders. On the right wall was a map of the world that I would invest time in, praying for different countries and missionaries that I knew. Then that crisp November morning, it blindsided me. There was an awesome, mind-blowing connection between the map on the *left* wall and the map on the *right* wall! I slowly rose as if on holy ground and stationed myself between the two maps. I could envision a pipeline going from the campus map to the world map. Eureka! The *key* to world evangelization was reaching, discipling, and mobilizing college students! It was so crystal clear it seemed as if I could reach out and touch it!

From that moment on my conviction became galvanized that the most effective and strategic use of my life was reaching college students to reach the world. It is a long and arduous process to take a student from a non-Christian to a world-changer, but seeing it happen over and over again not only brings tremendous fulfillment to my soul but also a smile to the face of God. Like raising children to the point where you finally launch them out into the world to stand alone and make a difference, you and I must embrace the same mission in our work with students. Some call this gradual building up and weaning off progression the "Four P's," and it is simply an overview of the process we've been going through:

> *Mobilization: Deploying an army of laborers to the frontlines where they order their lives around the Great Commission.*

48

The Four P's of Personal Ministry

A. Pioneering

As you begin your personal ministry, there may be no one to team up with—it's just you and God! When you go to your campus or ministry target, *you* are the one praying, meeting, greeting, and taking all the initiative. As you go door to door in the dorm or table to table in the cafeteria, introducing yourself and remembering names, some people will be skeptical, others will think you're downright weird! You might view yourself as the life of the party, but some students will suspect you're trying to butter them up to sell them something.

Either way, for the first few months, you are required to carry the ball in every introduction, every conversation, every invitation to get together. You are plowing new (and often hard) ground with your love, serving, and sharing. Don't give up during this first semester or two of pioneering, because you are laying the foundation for some great relationships and impact.

> *"You are about to walk on campus and the only ones you know are yourself and God. You have the opportunity to see the Lord build a ministry out of nothing except His leading and your obedience, faith, and prayer."*
>
> **Harvey Herman, Northeast director, Chi Alpha**

B. Parenting

Before long some of your efforts will begin to pay off, and students will acknowledge you and even smile occasionally! In our ministry, we get to move a person from the contact list to the friend list if they recognize us, greet us, and call us by name—a big step for some self-absorbed students! As relationships are formed, small groups started, the gospel is shared, and decisions are made, we move from a pioneer to a spiritual parent of those who respond. Growing bonds of friendship are being formed, and now *they're* calling and visiting you! Even though you work hard to get them plugged in to a local church and growth group, the responsibility of helping them mature is still laying at *your* doorstep. Each of the new and growing Christians needs months (and usually years) of intensive nurturing and establishing to move them from spiritual babies to mature believers. If you were to leave them at this stage, they may or may not make it.

C. Partnering

If we have paid the price in pioneering and parenting, we may be blessed with some key students who rise up, having gained the conviction that they want to colabor with us. Now you move from an inward focus of developing their spiritual foundation to an outward focus, equipping them to initiate their own ministry. If the goal of pioneering is to investigate and penetrate different campus groups, and if the goal of parenting is to concentrate on establishing the responders, then partnering has to do with saturating the campus with laborers in every target group. Leadership and ownership of the ministry is gradually being transferred to these faithful students as you spend one-on-one time building in the areas of knowledge, skills, character, and vision. You are thrilled at this team approach to ministry as the flame of revival spreads across your campus. But the cycle is not yet complete. . . .

D. Participating

You're always pioneering, parenting, and partnering with different students, but the final stage in this process is the complete release of this student leader to stand on her own. Just as parents hope to someday have their child totally independent and self-sufficient, this is also the goal we laborers are shooting for. Now you are in a supporting role, simply praying and encouraging, and your relationship with the student is as a friend and adviser that she may (or may not!) take advantage of. Don't get your feelings hurt if she zooms off without your permission or surpasses you in her achievements. Instead, take pride and joy in her success, knowing that your mission is accomplished, thus freeing you up to focus on other students who are moving through the "Four P's"!

Harvey Herman, a Chi Alpha regional director, describes these four stages in terms of transitioning roles that a staff person plays in the beginning of a campus ministry. The first year the staffer is the "Leader Pioneer," then as the months and years go by she shifts into the "Leader Catalyst," then the "Leader Equipper," next the "Leader Mobilizer," and finally, the "Leader Manager," where the staff person is resourcing student leaders who own the ministry themselves. Whatever stages or role titles you want to use, make sure that your end product is student laborer/leaders who will take personal responsibility for the Great Commission on your campus and beyond. If you will embrace this principle as your own, you will go down in God's history books as one who made a difference for eternity.

Principle #2: View Your Campus As a Sending Base

If a fire broke out on the roof of your dorm or apartment right now, you would have some choices to make. One option would be to scream, run outside to turn on the garden hose, and begin to squirt the blaze. You might slow down the burning of your building by two or three minutes due to your well-intentioned, but meager efforts, but in the end it would be futile. What if instead, you chose a second option wherein, at the smell of smoke, you called the fire department to come put out the blaze? Yes, it'd take five or six minutes for the firemen to arrive, hook their huge hoses up,

"The campus has more influence on the direction, morality, and overall fabric of society than any institution on earth. Will the campuses be a starting point in a spiritual awakening that will shake the earth? The answer is a resounding yes."

**Rice Broocks,
founder, Every Nation
Campus Ministries**

and begin spraying, but they'd be able to put out the fire and save most of your building. You and your tiny stream of water doesn't compare to waking up one hundred sleeping firemen to come and pour thousands of gallons of water on the fire.

You can choose to slug it out day after day on your campus, trying to witness to one here, encourage another there, maybe have a little Bible study or campus meeting, hoping to make a small difference in someone's life. But, what if you were to view your campus differently, with more eternal significance? What if, instead of having your lens glued on just that single room, floor, or dorm, you had one eye focused on the *entire* campus and the other on the world? Your whole perspective would be transformed, and your campus, whether it's a school of five hundred or fifty thousand, would now be viewed as a launching pad and every student a potential world changer! I have no doubt you can influence a few on your campus *and* the world all by your lonesome, but it is so much more effective to raise up one hundred sleeping (literally and spiritually!) students and send them out to have a much bigger, more powerful effect. It's the difference between addition and multiplication.

Our ministry has developed a tool we share with students, called The Vision. It's designed to challenge believers to take seriously the Great Commission, and it has been instrumental in recruiting many lethargic (or just uninformed) Christians in becoming disciples, making disciples, and ultimately taking the gospel to the world. Before we started utilizing The Vision, I would challenge believers to become disciples of Christ. Realizing that really wasn't a big enough challenge to warrant a total commitment of their lives, I raised the bar and began exhorting them to fulfill the Great Commission by making disciples. That was better, but it was still the means instead of the end. Until I started inviting students to exchange their *entire* lives to "glorify God by reaching the whole world for Jesus Christ" did I hit the hot button. Create your own version of The Vision or contact us for ours!

Never Underestimate College Students!

Dr. Bill Bright was right when he said, "Never in history have so many college students been more ready to receive Christ as Savior and follow Him as their Lord. They are waiting to be challenged and led in the greatest revolution in history—the fulfillment of the Great Commission in this generation." Students are looking for something bigger and beyond themselves to give their hearts to. The writer of Ecclesiastes, talking about how God has designed us, proclaimed in 3:11, "He has also set eternity in the hearts of men" (NIV). Don't challenge students with small dreams. Expand their vision by showing them their eternal marching orders that call them out of mediocrity to be an officer in a worldwide conquest for the glory of God, our great King and Commander, Jesus Christ! Small challenges receive small commitments, so don't embarrass yourself or the Lord by asking for too little.

You see, college students *are* different. They will go where others won't. They will believe it *can* be done when others doubt. They will *act* on their convictions when others are fearful to step out. They look to the future when others are living in the past. They want to join a *team* that is going somewhere significant when others are satisfied with the status quo. They are waiting for someone like you to love them, serve them, look deep into their eyes and say, "Would you like to join me in reaching the entire world for Jesus Christ?" That spark begins in *your* mind, but it can extend to an entire campus and the world if you'll be the fuel and let God be the flame!

Principle #3: Focus on Raising Up World Christians

When a New York professional sports team wins a championship they are honored with a huge ticker tape parade lined with millions of cheering fans. The athletes ride in a long line of convertibles that stretches out a mile, allowing each superstar to receive maximum adulation. The New Yorkers stand ten to fifteen people deep, hoping to catch a glimpse of their favorite athlete through the pressing crowd. Bit by bit the parade goes by, while each spectator only sees a small sliver of the action. Less than satisfied, they race home for the six o'clock news where they see it from a much better angle.

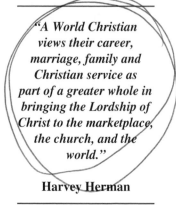

"A World Christian views their career, marriage, family and Christian service as part of a greater whole in bringing the Lordship of Christ to the marketplace, the church, and the world."

Harvey Herman

What if you were at the next parade and instead of wading into the mass of people, you were invited to view the mile-long procession from the top of the Empire State Building? You'd be thrilled because this time you could look down and see from the beginning to the end and every car and athlete in between. This kind of perspective, in a weak human way, describes the view that God has on the world and life. History *is* passing by like a parade, and He *does* see the end from the beginning and every detail in between! We may only be able to view a tiny bit of today's events, but history is truly *His story*. The Lord is fulfilling His plan for the ages, and nothing will deter it. We can either get on board with Him and view things from His eternal perspective, or we can live out our quiet little lives never reaching the God-ordained potential He had planned for us.

God yearns for us not to be worldly Christians (we have plenty of those!) but to be "World Christians." This is someone who not only views the world and life from God's perspective but also is passionate about what is on God's heart. According to John 3:16, at this moment and *every* moment, it is the world that is on His heart. David Bryant, former InterVarsity Christian Fellowship staff leader and author of *In the Gap*, tells us about the three stages in becoming a World Christian. Think of creative ways you can help your students catch, keep, and obey the vision that God wants every believer to possess.

A. Catch the vision

Continually expose your students to the world through mission conferences, biographies of missionaries, praying together over a world map, taking courses like *Perspectives on the World Christian Movement*, reading about world events in newspapers and magazines, befriending internationals on campus, doing Bible studies, and memorizing verses on world evangelization. We have a guest apartment at our house for the main purpose of providing visiting missionaries a place to stay. Our students and family are impacted by this firsthand contact with these men and women who have gone to foreign lands to share the gospel with the unreached.

B. Keep the vision

Fan the flames of mission fervor on your campus by forming world-mission prayer groups, holding a "Concert of Prayer" for lifting up the nations on a campus-wide basis, beginning small-group dinners and Bible studies for reaching out to internationals, or planning a mission trip to expose your students to the world during spring or summer break. Continue to pray vision and passion into the hearts and minds of your students, especially upperclassmen. Write down specific goals for how they can build their world vision now and when they graduate.

C. Obey the vision

Encourage your students not to leave campus until they have developed a world vision and, if possible, gone on at least one short-term mission trip with their church, campus ministry, or a mission agency. There is a trend right now where students around the country are taking a year off school to spend on an overseas mission effort. As you prepare your seniors for graduation and launching out into the world, make sure they know their role in Christ's global cause. Guide them toward cities, churches, ministries, job opportunities, and possible mates that will help them keep and obey the vision for reaching the world for Christ.

It seems as if everyone has mobile phones these days, with a variety of calling plans available to fit each need and pocketbook. Many choose the local plan, some the regional or national plan, and even fewer the international plan, allowing them to call anywhere in the world for one monthly price. Sad to say, but some people view Jesus' last command on earth with the same "pick and choose" mentality:

> But you will receive power when the Holy Spirit has come upon you; and you shall be My witnesses both in Jerusalem, and in all Judea and Samaria, and even to the remotest part of the earth. (Acts 1:8)

We may be given the option as to which phone plan we want, but Jesus Christ gives us no such choice when it comes to being His worldwide witnesses. We are all commanded to be on the "international plan," whereby we are simultaneously giving of our time, talent, and treasure to reaching Jerusalem *and* Judea *and* Samaria *and* the remotest parts. Like the bumper sticker on the hippie van that says, "THINK GLOBALLY, ACT LOCALLY," we are to build into the lives of our students that wherever they are, whatever they are doing, they're to carry out a world vision that, yes, even includes their next-door neighbors! I'm not saying every Christian should be a cross-cultural vocational missionary, but I am saying every Christ-follower should strive to be a "world Christian," a conviction that's caught much more than taught.

Principle #4: Seek to Build Self-Generated Leaders

I have tremendous respect for my friend, Curtis Tanner, the founder of Campus Outreach Ministries. Years ago he shared a goal with me I have never forgotten. His main ministry objective is to raise up fifty men who will go farther in their Christian walks and ministries than he will. In our dog-eat-dog corporate world where people are stepping on others to get up the ladder first, this kind of goal seems out of place. But Curtis truly gets excited about making other people successful and is well on his way to winning, building, and sending out solid Christian leaders who, in many ways, have already outstripped him. Is he jealous or angry that the students are "outshining" the teacher? No way! At the end of his life, and for God's glory, he'll be able to point to cities all over the world map, telling myriads of "war stories" about young men he had the privilege of empowering and launching into ministry. Certainly a life well lived!

> *"If a leader has no followers, really he is just taking a long walk by himself!"*
>
> **John Maxwell, author**

When I say these men and women are *self-generated* I don't mean that they are not relying on God's power or not plugged into the local church or not working with others in ministry. What I mean is that these sold-out disciples of Jesus Christ have such deep convictions, such quality training, are such men and women of F-A-I-T-H that you could parachute them down to any location on the planet and they would simply plug themselves into Jesus Christ, their power source, and begin to do what they have always done: win the lost and build the saved. These world-changing, ultra portable, disciplemaking generators need no outside pushing or pulling to get them to joyfully and faithfully serve Christ. Paul describes this kind of spiritual warrior for Timothy:

> No soldier in active service entangles himself in the affairs of everyday life, so that he may please the one who enlisted him as a soldier. (2 Timothy 2:4)

It's one thing to build a laborer, but how do you help them become an effective leader? It seems like I have read every book there is on leadership through my doctoral program in Church and Parachurch Executive Leadership. Of all the reams of religious and secular literature on leadership, one author I seem to resonate with is John Maxwell. His definition of leadership is "Influence—nothing more, nothing less." The real leader is often

> *"Are we preparing our students with principles and skills that will translate into the marketplace, or just giving them methods that will work during their four years of college?"*
>
> **Doug Nuenke,**
> **National Leadership**
> **Team, the Navigators**

not the person with the position or title, but the one who is able to motivate others with words and actions to take a particular course. Train your student to be an influencer, an initiator, a servant, a people person, or a man or woman of integrity—someone whom others respect and want to follow.

A whole book could be written on how to develop college students into leaders, so I'll just leave you with a simple description of a leader that Bobb Biehl, author of *Developing Your Leadership Confidence*, provides:

A. A leader knows what to do next
B. A leader knows why that's important
C. A leader knows how to bring appropriate resources together to accomplish it

Help your students become this type of individual, and they'll be on their way to leading (i.e., influencing) many toward the kingdom.

Principle #5: Prepare Them to Be Lifelong Laborers

To show you what a fossil I really am, I admit I was part of the Greek system during a time when guys (yes guys!) would gather around the piano after dinner and sing fraternity songs! I would sing a terrible backup baritone to everyone's sentimental favorite, "Not for College Days Alone." But looking back, the significance of my fraternity rituals *did* fade over the years, and the vision and passion we gain in college can slip away as well.

In the midst of those college years, I went to a conference

the fuel and the flame ♦

38

to hear Walt Henrichsen, former pastor, Navigator staff leader, author, discipler, and maker of audacious statements, speak. He stood before a hundred of us "green beret" type student laborers at a leadership summit and proclaimed, "Twenty years from now, only five of you will be walking with Christ and impacting others for Him with the same intensity you are today." I was stunned. "What?" I protested. "Who do you think you are? Only five out of a hundred are going to keep pressing on like we are now? Absurd!"

At the time I thought he was using reverse psychology on us, but I now realize he was simply speaking the truth. I haven't kept up with those one hundred students, but I have done informal surveys of many of the committed Christians I knew while in college. The dropout rate, especially in the first three years after graduation, is horrendous. Many take vows of lifelong dedication to Christ and the Great Commission, but as the trials and temptations of this world come along, many, if not most, bale out. Here are three choices (among many) that graduating laborers make that sometimes knock them off course:

A. Job choice

I have talked to so many students over the years who are accepting positions with companies based upon salary and climate. "Yeah," they might say, "I think I'm going to take the job with Dell Computers, because they're offering $3,000 more a year, and I like the warmer weather in Austin." Money and temperature are fine, but there are much bigger, more eternal factors to consider. I like to train our students to make decisions like this with two questions in mind: (1) Where can you go to continue to get the training

"I bring greetings from the real world. We're busy and we're tired. Please take advantage of your college years. You'll never have more time or energy than you do right now."

Tim Howington, Christian layman seeking to labor for Christ

you need to *keep* growing in your walk with Christ and personal ministry? and (2) Where can you go where you can make the greatest impact for the kingdom? I appreciate a little extra cash and a warm day, but if it means you have to sell your soul to a company, be cut off from people in some computer lab, or worse, have no idea where you're going to get the ongoing training you need to grow, you simply have to tell that company recruiter, "Thanks, but no thanks!" Teach students to listen to God, not the world, when making this very important decision.

B. Mate choice

I do seminars around the country for college ministries and churches, and, regardless of the topic, I am always compelled to fit this sobering thought into my message: Who you marry will make you or break you! Simple to say, hard to apply, especially when so many are pushing the senior panic button, realizing they might graduate without finding a spouse. Here's another profundity: You *will* marry someone whom you date. If this is true, and it is in America where we get to choose our mates, then only date someone who has the qualities you are looking for in a lifelong partner. Make sure they have the same goals, values, passions, and vision as yourself.

> *"God gives the very best to those who leave the choice with Him."*
>
> **Hudson Taylor**

Getting married is the scariest, most risky decision someone ever makes. Give that boyfriend or girlfriend of yours some time to develop a track record, because the only way you can be sure of what they *will* give themselves to in the future is looking at what they *have* given themselves to in the past. You need to teach your students to run the bases of life in this order: first base, Master (Jesus Christ); second base, Mission (Great Commission); third base, Mate (a partner who has also run the bases properly).

C. Lifestyle choice

I was twenty-eight years old and very impressed with my twenty-six-year-old "friend," Carol (my wife-to-be), to whom I was afraid to even mention the "M word" for fear of communicating something I couldn't follow through with. As we walked one night, I asked, "If we were to solidify our commitment someday, do you think you could live on $10,000 a year?" She said yes, and so I pressed on, "Do you think we could live on $8,000 a year?" (Remember, these are 1982 prices!) She shook her head in the affirmative, and so I added, "How about $6,000?" Finally, when I got her down to $4,000 a year, she blurted out, "It doesn't matter how much you make, I would not be marrying you for the money!" Well, I breathed a huge sigh of relief, because I had always been afraid I would marry someone who claimed to love God and want to reach the world for Christ but five to ten years into the marriage would be more interested in houses, cars, clothes, and vacations. I'm not saying you have to live at the poverty level to please God. But, according to Roberta Winter (cofounder of the U.S. Center for World Missions), every believer is to live a "wartime lifestyle," evaluating every expenditure in light of the worldwide spiritual battle we're engaged in.

Be a Finisher!

If you choose a mate with different values, if you go into big-time debt, if you gravitate toward accumulating things rather than giving your life away to others, it's just a matter of time until the fruitfulness in your life will be choked out. Instead of making job, mate, and lifestyle decisions like the world does, why not team up with some of your closest colaborers, move to a city with a great church and community ministry, find good, flexible jobs where you get to be around people and, finally, plug in and become self-generators for Christ? As you follow Jesus as

Tag the bases of life in this order: Master, Mission, Mate.

master and commit yourself to His *mission*, it's amazing, even as He did with the sleeping Adam, how the Lord has a way of bringing a *mate* along when you least expect it!

Because the attrition rate *is* so high, it's sometimes hard to measure your long-term effectiveness until your graduating students are three, five, even ten years out and have had a chance to really live out their convictions. One vital sign that can tell us whether our student's commitments are not for college days alone is to note how many of your *undergraduates* have actually made a disciple. This will be a good indicator of how many will continue on. Because if we have a student who can't or won't make disciples as an undergraduate, what makes us think he's going to once he gets out of school? It will be rare for him to find a person, ministry, or local church that will give him the *individual* training he needs to learn how to make disciples. A graduate will have less time and more responsibilities, and if she didn't learn and apply these principles in college, it becomes increasingly difficult to once she's out—and very few do.

Principle #6: Develop the Whole Person

A lot of students today come from broken or dysfunctional homes, many times with parents who have not taught their children the essentials of basic living. If you really care about your students and want them to be successful in *all* areas, you will probably have to help them in a number of the seemingly basic areas of life. Some of these you can teach in a group setting or even in a conference workshop, but some of the areas need to be communicated on a private, one-on-one basis. Below, in no particular order, is a sampling of areas you might need to help them in:

A. Family/marriage
   How to prepare for marriage
   How to raise children
   What birth control options are available
   Why and how to put a filter on the Internet

How to safeguard against impurity in relationships
How to honor and care for their parents

B. Finances
How to make a budget and use a credit card wisely
What kind of car to purchase and how to care for it
How to build a good credit rating
How much to give and where
How to save, invest, and borrow
How to raise support if they need to
How to buy insurance
Why to pay every bill on time

C. Personal gifting/talents
How to discover their spiritual gifts and use them
How to discover and develop a hobby
How to understand their personality type

D. Physical
How to maintain good exercise and diet
How to have a healthy self-image
How and where to get regular checkups

E. Professional
Why and how to read a daily newspaper, magazines, journals
How to dress modestly
How to choose a career
How to be a good employee
How to exercise business ethics
How to select a graduate school or full-time ministry opportunity

F. Social
How to develop good manners
What kind of person to date

How to maintain personal hygiene

How to relate to people of all ages

How to get involved in a single's or couple's class

G. Spiritual

How to find a good church

How to continue in Scripture memory

How to find an accountability partner

How to use Bible study reference tools

How to handle cults and false teaching

H. Ministry

How to be hospitable

How to have a house ministry

How to reach and disciple laymen as opposed to students

How to find resources for ministry materials

The list goes on and on, including how to manage time, make priorities, set and reach goals, and balance work, family, and ministry. Because life is complicated and we as Christian laborers are held to a much higher standard than most, any one of these ares if not attended to properly, could have negative, even devastating, effects on us and the people around us.

Luke 2:52 says Jesus increased "in wisdom and stature, and in favor with God and men." If Jesus felt the need to develop Himself mentally, physically, spiritually, and socially, how much more should we? Commit to a holistic ministry in your students' lives, but don't think you can do it alone. Even this morning (at 6:30!), I brought in Bill Smith, a godly sixty-three-year-old Little Rock businessman, to talk to our key students about following Christ and making disciples over the long haul. Our goal is to address areas of personal life and ministry that will help their transition from college to the real world. Make it a team effort and involve others from your church, campus ministry, and community, together seeking to produce *balanced* laborers for Jesus Christ.

3 2

Principle #7: Guide Them into Their Calling

"Most students come out of college, out of church, out of their campus ministry with both feet firmly planted in mid-air!" so says renowned Dallas Theological Seminary professor, Dr. Howard Hendricks. Your response to the prof might be, "But I thought college was supposed to guide us in the right direction to go in life!" I have seen this combination of fear and feeling lost played out many times as students finish high school, college, and even graduate programs. School was safe and secure, but now that they are leaving the nest, and many students have no idea which way to fly.

One of the biggest favors you can do for your graduating students is to help them work through a personal purpose statement. Once they have biblically and prayerfully put it together, show them how to use it as a grid through which to run every decision, job offer, dating prospect, and financial situation to see if it lines up with God's will. Help them to look at the future positively, not pessimistically, viewing life as a glass half full, not half empty! It's an opportunity of a lifetime to graduate from college and go and accomplish *anything* they put their minds and hearts to. After you share all the good news, slip in the bad, too. Warn them against some of the toxic options that could slowly poison their lives and future. Here are three common ones:

A. The rocking-chair mentality

Many American Christians, out of a misapplied view of God's sovereignty and our lack of responsibility, don't embrace the unbelievable partnership the Lord is offering us in the Great Commission. Instead, they choose to spend their college and adult years patiently rocking away, watching God's "kingdom-building parade" pass by. Maybe it's not their theology that paralyzes them but their laziness, ignorance, or preoccupation with the things of this world. Whatever the reason, don't let your students waste their lives doing nothing, someday to face a Creator who will ask them to account for how they filled their years on earth.

B. Climbing the wrong ladder

These are the ambitious people who are not satisfied to just watch history happen; they want to make history. Only problem is, they don't know how! Convinced that hard work, perseverance, and getting the right breaks are the keys to their success, they'll spend the better part of their lives scrambling to the top of the ladder, only to look back and realize they were climbing the wrong ladder! My dad had this disheartening experience after he spent thirty years rising in the ranks of an international company, retiring early with a big pension, then going to his retirement party, complete with cake and watch. That first day on Easy Street was when he finally had a moment to look back at his life. And the result? He went into depression, realizing that he had nothing of real, lasting value to show for his efforts. He soon committed his life to Christ and completely revamped his definition of success. Help your students get on and stay on the right ladder!

C. Dabbling at forty things

Christians who were busy in college may once again find their schedules about to explode once they start their careers. Working from the equation that busyness equals importance, they not only volunteer for extra assignments at work but also join every civic club, sports team, Bible study, and single's class. In their "spare time" they help with the youth group, church greeters, and soup kitchen. Hoping that this whirlwind of activities will somehow please God and make disciples, these "dabblers" are stretched to the point of breaking. Quality time with the Lord and their ministry suffers. Guide your students to focus on a few things and do them well. You may want to teach them now how to say no on a daily basis, just to keep in practice!

the fuel and the flame

30

Have You Been "Called"?

The concept of calling is a hard one to get your hands around.
The greek word *kaleo* means to call, summon, or invite. All of us
are called to become like Christ, to abide in Him, and to bring glory
to Him through our lives and personal ministries, regardless of what
our vocation happens to be. But God *has* made us all different, and
our personalities and giftings will each be suited to a unique calling.
One of my first experiences with this idea of calling was on my first
day of seminary where, in each of my classes, I would grab a seat on
the second row then wait for the prof to introduce himself and orient
us to the class. It turned out to be a "get to know you" day, as each
instructor posed the same question at the beginning of class, "What is
your name, and how were you *called* into the ministry?" As I sat and
listened to story after story, I was amazed. The first guy talked about
running from God and finally surrendering, the next about walking
the aisle after breaking down in tears, another retold a vision he
received in the middle of the night, and on and on.

By the time it was my turn I didn't know what to do. I was
tempted to say "pass" but instead confessed, "Well, I became a
Christian in high school and found out the Bible commanded us to
share our faith and make disciples. So I went to college and started
winning some of my fraternity brothers to Christ and discipling
them. I enjoyed it so much that I thought I'd like to witness
and disciple *all* the time and just thought taking some of these
seminary courses might make me more effective in my ministry."
Being the only one the prof did not affirm with nods and amens
made me a *little* uncomfortable, but the follow-up question was
the real stinger: "Yes, brother, but how were you *called* into the
ministry?" It was obvious my first response did not satisfy him,
but I had no other answer, no dramatic story, no tears or surrender,
no liver quiver to tell me (or persuade him!) that I had really,
really been called!

Reflecting on that day and the way some of my profs and
classmates reacted to me made me a little frustrated. If God calls

all of us to follow Him and embrace the Great Commission, why would I need an emotional experience to confirm this calling? To me it was a clear command from Scripture, right there in black and white for all of us to see and obey. Was I being pressured to place my experience as a higher authority than the Scriptures? I couldn't help but remember what one of my heroes of the faith, Dr. Sidlow Baxter, once said: "God will not do His deepest work in our most shallow part." I'm not saying emotional experiences are bad or that God will not use them in our lives, but help your students understand that God is looking for obedience more than goose bumps, and that the heart *and* the mind need to work together to discern His will for our lives.

Should You Go into Full-Time Ministry?

Many Christian laborers in college wrestle with the question of whether they should go into full-time ministry, the secular work force, or (much to the detriment of their parents' retirement savings!) go on for more education. I usually encourage these graduating seniors to apply the traditional means of praying, reading Scripture, getting counsel, making pro-and-con lists, etc., but I also include one question that has tremendous bearing on this issue of discovering God's will. With excitement and anticipation in my voice I ask, "If you could do *anything* in the world with your life, what would it be?" I give them a blank piece of paper and ask them to write down what they could get most excited about doing.

I admit I probably have a "wide open" view of helping a person discover God's direction for his or her life, but I believe this exercise helps them understand what they were designed to do. Psalm 37:4 says, "Delight yourself in the LORD and he will give you the desires of your heart" (NIV). If a student is truly seeking to please God in all of his ways, then the desire of his heart will certainly line up with God's desires. Besides, he will only be 100 percent motivated doing what he truly *wants* to do. If your student *really* possesses a love for God, a love for people, and the vision and training to build upon those two loves, he *will* find a way to bring glory to God through fulfilling the Great Commission—wherever he goes and whatever he does. The more men and women you launch out into the world with these convictions, the more you'll be exporting the flame that burns on your campus to a world in desperate need of the light that only Jesus Christ and His laborers can provide. ⚘

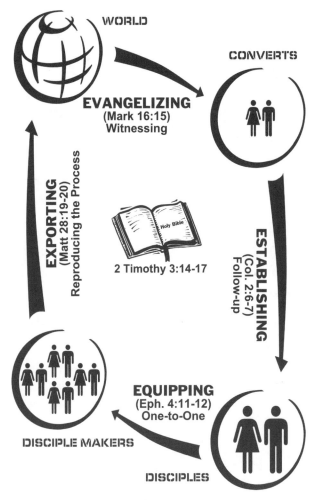

Discussion And Application Questions

1. What can we learn from Charlie's story? What does it mean to export laborers?

2. What does Steve mean when he says he shifted from his ministry to Charlie's ministry?

3. What is mobilization, and why is it the key to evangelizing the world?

4. On your campus or with your campus group, how can you move students through the "Four P's"?

5. How could God touch the world through your campus? What is the potential of just one student?

6. What is a World Christian? Are you one? If so, why do you call yourself that? If not, how can you become a World Christian?

7. What is the key to raising up World Christians on your campus? How do you do it?

8. What is a self-generated leader, and how do you develop one?

9. Preparing students to be lifelong laborers for Christ involves helping them make the right choices in critical areas like:

    A. Their career
    B. Their mate
    C. Their lifestyle

    Have you seen Christian students make bad choices in these areas? How can you help them to make the right choices?

10. As you look at the list of topics to help build a whole person for Christ, which area do *you* feel strongest in? Why? Which area do *you* feel weakest in? Why? What can we do this month that will help prepare you in this area?

11. Why do so few students who witness and disciple in college continue to do so in their adult years? What can you do now to ensure that in ten, twenty, forty years from now you'll still be witnessing and discipling? What can you do with your key student(s) now to try to ensure they will be lifelong laborers for Christ also?

12. Has every believer been called into ministry? Why or why not? How do you know if you've been called?

13. What does it mean that your campus could become a sending base? Make a list of all the disciples and disciplemakers on your campus. What can you do to help launch them (individually *and* corporately) to become lifelong laborers for Christ, stateside and/or overseas?

Read your applications and pray together that God would use you to raise up and send lifelong laborers all over the world.

chapter 10

remember to always keep the world in clear focus

iranda came from a middle-class family near St. Louis that loved her, took her to church, and did their best to instill good values in her. She was never quite satisfied, though, with her station in life. She was always comparing herself with others, wishing she could have nicer clothes, a sportier car, and a charge card to do with as she pleased. When she got to college, she turned her back on God and on her parents' upbringing and, instead, chose to run with the fast crowd. This group of hedonists were into seeking thrills, obtaining material possessions, and arrogantly flaunting their "It just doesn't get any better than this!" attitude to others. Miranda spent two years chasing this dream, trying to fill the emptiness in her soul, only to come to a dead end one day when, after receiving a notice that her $10,000 credit card limit had reached its max, she purposely got drunk and ran her convertible into a tree.

Now laid up in intensive care, Miranda had plenty of time to reflect on her life and the choices she had made. When she was released from the hospital, she went back to her campus apartment, got down on her knees, and determined to return to God and start searching for *real* meaning in her life. A high school friend had been bugging Miranda to come to a Wesleyan Center meeting with him, and she decided now was the time to quit making excuses. The program that evening consisted of a visiting band of missions mobilizers called The Traveling Team that went from campus to campus sharing the story of God's heart for the nations.

Miranda had grown up in church, been a leader in Fellowship of Christian Athletes, and had even read *National Geographic* growing up, but she had never heard passages or stories like the ones the speaker was unfolding that night. She sat mesmerized, learning that God had given her all these different blessings in life (health, education, finances, technology, salvation, the Bible, etc.) not to horde for herself but to give away to others. She realized she had basically been a "taker" rather than a "giver," and she became resolute about making a real difference in the world she was hearing about. That night, she set up an appointment to meet with one of The Traveling Team representatives in the student center the next morning. As they chatted Miranda started to see her whole life flash before her, and this confident, self-sufficient girl broke down crying, repenting of her selfishness, her ego, and her "bless *me* Lord!" inward-focused Christianity.

She Came Back to Campus a Changed Woman

The Traveling Team rep plotted out a timeline for spiritual growth and mission involvement for Miranda and then connected her with a Wesleyan Center staff woman. Together, they started meeting for quiet times, Bible study, and working through "12 Lessons to Become a World Christian," which the Traveling Team rep had given her. A year later Miranda finally had the chance to go with a summer missions team to Kiev, Ukraine, where she spent two months getting to know students, sharing her faith, and leading them to the Savior. By the fifth week she was hooked. This was exactly what God had created her to do. She no longer cared what others possessed and what she didn't. Instead she became eternally grateful for all that God had blessed her with and purposed to spend her life giving it away to the desperate and separated from Christ.

Miranda came back to campus that fall a changed woman, serving and sharing the Lord with every international student she could and immersing herself in giving rather than taking. Now Miranda is about to graduate and has been offered a high-paying position with a huge advertising firm. But instead Miranda is trying to figure out a way to become a university English teacher in a closed Third World country. The difference now is that she has real, lasting peace and fulfillment in her heart. She's found an endless source of joy that only comes when we say no to ourselves and yes to God.

Five Applications to Reach the World through Students

If you, too, want to reach students in order to reach the world, then read and heed these five applications you and your students will need to embrace and implement to have maximum, worldwide, impact.

Application #1: We Have Been Blessed—to Be a Blessing!

In the early 1980s I started getting phone calls from a persistent guy named Bob Sjogren, who worked with Frontiers mission agency. He along with Greg Fritz's Caleb Project ministry, had launched some traveling missions mobilization teams that moved from campus to campus every night giving world missions talks and challenging students with practical application steps. During those frequent calls that first year, I patiently listened but wondered, "Why is Bob calling *us*? We know *all* about missions." As pastor of students at our church, I turned him down, as I did so many of the groups that wanted to pitch their stuff to our 800-plus students. Bob would not give up, though, and I finally decided to humor him and let him and his vanload of "mission fanatics" give their little presentation.

I was *blown* away! I had studied at the largest denominational and non-denominational seminaries in the world, and I'd never heard this biblical perspective. The Great Commission in the Old Testament? God's promise to bless all nations? The Lord forming a people from every ethnic group on the planet to spend eternity with Him around the throne? My mind and heart were on overload because, for the first time, I was looking at the Scriptures and the world from *God's* perspective—not mine. I later realized Bob didn't want to get to our 800 students *nearly* as much as he wanted to get to me. He was applying the old mission field strategy: win the chief, and you'll win the tribe!

That summer Bob talked me into packing my wife and nine-month-old daughter in the old Volvo and making our way out to Pasadena, California, to take a month long *Perspectives of the World Christian Movement* course at the U.S. Center for World Missions. Since I fancied myself to be the next Billy Graham, and still thinking I pretty much had my "missions ducks" lined up, I wasn't prepared for the radical transformation that God had in store for my wife and me.

"My Heart Is So Full, It's about to Burst Wide Open!"

By day, world renowned missionaries were piercing our hearts with supernatural stories of mission field conquests, and, by night, through our readings, we were filling our minds with passages and principles of expanding the Kingdom of God here on earth. The powerful combination of inspiration and information over a four-week period just about did me in. Three days before the course was over, I went to the facilitator and said, "I *have* to go." Confused and maybe thinking I was asking directions to the bathroom, he blurted out, "What?"

"I have to leave the class *right now*. I can't stand it any more!"

Startled, he gently pleaded, "Did we offend you in some way? Is something wrong?"

"No, no. That's not it," I laughed. "It's just that my heart is *so*

the fuel and the flame ♦

full it's about to burst wide open. I *have* to get back to Arkansas and get started!"

I immediately repacked my wife and now ten-month-old daughter in the old Volvo and rushed back home to apply the things God had shown us. Two months later we had our first missions conference ever, and Dr. Ralph Winter, founder of the U.S. Center for World Mission, agreed to speak. That spring we had our first ever Perspectives course, and you'd have thought a second Pentecost had come down! After saturating their minds from the life-changing Perspectives reader each week, sixty "chomping at the bit" college students would come for three hours every Thursday night, cram into a little library room, feast on the Scriptures, and hang on *every* word the visiting missionary speakers uttered.

As a result, we were no longer interested in just "touching" our little campus. Our university, as well as every other college within our reach, had now become a launching pad to impact the entire world for Jesus Christ! Students from that first and subsequent Perspectives courses are now all over the planet, fulfilling the vision God implanted in them during those late night sessions where they grappled with the most eternal issues known to man.

Tomorrow morning turn to Psalm 67 for your quiet time to get a feel for how much God yearns for "the nations" to bow down to Him in adoration. The final verse of the chapter is the crescendo, where the psalmist cries out, "God blesses us, That all the ends of the earth may fear Him." Certainly, God has blessed us in every sense of the word, but He has poured out His grace and revelation on us for a reason. Peter uses some Old Testament language to describe what we New Testament believers are to do with the blessings:

> But you are a chosen race, a royal priesthood, a holy nation, a people for God's own possession, that you may proclaim the excellencies of Him who has called you out of darkness into His marvelous light. (1 Peter 2:9)

We are to "proclaim the excellencies" of Christ, the One who has turned our darkness into light. But if we horde this light, God will find another way, another person, to get it to those in need. We are to be His "proclaimers," yes; but if our *total* focus is on the enormous need for laborers or on diagramming neat ministry strategies or even bringing nations to the Lord, we have missed the point of exalting Christ and His excellencies.

Missions Is Not the Ultimate Goal of the Church

Author and pastor Dr. John Piper reveals the real objective of swapping a man-centered theology for a God-centered theology in his book, *Let the Nations Be Glad:*

> Missions is not the ultimate goal of the Church. The glory of God is the ultimate goal of the Church because it is the ultimate goal of God. The final goal of all things is that God might be worshipped with white hot affection by a redeemed company of countless persons from every tribe and tongue and nation. Missions exists because worship doesn't. When the Kingdom finally comes in glory, missions will cease. Missions is penultimate (the next most important thing); worship is ultimate. If we forget this and reverse their roles, the passion and the power for both diminish.

Turn the eyes of your students toward bringing glory and honor to our excellent Lord and His worldwide objective of recruiting the nations to be His "white hot" worshipers, and your young disciples will soon forget the pitiful, transient allurements of this world. Besides, they will be spending all of eternity worshiping Jesus Christ, why not get them started now?

Finally, have some fun with your students sometime by sending them into some of the local Christian bookstores to ask the clerk a couple of questions. Question 1: "Could you please tell me where your missions section is?" Watch the clerk freeze, his mind racing and eyes glazing over, and then after a few awkward seconds of silence he'll reply, "Wait a minute, I'll go ask the manager." Next comes question 2: "Can you please tell me where the Christian romance novels are?" Watch him immediately smile and say, "Right this way," proudly walking you to two full aisles of Christian fiction that would put Tom Clancy and John Grisham to shame. No need to embarrass the clerk any further by quizzing him about the evangelism section or books for college students. Besides, he may be too busy straightening up the Christian self-help shelves! Let's face it: Christian bookstores reflect the craving of our spiritual appetites; they simply stock what people want, and the sugar-coated, fantasy fiction along with the inward focused, "bless *me*, Lord," self-help titles are making a killing!

> *"Instead of living from birth to death seeking that which is safe, soft, and comfortable, live with a purpose: the purpose of glorifying God!"*
>
> **Bob Sjogren, president, UnveilinGlory Ministry**

Application #2: The Task Remaining Is of God-Sized Proportions

I will never forget the first time I stepped off the underground metro in Kharkov, Ukraine, and was confronted by thousands of quick-walking, dark-clothed, grim-faced, Russian-speaking people hurrying past me. I stood there speechless, overwhelmed, and slipping into depression. What difference could I make in this huge throng of foreigners, in a country of millions aimlessly rushing through life without Christ? At that moment, my Scripture memory paid off, as the Lord brought to mind John 15:5 where Jesus reminds us, "Apart from Me, you can do nothing."

I realized that *only* God can complete this task of world evangelization. Yes, He has chosen us as His method, but if we *ever* get the idea that we can somehow finish the job on our own, He has ways of showing us our pride and stupidity! I can't count how many times I have fallen flat on my face because I clung to

remember to always keep the world in clear focus   235 the first part of Philippians 4:13, "I can do all things," but left out the second part, "through Him, who strengthens me." Please don't make that same mistake!

Let the Facts Enflame You!

We live in unprecedented times. There are more people alive today than there have been throughout all of history. I don't understand why, but if you were to put all the people who have *ever* lived and died in stadium A and then place all the people who are alive today in stadium B, the second stadium would have *more* people! If there was ever a time to make (and even change) history, now is that time. God has picked us to be His ambassadors to this generation, and I for one want to be "looking for and hastening the coming of the day of God" (2 Peter 3:12). Can you and your students make a difference among the billions of people on our planet who do not know Christ personally? The way to begin answering that question is to find out what the needs are and, as my pastor says, "let the facts enflame you!"

The world we live in is made up of thousands of people groups. A "people group" is not a country but a nation (translated *ethne* in the Greek language). When Jesus said to "make disciples of all the nations" in Matthew 28, He could not have meant countries (those boundaries and names have changed hundreds of times since then), but *ethne* or ethnic groups (bands of people who share the same language, customs, dress, appearance, religion, etc.).

> "Do not say that God allowed the flame to wane. Have you fed the fire? Information is the fuel. If the fire has died for lack of fuel, it is your own fault."
>
> **Robert Wilder, student volunteer movement leader**

Although there are about 225 countries (as of today!), there are approximately 24,000 unique cultural affinity clusters around the world ranging from 2,500 to 25 million people in each one.

Almost two-thirds of these groups are "reached" (that is, they have an evangelistic, indigenous church with national leadership capable of reaching out to its own people), while one-third are "unreached" (that is, they are still waiting for cross-cultural missionaries to come and plant an evangelistic, indigenous church). There are lost people all over the planet and excellent mission efforts being carried out on each continent, but most of these unreached people groups lie within a certain area of the world called the 10/40 Window.

The 10/40 Window

We live in a world with many areas cut off from the gospel, but none are as blatantly isolated as the nations in the 10/40 Window. Ten and forty degree latitudinal lines above the equator, stretching from North Africa across the Middle East and including just about all of Asia—this is truly the final frontier. Estimates are that well over half the world's population lives in this box with over one billion Muslims, one billion Hindus, and one billion Buddhists, secularists, tribals, and animists combined. It's not only the least evangelized and most illiterate, the poorest of the poor with hundreds of millions starving, but also the part of the world where, each year, many of the 150,000-plus Christian martyrs worldwide are killed for their faith. Satan has a stronghold on this portion of the world like none other, intimidating the Christian church to such an extent that no more than 5 percent of the world's missionaries dare go there to live and minister.

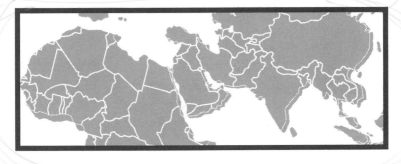

Almost half the world lives in cities, and missiologists have identified one hundred metropolitan areas within the 10/40 Window that are strategic population centers. Most of these large cities contain well over one million people and represent a melting pot of people groups in that region. Experts believe that planting an evangelistic, indigenous church in each of these cities would be the key, or gateway, to reaching the majority of the unreached people groups throughout the 10/40 Window. As an example of a creative way to make a difference in these unreached urban areas, my friend, Mike Compton, along with some Christian businessmen, is raising money to buy houses next to college campuses to rent to ministry-minded college students and funnel all the monthly rent money toward a church planting effort in some of these one hundred gateway cities.

Mike and his ministry are fantastic, but he will tell you that the real obstacle to finishing this job is not a lack of money, knowledge, materials, or even opportunity. It has, is, and always will be workers—men and women willing to go to one of these cities or people groups and lay down their lives to see a church planted and the Kingdom established. Why, 2,000 years after the command was given to preach the gospel to every person, are there still so many people who have never heard the name of Jesus?

What Is the Need of the Hour?

A number of years ago, someone was wondering the same thing and asked Dawson Trotman, founder of the Navigators, "What is the need of the hour? Some say it's larger staffs, better facilities, better communication, transportation, or literature. Some say if we just had more money or workers who were younger or older, then we'd get the job done. What is the answer?" With a burning heart Trotman responded, "What is the need of the hour, you ask? God is the God of the universe and He will supply every need we have to pull it off. The need of the hour is an army of soldiers dedicated to Jesus Christ, who believe that He is God and that He can fulfill every promise He ever made, and that nothing is too hard for Him. The need of the hour is men who want what Jesus Christ wants, and who believe He wants to give them the power to do what He has asked. Nothing in the world can stop these men."

> *"God is not looking for nibblers of the possible, but for grabbers of the impossible."*
>
> **C. T. Studd, leader of the "Cambridge Seven"**

How about you? Are you willing to rise up in this hour of need and be a dedicated soldier of Christ who wants *only* what He wants? Trotman believed that kind of laborer would not (and could not) be stopped until the job was done. Although Trotman never got past one semester of college, supported himself as a gas station attendant, and weighed only 125 pounds, he had a contagious passion for the world that couldn't be contained. When he zeroed in on the men he was discipling, slammed his fist into his hand, and with a booming voice proclaimed, "The world for Christ!" they knew he believed it with *every fiber of his being*. After Trotman drowned in 1956 while saving the life of a young girl at a lake, Billy Graham preached at his funeral and declared that he had never known *anyone* who had touched more lives for Christ than Dawson Trotman.

Does the world burn on your heart? If it does then you will infect your students with the real disease. They will catch the vision, keep the vision, and ultimately obey the vision, and *nothing* in the world can stop them! This powerful, uncontrollable fire will multiply, passing from you to them and finally to the world.

Application #3: Each Believer Has a Role in the World Christian Movement

Every believer is to pray, give, witness, and disciple, but are we called to do more, to find a specific role (or calling, if you will) in Christ's global cause? The answer, of course, is yes.

As you consecrate yourself to God to be used in any way He

sees fit, try one or more of these four world-Christian roles on for size. One size does not fit all, and you may end up wearing several different ones at various stages of your life. In a sense, these are simply four "habits" to develop in your life; but ask the Lord whether your primary role right now is as a goer, a sender, a welcomer, or a mobilizer:

A. The Goers are the Frontline Warriors

In reality we are all goers—all frontline warriors. Jesus gave us the command to "go and make disciples of all nations." From man's perspective, though, it would appear that God's distribution plan has not worked out so well! It is estimated that up to 95 percent of the world's trained Christian workers live in the good old United States (where only 6 percent of the planet's population resides!). Many people are willing to go but are planning on staying. We need folks who are planning to go but are willing to stay if that is the most strategic thing to do for the Kingdom. Most are waiting for an emotional calling, a voice from on high telling them to be a missionary. It's amazing that this is just about the only area of life that we apply this lightning bolt-calling concept to! There are about 600 million active Christians in the world today. Approximately 150 million of them are between twenty-two to fifty years of age. The estimate is that we need only about 20,000 to 30,000 of them to be cross-cultural missionaries to finish reaching every unreached people group. That means we only need one volunteer from every 5,000 people in this age group! With 600 Bible-believing local churches for every one unreached people group in the world, you would

> *"For years we have been trusting God for every student. Now for the first time in history we have access to every student. Today, no person, no administration and no government can stand between a college student and the good news of Jesus."*

Steve Sellers, Campus Crusade's director of Global Campus Ministries

think together we could recruit enough goers to complete this task! Let's get our people praying Matthew 9:36–38, and ask the Holy Spirit to fill this quota!

B. The Senders are the Vicarious Rope Holders
These are people who would like to be overseas but feel called to stay and hold the ropes for those who do go. Out of the 100,000 students who volunteered for missions from 1890 to 1930, about 20,000 actually went and 80,000 stayed at home to help fund them. Imagine applying that ratio today, having four laymen team up and each cover one-fourth of a missionary's support. This kind of sacrifice would allow us to make tremendous strides in getting funds to the frontlines, because currently 96 percent of all the money we give to Christian causes stays in North America! Amazingly, the combined annual after-tax income of American Christians is well over a trillion dollars, but collectively we only give two billion to missions. That may sound like a lot, but it represents only one-sixth of 1 percent of our income. We spend 10 billion each year on weight reduction programs and even more on cosmetics and dog food! To be a financial sender you may have to take a look at your lifestyle in order to radically scale it back and give more to God's work around the world. Senders not only give but also pray. They can impact the world right from their dorm room, daily shooting prayer arrows around the world asking God to raise up laborers, to empower those who are laboring, and to bring about fruit in the unreached areas of the world. Lastly, senders are involved in personal ministry, where they disciple others with a world vision and seek to send them into the harvest field. World-Christians beget world-Christians!

> *"Eight out of every ten dollars held by Christians are in the hands of American Christians."*
>
> **George Verwer, founder of Operation Mobilization**

C. The Welcomers Are the Ministers of Hospitality

It's like the Lord told us to go to the world and gave us all these resources, but we, instead, chose to stay and enjoy the comforts of America. "Well," God said, "if you won't go to them, I'll just bring them to you. Is this close enough?" There are close to 750,000 international students from almost 200 countries in the United States. Our country has become an international melting pot, and yet we neglect to reach out to these foreigners who are all around us. Statistics show most international students come to the States to study for four to six years and *never* even enter an American's home. They want to, of course, but are not invited. How would you feel if you spent four to six years in another country and never even ate a meal in a family's home there? This is one of many reasons why these internationals get bitter and cynical toward our so-called Christian nation. We can impact the world right here in our backyard, because the nations send their best and brightest (the future leaders) right to our doorstep. You can adopt one or more while they are here. Pray for them, love on them, share your life and faith with them. Let them see what you, your family, and your faith are all about. The ministry of International Students Incorporated (ISI) encourages us to try it and see what God will do. You just might end up sending them back with a vision to reach their own country for Christ. That's definitely the most strategic (and cheapest!) way to infiltrate the nations with missionaries.

D. The Mobilizers Are the Strategic Motivators

These are the ones who yearn to be on the field, but they feel called to stay behind to rally the troops and to "stir the pot" stateside. They form mission committees at their churches; plan missions conferences; recruit people to pray, give, and go; organize short and long-term mission teams; and attempt to get books and materials into every Christian's hands. As a result, they are sometimes called pests or fanatics behind their backs! Dr. Ralph Winter, founder of the U.S. Center for World Mission, says a high priority within the body of Christ is for more mobilizers—more men and women in every church, every town, and every campus who will help open people's eyes to what God is doing around the world and aid believers in finding their world-Christian role as either goers, senders, welcomers, or mobilizers.

Dr. Winter claims that no less than 100,000 sincere, envisioned people write each year to one or another of the various mission agencies in this country asking for information about possible service. The estimate is that less than 1,000 of those will ever make it to the field. Why? There is no one to nurture and guide and equip them to complete the process. In other words, the workers are plentiful, but the mobilizers are few! Dr. Winter asserts, "Anyone who can help 100 missionaries to the field is more important than one missionary on the field. In fact, mission mobilization activity is just as crucial than field missionary activity." You may or may not agree, but read on!

> *"Millions of Christian students casually pass through four of the most important years of their life. Many are involved in ministries, and yet the uttermost remains the uttermost. Why? Very few students have been introduced to the fact that 3 billion souls are without Christ. Even fewer students realize that their lives can be used to impact the eternal destiny of these people. We need to be people who can motivate students by sounding the trumpet that life is about more than just themselves."*
>
> **Todd Ahrend,**
> **international director of**
> **The Traveling Teams**

Standing before a crowd of university students, Dr. Winter challenged them, saying, "Suppose I had 1,000 graduating seniors in front of me who asked me where they ought to go to make a maximum contribution to Christ's global cause. What would I tell them? I would tell some of them to stay home and mobilize." How in the world can this former missionary say this with a straight face, talking people into *not* becoming missionaries? He answers, "Because the need to sound the alarm is so great. Some will go as pioneer missionaries. Still others will be able to exercise the even *more* unusual faith to stay back from the field and assist this entire U.S. mobilization process to succeed."

Application #4: Unleash Students to Spearhead the Charge

Like a car that makes a ninety degree right turn going sixty miles per hour, college students have the innate ability to make quick decisions and instant life changes. Jordan grew up camping, hiking, and rock climbing with full intentions of passionately pursuing these loves when he entered the University of Arkansas, but God had a hard right turn in store. Almost from day one, a Campus Crusade staff member plugged him into a small group and their leadership training track. Although he became a Christian at an early age, his walk with the Lord didn't take off until he attended a CCC summer project in Branson, Missouri. After that experience, his new focal point was to become a *Christian* physical therapist, that is until he met Pete Kelley, a CCC staffer in Estonia, where Jordan had gone for another CCC summer mission project. When Pete challenged Jordan to consider full-time ministry as his vocation, he came back, prayed hard, and made another right turn by changing his major to graduate sooner, raise support, and head to Thailand for a year-long mission assignment.

> *"The most important work of any kind in the world today—greater than all of the problems facing men and nations—is the recapturing of the great universities of the world for Jesus Christ."*
>
> **Dr. Charles Malik, former president of the United Nations**

Jordan's mentor, CCC veteran David English, sent me his e-mails from the field, and they read like a modern-day replay of the book of Acts. He describes one adventure of taking the *JESUS* film to an eager tribe of natives who had never even seen a movie: "My group was going to the most remote village around and the terrain was so hilly that at times we had to pull the truck (full of equipment) up the hills using a rope!" Once Jordan and the team got set up, a neighboring tribe saw the lights and walked an hour and a half to see the film. There were many who received Christ that night as their eyes were glued to the screen. Jordan was impacted too, sharing, "The Lord really spoke to me that night. My dreams were coming true: being out in the wilderness and showing the *JESUS* film to those who have never heard. Just to look at the people's eyes during the film was amazing. It was one of the greatest nights of my life."

His main ministry, though, is among the almost one million college students in the bustling, pollution-filled city of Bangkok. After overcoming culture shock from the abject poverty, the putrid smell, and the swarms of stray dogs everywhere, he was able to build relationships with Thai students. Jordan is sharing the gospel on a daily basis, seeing some receive Christ and others reject Him because of their Buddhist beliefs. He agonizes over the hardened hearts of many of the male students. When one guy responded to his gospel message with, "I don't need Jesus," Jordan just about broke down and cried. It's hard to believe that this happy-go-lucky kid from Harrison, Arkansas, who had his life all planned out, is now half-way across the world pouring out his life for the lost in Thailand. The moldable, pliable, flexible heart of a college student is a beautiful thing in the hands of the Lord. For students, this is *the* opportune time in their lives for us to pray, challenge, recruit, and send them to a world in desperate need of workers.

This just in: Jordan just signed up for another year in Thailand!

Even though *students* have led the way in evangelizing the world, they have done it, many times, without the help of *churches* and *mission agencies*. Just as the roots, trunk, and branches serve one another to produce a healthy tree, an incredible synergy could be created if these three groups could coordinate their efforts, drawing upon the strengths of each to be church-based, student-focused, and agency-linked:

A. Church based

This is the place where the workers are nourished, fed, and

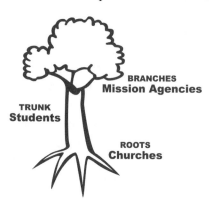

prayed for. These are the rank-and-file believers who intercede, give, and send. Just as the roots of a tree provide the stability and resources for the trunk and branches, world-Christian churches do the same for student groups and mission agencies. Parachurch campus min-istries must not try to take the place of local churches, but work in partnership as a complement to them.

B. Student focused

Virtually every major missions movement in history has been instigated and fueled by college-aged young people. Then and now, they are the primary suppliers of crucial personnel for the over-ripened harvest. Xavier, the pioneer missionary, told students centuries ago to "give up their small ambitions and come eastward to preach the gospel of Christ." The winning, building, and sending of collegians must be a primary focus of churches if the workers are going to get to the field.

C. Agency linked

We don't need more mission agencies—we've got hundreds of excellent ones ready and able to penetrate every unreached people group. But they are waiting for student ministries and local churches to wake up and provide them with the needed workers and the resources to turn them loose. The roots or the trunk can't reach up into the sky to heights unknown; only the branches are designed to do that.

Right now you might be thinking, "Gosh, I would like to raise up some Jordans too! Just *how* do you get students to develop a heart for the world?" As we've seen, it requires teamwork and, it begins, ends, and is covered with deep, consistent intercessory prayer. This role of "world prayer warrior" is only as effective as the specific information that we have to pray back to our heavenly Father. Patrick Johnstone's book, *Operation World,* is the best tool I've seen that gives, what I call, detailed "prayer fodder" about the demographics, needs, and prayer requests of every country and, most of all, the people groups within those countries. Use it in your own devotional time each day to build a heart for the world. Take it with you when you have quiet times or concerts of prayer with your disciples. Train your students to use their *Operation World* along with their journals and Bibles on a daily basis.

The Sneakiest Verse in the Whole Bible

In Matthew 9:36–38 (NIV), Jesus gave us an awesome plan for raising up world-Christians. But beware, it is easily the sneakiest passage in the whole Bible! Here it is:

> When he saw the crowds, he had compassion on them, because they were harassed and helpless, like sheep without a shepherd. Then he said to his disciples, "The harvest is plentiful but the workers are few. Ask the Lord of the harvest, therefore, to send out workers into his harvest field."

You look at this verse and realize that the bottleneck is *not* with the harvest, it's with the workers! Jesus doesn't tell us to get out there and start witnessing, nor does He say to start praying for the lost. The Lord simply commands us to *ask Him* to raise up Christian laborers to work among the unreached of our world. Let's say you've completed your inductive Bible study of this passage and you are now ready to make an application, doing exactly what it says. You get out your trusty *Operation World* and flip to today's entry, which lists the kingdom of Morocco in North

Africa. You casually read some of the basic country information: "Total population: 30 million; Urban population: 51%; Arabic speaking: 65%; Berber speaking: 34%; Literacy: 30%; Annual income per person: $1,260."

This reminds you of your old high school geography class and you're getting a little bored with this information, so you glance at the religion statistics and suddenly you're stopped dead in your tracks! What? 99.85 percent of the whole country is Muslim? Less than 500 believers out of 30 million people? And many of those believers aren't even Moroccan? It must be a misprint! How could *any* country in the world only have one Christian for every 60,000 people? You bear down and look closer at the text, carefully reading that Sunni Islam is the *state* religion, that witnessing and church planting are not tolerated, and that this country is the tenth worst persecutor of Christians on the planet. How could this be? You never heard about this in church, much less geography class! Out of frustration and burden, your mind races to figure out a way you can right this wrong.

Then you remember Matthew 9:36–38, where Jesus gave you the solution to this dilemma, and so, on bended knee you begin, "Lord, You told me in Matthew 9 to ask You to raise up laborers to go to the harvest fields. I'm right here just doing what You told me. I ask, Lord, that You search out workers who will go to Morocco and boldly tell those people about Jesus. Oh God, please find men and women who will heed Your call to go. You said that the harvest is plentiful, and I believe it Lord. So I'm asking You, Father, just like You told me, to send workers to Morocco quickly. Amen."

Let's say that day after day, week after week, you decide, even though at times you don't feel like it, that you're going to obey the command

> *"God is amazing, unrivaled, glorious, central everywhere in the universe, yet in large measure His praise is absent from the campuses of our nation and world. Anyone passionate for His fame longs to see that change."*
>
> **Louie Giglio, director of Passion Ministries**

the fuel and the flame ◆

Jesus gave us in Matthew 9 and continue to plead with God to raise up and send workers to this spiritually desolate country of Morocco. Then early one morning, while on your knees, you unexpectedly get what I call "the divine tap" on the edge of your shoulder. A still small voice speaking to your heart calls you by name and says, "I have answered your prayers." Your heart leaps and you cry out, "Thank you, Lord, thank you. I have been *so* diligent to pray, just like You commanded, for laborers to go to Morocco; and now you've responded. Praise you, Jesus!" "Yes," the small voice replies, "I have answered your prayers, and *you* are the answer to your prayers!" "Oh, no, Lord," you cry out, "I didn't mean send *me*. I was praying for You to send someone else! There must be a mix up!"

This little drama would never end this way because if you *really* had been toiling in prayer for weeks or months over Morocco, and if the Lord *did* speak to you about going, your heart would have been prepared for His call. The reason this is the sneakiest verse in the Bible? Because Jesus knows full well that you will become deeply burdened about *whatever* you labor over in prayer. This passage serves as the crux of God's missionary recruitment strategy. If He can get you and your students to obey the command of Matthew 9:36–38, He knows it is just a matter of time before your heart will be so full, so weighed down, that you will be willing to do *whatever* He tells you. That makes these Matthew 9 verses not only the sneakiest but also the most dangerous in the Bible. WARNING: Do not obey this passage if you do not want to become a laborer in the harvest!

If we will be faithful to intercede for the nations, our prayers will break down strongholds of sin, soften the hearts of leaders, open the doors for missionaries, and pave the way for nationals trying to win their neighbors. Dick Eastman, author of *The Hour That Changes the World* claims that prayer is the most powerful and effective weapon we have to bring about real, lasting change in people and nations. As Eastman says, "To pray for world evangelization is to serve on a 'Great Commission Fulfillment

Committee' that meets daily in the courts of heaven." We can huff and we can puff trying to blow a nation over for Christ, but unless we look to *His* power (through prayer) and not our own, we will be ministering in vain.

Application #5: You're in the Race, and the Baton Is Passed to You!

Growing up, all the men in my family were pole-vaulters, except me (the Shadrach strength and speed genes skipped me!). But I did enjoy cheering them on at track meets. One memorable Friday night conference meet in Dallas featured the world-record holding Lincoln High School mile-relay team. It was standing room only for this final event of the evening, everyone hoping that maybe the four Lincoln runners would set a new record in front of a hometown crowd.

See if you can imagine this scene: When the gun sounded, Lincoln's first leg sprinted to the front and maintained his lead around the track before handing the baton to the second leg, who increased Lincoln's lead even more. As the third man received the baton and raced around the 440-yard track, thousands of cheering fans knew they were witnessing history being made. With a huge lead, the third leg came cruising into the handoff zone to pass the baton to the anchorman, the final and fastest leg of the team. As the fourth man started his sprint and held his hand out for the baton, disaster struck. Even though they had practiced the handoff thousands of times, that night there was a bobble, and the baton fell to the ground. Everyone in the stands froze as we watched the runner lean down to pick it up, only to accidentally kick it into the infield. Now the young man was on all fours, crawling toward the baton, while the paralyzed crowd was hyperventilating!

> *"I have found that there are three stages in every work of God; first, it is impossible, then it is difficult, then it is done."*
>
> **Hudson Taylor, 1865**

By the time he got the baton and ran back to the track, every runner had passed him. Starting from a dead standstill, Lincoln's anchorman put it into a gear that no one knew he had. His adrenaline pumping wildly (along with ours!), he caught up and passed the last man, then the second to the last, and the next, and the next, until finally, with a photo finish at the tape, he beat the lead runner and won the race! The disbelieving crowd erupted with an ear-shattering cheer, realizing that we had seen history being made, but it was very different than we'd expected. It was certainly a night to remember—and learn from.

I don't know who led you to Christ, who followed you up, who discipled you, or who instilled a world vision in you. Or, maybe you're a spiritual orphan who had to figure out all these things on your own, with no one to pass the baton to you in a solid, effective way. Whether or not there has been a person or ministry to hand off the necessary knowledge, skills, character, and vision to help you run (and win) this race does not excuse you from picking up the baton and running with all of your heart, soul, and mind. The purpose of this book is to provide you with a good baton pass, share some basic principles that anyone (regardless of background) can apply to life and ministry.

Get Up, Strip Down, Dig In, and Move Out!

By now you've realized the Great Commission is not a spectator sport. You need to get out of the stands and onto the track and find the race that God has for you. In fact, Hebrews 12:1–2 exhorts us to get up, strip down, dig in, and, move out:

> Therefore, since we have so great a cloud of witnesses surrounding us, let us also lay aside every encumbrance and the sin which so easily entangles us, and let us run with endurance the race that is set before us, fixing our eyes on Jesus, the author and perfecter of faith, who for the joy set before Him endured

the cross, despising the shame, and has sat down at the right hand of the throne of God.

Not only are Moses, Abraham, Paul, and Timothy our witnesses, but so are the pioneer student world-changers like Samuel Mills, Hudson Taylor, and Grace Wilder—men and women who ripped out every stronghold of sin in their lives, every attachment to this world that might choke out their spiritual power, in order to run the race. One student volunteer, world-class sprinter Eric Lidell of *Chariots of Fire* fame, felt led to give up his sports career to be a missionary in China so he could keep his eyes fixed on Jesus and experience "the pleasure of God" in his life.

> *One definition of a football game:*
>
> *22 men on the field in desperate need of rest being watched by 50,000 people in the stands in desperate need of exercise!*

What Can One Student Do?

I know of a student who didn't quite have this vision yet. John indulged himself in the party life, mocking the Christians who witnessed to him at every turn. At the end of his freshmen year, John decided to transfer to Cornell, an Ivy League school that he'd heard could *really* supply the kind of night life he was looking for, without all the pesky religious nuts constantly trying to convert him. When he arrived on campus that fall, who was there to help him unload, unpack, and get settled into his dorm room, but a group of men from a local campus ministry! He could run, but he couldn't hide; for these students persisted in inviting John to their weekly meetings.

Finally, to get them off his back, he agreed to come to one of their gatherings, but he showed up late so as not to appear too interested. As he slipped in through a side door, he was surprised to see a packed-out auditorium and every student intently listening to each word that the lecturer, a British sports hero, was saying. As

John started to tiptoe to the back, the speaker suddenly cried out, "Young man!" John turned, thinking he had been caught. "Are you seeking great things for yourself?" the loud voice boomed. John stood speechless, unable to move and in a stare-down with this hulk of a man at the podium. "Seek them not!" the speaker added, "Seek first the Kingdom of God!"

John regained his composure, then lost himself in the back of the crowd. But he could not sleep that night, wondering if it was the visiting speaker who was addressing him, or if it could be God Himself trying to give him a message. The next morning, John tracked down the British guest and set up an appointment to talk. The speaker, he learned, was J. E. K. Studd of England, who, along with his brother, was giving away his family fortune and turning down lucrative sports contracts to be a missionary in China. Studd's conviction about sacrificing all for Christ and His worldwide mission cut John to the core. That very day John humbled himself, repented, and turned his life and future over to the God he always knew was patiently waiting for him.

Soon after, John was invited to a summer project in Massachusetts to study the Bible and grow in Christ. He attended with about 250 other guys, not realizing the Lord had another big step for him. Midway through the project, a challenge was issued to the group, asking them to dedicate their lives to reaching the world's unevangelized, inviting each man to sign a declaration stating their intent. John was one of 100 men who put their names on the document, making a covenant with God to give their lives to doing whatever they could to see the world come to Christ.

Reaching Students to Reach the World

Because John had been impacted by a visiting missions speaker during his undergraduate days, he volunteered to travel from campus to campus challenging students to embrace Christ's global cause. He never actually became a cross-cultural missionary himself, but over the next sixty years he traveled the world, recruiting over 100,000 students to the job of world evangelization. After winning the Nobel Peace Prize in 1946 as one of the greatest missionary statesmen in all of history, John reflected, "Across the years this work among students, first in one's own country and then throughout the world, was always my first love." At the end of his life, looking back at the different people and events that shaped him, John could not forget the short appointment he had sixty years earlier with the visiting British sports hero turned mobilizer. He paused, looked at his biographer and stated, *"It was the decisive hour of my life."*

John R. Mott may have started out as a rebellious sophomore at Cornell University in 1885, but God awakened in him a heart for reaching students to reach the world and, in so doing, spearheaded the greatest mobilization effort ever, the Student Volunteer Movement. Right now, trying to type these words through my tears, I ask you the same questions I

> *"At first glance, it might seem like all the pioneering has been done. But the marathon is still on and the baton has been passed to us."*
>
> **Patti Burgin**

am asking myself. What difference can one college student make? What is the potential of one individual sold out to the person and purposes of Jesus Christ? Is this cause worth exchanging *your* life for?

Know this for sure: If you will give yourself as the fuel, God will ignite the flame for worldwide impact. *You* are responsible for reaching *this* generation of students. Experience the pleasure of God by investing your life as a co-gatherer with Him, reaching people from every corner of the earth to spend eternity worshiping Christ around the throne.

> After this I looked and there before me was a great multitude that no one could count, from every nation, tribe, people and language, standing before the throne and in front of the Lamb. They were wearing white robes and were holding palm

branches in their hands. And they cried out in a loud voice: "Salvation belongs to our God, who sits on the throne, and to the Lamb." (Revelation 7:9–10, NIV)

This passage tells us what to pray for and work toward in life: always keep your eyes focused on *that day*. It is the glorious culmination of all of history, as well as the final exam on what we gave ourselves to during our brief stay on earth. Decide *now* that you will not be at the throne alone, but with a throng of individuals who came to college as students but left as world-changers as a result of *your* life and ministry.

Are you ready to give yourself totally to this purpose?

Could this be the decisive hour of *your* life?

The baton is being passed to you.

Take it and run!

Discussion And Application Questions

1. What can we learn from Miranda's story?

2. What changes took place in Steve's life after he took the *Perspectives* missions course? What actions did he take as a result of those changes?

3. If missions is not the ultimate goal of the Church, what is?

4. What remains to be done to finish evangelizing the world? What is the 10/40 Window, and why is it called the final frontier?

5. Read 2 Peter 3:12. We are commanded to look for and hasten the day of His coming. Are you anxious for Christ to return, and is there a role you can play to hasten His coming?

6. Listed are four different roles we can fill in the world Christian movement. Explain each and tell us which one(s) you feel drawn to:
   A. Goer
   B. Sender
   C. Welcomer
   D. Mobilizer

7. Are you most closely associated with a local church, a parachurch campus ministry, or a missions agency? How can you work with the other two groups to finish the task of world evangelization?

8. Read Matthew 9:36–38. Why does Steve call this the sneakiest, most dangerous verse in the entire Bible? Do you have the courage and obedience to start praying this prayer regularly? How could you get started?

9. Is there any baggage in your life that is keeping you from taking the baton from the Lord and running with all of your heart, soul, and mind?

10. Nineteenth century evangelist D. L. Moody once said, "The world has yet to see what God can do through one person who is totally yielded to Him." What do you think is the potential of just one student?

11. How did God touch John R. Mott's life while in college, and, as a result, what did John do the rest of his life? How does God want to touch your life while in college? What would He have you do with the rest of your life?

12. Read Revelation 7:9–10. Start with the end in mind and work backwards. If this event is the *final* culmination of history, and you desire to be there, surrounded by the people(s) you touched for Christ, what is your plan to get you from here to there?

13. Share what changes God has brought about in your life as a result of reading, discussing, and applying this book.

Read your applications and pray together that each of you would take the baton, keep the world in clear focus, and someday meet up at the throne, each bringing a multitude of peoples from around the world that God touched through you.

appendix

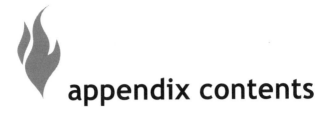

appendix contents

appendix 1

the three kinds of students on every campus

All students are different. They come to college with a preformed package of gifts, personality, family pluses and minuses, goals, and interests. They are also at different stages of social and emotional maturity. If a person comes to Christ and has a strong self-esteem because of her social and emotional maturity, she can grow in Christ rapidly and is able to reach out to others immediately. Those who come to Christ and who aren't as strong socially or emotionally normally have a harder time taking off spiritually. They may find it difficult to get beyond their feelings of inadequacy and reach out to others. These three categories following are very broad ways of how students might be broken into groups based on their social and emotional maturity. Obviously not everyone fits one of these descriptions.

A. The Influencers

These are "mainstream" students who choose their university based upon the reputation of its campus life, thus giving them a chance to socialize with others they consider "equals." Like high school, they start building a web of friendships from day one, seeking involvement in student government, Greek chapters, athletics, or clubs. They don't necessarily have a cause they're pursuing; they simply want to be in the middle of whatever is happening on campus. Their desire to be accepted and to influence guides their decisions about time and involvement. Because they are naturally able to bond with and attract others, recruiting one of these individuals could allow you to affect a large number of students. When you hold a study break (i.e., food and talk as an intro into a Bible study) for a group of students in a particular dorm wing, it won't take ten minutes to see which student is the ringleader.

B. The Interested

These are "midstream" students who were never big fish in high school but are now trying to find a place to plug in. They have strengths to offer and want to get involved and make friends; they just don't have as much confidence or experience yet as the influencers. They will usually gravitate toward one of the official or unofficial groups attached to the influencers. Even though they may not have as much natural leadership, they can be trained to influence others if someone takes the time to befriend and believe in them.

C. The Isolated

These are "out of the stream" students who are tucked in a cove away from the influential and interested. They might go to a major institution because of a certain academic program, but many will choose a lesser-known or smaller college because it's not as intimidating. A high percentage want to stick close to home and enroll in a nearby school, because they're kind of checking college out to see if it's for them. They may come from a dysfunctional home where a foundation of love and nurture wasn't established and, consequently, struggle with forming multiple friendships. Not desiring to socialize in large groups, they are still willing to be influenced, but they may be turned off by the popular or outgoing leader type. They can end up being lonely, but curious students who will simply be observers until someone pulls them into campus life. As they mature spiritually, they can progress socially and emotionally too, gradually reaching out beyond themselves to minister to others.

Why Do You Work with the Students You Do?

A lot of campus ministries may subconsciously gravitate toward the interested and isolated students, because they appear less intimidating and are usually looking for a spiritual or social refuge while at college. As needy as these students are, many times they do not represent the heart of the campus, the movers and shakers who influence which direction a campus is going. I would encourage you not to minister by default (that is, working with whatever students happen to cross your path) but to purposely choose the students you believe God wants you to reach in order to have maximum impact on your campus.

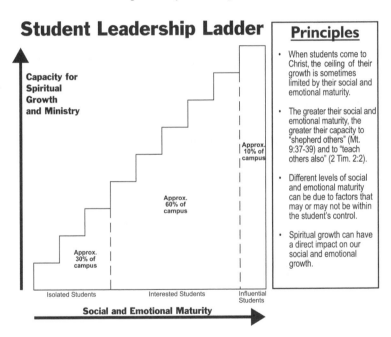

Student Leadership Ladder

Capacity for Spiritual Growth and Ministry

Approx. 30% of campus

Approx. 60% of campus

Approx. 10% of campus

Isolated Students   Interested Students   Influential Students

Social and Emotional Maturity

Principles

• When students come to Christ, the ceiling of their growth is sometimes limited by their social and emotional maturity.

• The greater their social and emotional maturity, the greater their capacity to "shepherd others" (Mt. 9:37-39) and to "teach others also" (2 Tim. 2:2).

• Different levels of social and emotional maturity can be due to factors that may or may not be within the student's control.

• Spiritual growth can have a direct impact on our social and emotional growth.

Over the years I have done some informal surveying of church and parachurch ministries on a variety of college campuses. As I quiz them about the numbers involved with their ministries along with the kinds of students who are coming, I've learned that a maximum of only 2.5 to 5 percent of any given student population are involved in campus ministries, and that most groups have few, if any, influencers participating. Although there may be anywhere from three to fifty different ministries on a particular campus, many times they are all focused on the same groups—primarily interested or isolated students. As a result, it is difficult for ministries to get influencers to come over or stay at their meetings, because they want to associate with others like themselves.

Rick Warren, pastor and author of *The Purpose Driven Church*, says that first time visitors make a decision about whether they will come back to a church in the first *ten minutes* of being there! When a newcomer walks in the doors, he looks around the group and makes an almost immediate value judgment as to whether "these are my kind of people" or not. Birds of a feather *really do* flock together, and it's human nature to want to associate with those we perceive are most like us. Warren and his mega congregation at Saddleback Valley Community Church in southern California have gone so far as to identify the characteristics, values, and lifestyle of the "people group" they are going after. He chose to build his leadership core around influencers, even including example pictures of what "Saddleback Sam" and "Saddleback Sally" look like! Now, I don't know if you want to put wanted posters up around campus with photographs of the kinds of students you are looking for, but it is good to know which group you're targeting!

You must decide which campus groups the Lord wants *you* to focus on. What I described is just one strategy I've observed having a powerful effect over the last twenty-five years. Still, obedience to Christ is the key, not copying others' strategies.

appendix 2

eight principles for reaching the influencers

If you desire to raise up strong generations of student leaders, to boldly plant the flag of Jesus Christ in the heart of your campus, and to help change the very direction the school is headed, you may want to consider focusing much of your prayer and efforts on the student influencers. If so, here are some principles you can apply to your ministry.

1. Select individuals who can "teach others also."

Paul told Timothy to be very careful about which individuals he selected to work with. He narrowed down the pool of potential laborers significantly because they not only had to be faithful but be "able to teach others also" (2 Timothy 2:2). They were to be men able to focus on others' needs, and not their own. They needed to have a desire to influence others and the confidence and gifting to succeed. When Timothy found such men he was to entrust his life and teaching to them so that they could become multipliers—and pass it on to others.

2. The mature can relate to a broader spectrum of people.

Paul didn't *have* to relate to anyone, but he chose to. He was free from all men, but he was willing (and able) to relate to and reach different kinds of people. Whatever religious background or personality traits a person possessed, Paul adapted himself in order to reach him for Christ (1 Corinthians 9:19–23). Usually people are only able to relate effectively to those who are like them (or below them) spiritually, socially, or economically. It takes a lot of maturity and confidence to think you can relate to, understand, witness to, and win *any* person no matter how high and mighty they might be in the world's eyes. Paul possessed this perspective of himself and ministry. So should we.

3. Jesus said to focus on shepherds more than the sheep.

The Lord told us there's a vast harvest and that the majority of the world's people are part of the wandering group of distressed and downcast sheep. The need is not for more sheep but for people who can be raised up to shepherd and work among them. They must be raised up from within the flock, not outside it. They must have the spiritual, social, and emotional maturity to go beyond themselves and care about the needs of others. Jesus told His disciples not to pray for more sheep but to pray for more shepherds. The cry of His heart was for more laborers (Matthew 9:36–38), not more followers, but more leaders—people who could be part of the solution rather than part of the problem. It is not exclusivity or favoritism that we select and develop these individuals. Not only is it in obedience to Christ, it is what He modeled Himself.

4. Win the chief, win the tribe.

This is part of the "people group" concept that missiologists finally discovered in the mid-twentieth century. To try to win the tribe *before* the chief will backfire, but if the chief makes a genuine decision, then the whole tribe will make a decision also. I saw this so clearly when I was witnessing to a group of ten college students in a Ukrainian dorm room. They listened closely, but when it came to decision time they took their cues from the leader of the pack. He hesitated to commit himself—and then, one by one, I saw the others follow suit.

5. The heart of the campus is the most unreached segment.

Most ministries are nibbling around the edges of a campus, focusing on interested or isolated students because it is less threatening and they are more available. Seldom will an influencer feel the need to come into a church or campus-ministry building. If they are going to be reached, it will be because the worker goes to them, on their turf, to build rapport and win them. Few campus workers are willing to take the initiative, break through the mental barrier, and approach a student who *appears* to have it all together. Even though some of the influencers have insecurities (and deep down are waiting for someone to break through to enter their world), they are easily the most unreached segment of students on any campus.

6. The core of the movement must be made up of influencers.

Everyone yearns to have a growing, dynamic large group with lots of excitement, momentum, and relationships. For this to happen, the core of at least ten to twenty students has to be influencers. They are the magnets who attract other influencers, the interested and the isolated to the ministry, and they are also the glue that cause them to stick. If the core is primarily interested or isolated students, then a movement will never get off the ground. Your group will struggle with: (1) relating to each other, (2) being able to have personal ministries, (3) attracting others to the movement, and (4) influencing the campus. When influencers are at the core, recruiting to meetings, conferences, and summer projects is revolutionized. If the key leaders are going, everybody wants to go. The body goes where the heart goes.

7. Focus on influencers and you'll indirectly affect more of the interested and isolated.

Jesus loves all students the same, and so should we. How can we impact the greatest number of students regardless of what grouping they might fit into? If our core is interested or isolated students, the movement may remain small and impotent. If a staff person will spend the first two years forming a core of influential men and women, the ministry will be able to do anything they want the third year (i.e., start a large-group meeting, small-group studies, etc.), and the campus will follow their lead. Sixty percent of the campus are interested students who are waiting to follow and get involved. Thirty percent are isolated students who are curious or lonely enough to at least check out what is going on and consider participating. Quality begets quantity, and the level of spiritual, social, and emotional maturity at the core will determine the ultimate quality *and* quantity of a campus movement. If you have a heart for reaching the interested and isolated students, consider focusing on the influential—they will draw the others in.

8. If you want influential staff, you must focus on influential students.

The students we focus on and build into will be the ones who join our team. A ministry staff that is made up of interested or isolated individuals will have a hard time recruiting an influential leader to join its staff. As crass as it may sound, John Maxwell, in his book *21 Irrefutable Laws of Leadership,* places a number next to each person, rating their leadership abilities with one being the lowest and ten the highest. His premise is that we can only attract and influence those who are equal or below us in the leadership chain. A six can recruit and lead fours, fives, and sixes; but a nine can lead sevens, eights, and nines, etc. If your ministry is full of bold visionaries who are not afraid to go straight to the heart of the campus, you will draw stronger leaders to your team. We reap what we sow, and leaders attract leaders.

Sometimes I wonder whether a ministry ought to be "targeting" *any* student group. If a student crosses your path, isn't that a sign from the Lord that this person deserves your ministry time and energies? Well, maybe and maybe not. He might appear faithful, but it may be that he doesn't have any friends, so he will surely respond to *any* attention you give him! It could be that he doesn't really have anything better to do, so why not hang with you? And yes, he seems very teachable, but is it because his self-esteem is so low he'll listen to anyone?

Mike Hearon, director for the Campus Outreach ministry headquartered in Augusta, Georgia, gives us some perspective on selecting students. He says, "Campus workers are already selective, it's simply a question of how selective. They're not working with the homeless, mentally impaired, unwed mothers or anyone who is *not* a student. So, they have already selected a mainstream group by choosing the college campus because most people can't or don't go to college."

Hearon encourages his staff and student leaders to take these facts into consideration when deciding where to invest their limited amount of time and energy. He wants to reach as many students on campus as possible and believes that focusing on the influencers is the key: "We must see our apostolic calling and realize more people can be reached by investing in those who will be able to teach others also." When asked how long it takes to develop an individual who is not already a leader into a campus leader, Hearon responds, "It probably won't happen in the short period of time they are in college. They can eventually become a force for God, but it will probably take five to ten years. A staff person must 'restock' the movement each year in order to perpetuate the impact on the campus, so the staffer must be selective in leadership investment." In short, if your goal is to raise up students who can reach out to other students, it will be much more difficult if you start with just interested or isolated students. Pray about going after the most unreached on your campus: the influencers.

appendix 3

the dynamics of starting a weekly large-group meeting

Every ministry longs to have an ever expanding large-group meeting with lots of enthusiasm, momentum, and impact. In fact, many ministries and churches measure their success by how many people come to their meetings. As important and valuable as a large-group meeting can be, we dare not make that the highest measure of success. Experience tells us that some of these meetings (and ministries) can have a lot of breadth but very little depth.

Why Start a Large-Group Meeting?

This is the key question you must answer on a semester by semester basis. Most ministries start a large-group meeting, but cannot clearly identify its goal. The fog of confusion and tyranny of the urgent can roll in fast, and the unspoken objective can evolve into simply seeing how many people you can get into the meeting room each week. That doesn't stop some ministry leaders who, once they've lost sight of their goal, redouble their efforts! Why the students are there or where you plan on taking them as a result of the meeting are questions that ought to be addressed constantly, but usually aren't.

Here are some possible reasons to start and sustain a regular large-group meeting. Several of these may be reasons you choose to initiate a meeting.

1. Builds Momentum

A well-attended, regular, large-group meeting can be like a huge funnel that attracts more and more students. If you will then initiate one-on-one gospel appointments and guide students into small groups, the momentum can be properly harnessed.

2. Creates an identity for the ministry

Many students seek out a meeting with a certain kind of student or worship or teaching. If the large-group creates an attractive front door to your ministry, it can enhance your recruiting efforts on campus.

3. Trains student leaders

Seek to use every responsibility, from planning to recruiting to leading worship to cleaning up, as opportunities to develop and train student leaders. The more students own and lead the large-group meeting (and any aspect of the ministry), the more committed they will be, and more responses you will see.

4. Fellowship

The meeting can be used to bring believers together for encouragement and the deepening of relationships. Every student desires to be part of a group that loves and accepts them. This can serve as the body of Christ on campus.

5. Evangelistic

Depending on the purpose, your meeting can be a seeker-friendly atmosphere where non-Christians feel welcomed and witnessed to. Whether or not there is an evangelistic message or appeal, believers can still use the meeting to reach out to the non-Christians there.

6. Teaches students the basics

Some groups focus the topics and testimonies on building the basics of the Christian life into students. These can either be topics students may not normally hear at their church or topics that reinforce what they are getting at church.

Noble Bowman, a campus pastor for Chi Alpha Ministries, started and led a dynamic large-group weekly meeting that sustained its purpose and vitality for many years. The secret? He uses his meeting for three things:

1. A corporate *worship* gathering where students are led into an intimate encounter with the person of Christ.
2. A corporate *teaching* gathering where the ministry leadership teaches and leads students into studies on various topics.
3. A corporate *vision-casting* gathering where the ministry leadership casts vision to the students.

The answer to the "Why are we having this meeting?" question will *always* determine the meeting's location and content, including speakers, topics, worship style, and etc. Noble Bowman will tell you that one danger of a large-group meeting is that it takes so much energy and focus from the staff and student leadership that there may be little time left for evangelism and discipleship. Remember, Jesus didn't tell us to go into all the world and hold meetings, He said to "make disciples" of all the nations. A large-group meeting has the potential to aid in the overall discipling process, but, believe it or not, the meeting can also be the *main* obstacle in fulfilling the Great Commission on your campus!

When to Start a Large-Group Meeting

The very first agenda item for most new ministries is to start a weekly large-group meeting. I wish, though, that campus ministries knew what most church planters know—that solid lay leaders and several healthy small groups are essential prerequisites for launching a high profile, weekly church service that will effectively attract others from the community.

In our mind's eye, all of us dream of having hundreds of spiritually growing students coming to our weekly meeting, most of them having been won to Christ by someone in our ministry, and plugged into small discipleship groups and good local churches. For this vision to become a reality, a couple of critical first steps have to take place.

1. Focus on grassroots ministry

If you want your students to win other students to Christ, then you will have to model that. If you just gather as many believers as you can to start your large-group meeting, that is also the way your students will operate in years to come. However those initial students are recruited to your movement will determine the DNA of your ministry in the years to come. Students will either (1) just invite other Christians to meetings or (2) evangelize in their relationships and living groups. It all depends upon how much evangelism and discipleship you do *before* you start a large-group meeting. Lastly, your decision to focus your grassroots ministry efforts on isolated loners or mainstream leaders will determine who (and how many) will ultimately be part of your large-group meeting.

2. Wait for a solid core to emerge

It will be difficult, but try to exercise self-control over when you launch the large-group meeting. Wait until there are several small-group Bible studies operating and a growing number of student leaders who are taking personal responsibility for ministry. When you have developed fifteen to twenty key students who have a love for Christ and the emotional and social maturity to reach out to others, then it may be time to think about a large-group meeting. These key students (I sometimes call them influencers) will be the magnets who attract other influencers, interested, even isolated students to your meetings. Give them as much ownership as possible in the creation of the name, location, format, and topics, all based, of course, on the clear-cut purpose of the meeting you and your leaders have agreed upon. Whether you like it or not, your ministry will never grow beyond the quality and quantity of your student leadership.

My Ten Commandments of Large-Group Ministry

1. Get all of your key students committed to planning, leading, attending, and recruiting to the meetings.

2. Be crystal clear as to the purpose of the meeting. (Keep that focused in the minds of your students.)

3. Bathe the purpose, people, and program in prayer on a weekly basis.

4. Rely mainly on your core of student leadership to invite and bring others to the meeting, rather than signs and banners.

5. Choose an on-campus location that is slightly smaller than the number of people you are expecting at your meeting. (One hundred students in a room designed for seventy-five creates a lot more excitement and momentum than one hundred and fifty students in an auditorium that holds six hundred.)

6. Have a well-liked, well-prepared student emcee the meetings. Make sure he is a committed believer.

7. Develop a high-quality, high-energy worship band made up of godly students.

8. Use student-designed, student-led skits and testimonies to reinforce the point of the talk or the purpose of the meeting.

9. Choose speakers and topics that are biblical, relevant, and impactful.

the fuel and the flame ❧

10. Use the meeting to create momentum for your ministry and to funnel as many students as possible into smaller, student-led discipleship groups.

I am convinced the main reason students come to a large-group meeting (or to any activity) is because of *who* is there. As great as the worship, message, or refreshments might be, the primary question they are asking as they first look around is, "Are these *my* kind of people?" Like magnets the number of spiritually, emotionally, and socially mature students you have at the core of your ministry usually determines the kind and number of people who come to (and then stick with) your movement.

appendix 4

scripture memory verses

On Discipleship

I. **Discipleship Characteristics**
   A. Puts Christ before family   Luke 14:26   Mark 3:35

   B. Puts Christ before possessions,
   things, status   Luke 14:33   Phil. 3:5-7

   C. Gives priority to Word
   1. Quiet time   Mark 1:35   Ps. 63:1
   2. Love for Word   Ps.119:97   Ps. 119:20
   3. Obeys Word   Ps. 119:59-60   Isa. 66:2
   4. Consistent in Word   John 8:31   James 1:25

   D. Bears fruit   John 15:8   Col. 1:10

   E. Is a learner   Isa. 50:4   Job 34:32

   F. Presses on   Isa. 50:5, 7   Phil. 3:13-14

   G. Is known by His love   John 13:34-35   1 John 4:20

   H. Is openly identified
   with Christ   Matt. 10:32   Mark 8:38

II. **Relationship to Body**
   A. To one another
   1. Love   Col. 3:14   Col. 2:2
   2. Unity   Eph. 4:2-3   Matt. 5:23-24
   3. Serve   1 Cor. 16:15   Heb. 6:10
   4. Forgive   Luke 6:37   Mark 11:25-26
   5. Clear conscience   2 Cor. 4:2   2 Cor. 1:12
   6. Identify   1 Cor. 12:25-26   Heb. 13:3
   7. Employ your gift   1 Peter 4:10   1 Tim. 4:14

| B. To leadership | Heb. 13:7, 17 | 1 Thess. 5:12-13 |

B. To leadership   Heb. 13:7, 17   1 Thess. 5:12-13

C. To opposite sex
  1. Maintain purity   1 Thess. 4:3   Matt. 5:8, 28
  2. Guards his heart   Prov. 4:23   Jer. 17:9
  3. Waits for God to act   Isa. 30:18   Song 8:4
  4. Marries within the body   2 Cor. 6:14   Neh. 13:26

III. **Handling Life's Circumstances**
  A. Knowing God's will through
    1. Being yielded to God   Phil. 2:13   John 7:17
    2. Word of God   Ps. 119:105   Prov. 6:22-23
    3. Prayer   James 1:5   Ps. 143:8, 10
    4. Counsel   Prov. 15:22   Prov. 3:5-6
    5. Circumstances   Rev. 3:8   Gen. 24:14
    6. Deep, inner peace   Isa. 32:17   1 Cor. 14:33

  B. Handling pressures   Ps. 138:7   Matt. 11:28

  C. Handling suffering   1 Peter 1:6-7   Rom. 5:3-5

IV. **A Disciple's Promises**
  A. God's leading   Ps. 32:8   Isa. 30:21

  B. Security in Christ   1 Peter 2:6   Ps. 62:6-8

  C. God's love   Jer. 31:3   Isa. 43:4

  D. God's presence   Josh. 1:9   Heb. 13:5

  E. Prosperity   Ps. 1:2-3   2 Cor. 9:7-8

On Disciplemaking

I. **WHAT** is a Disciplemaker?
  A. He is a teacher.
    By sharing what he's learned   2 Tim. 2:2
    By sharing himself   1 Thess. 2:8
    By pacesetting   1 Peter 5:3

  B. He is a follower.
    1 Thess. 1:6-7   Phil. 4:9   Mark 6:30

C. He is adaptable.
    1 Thess. 2:11-12   1 Thess. 2:7   John 15:13

II. **WHERE** does a Disciplemaker work?
    Luke 24:47   Acts 20:20   Deut. 11:19

III. **WHEN** does a Disciplemaker work?
    1 Thess. 3:10 2 Tim. 4:2   Col. 1:29

IV. **WHO** can be Disciplemakers?
    Phil. 1:23-25 2 Peter 1:12   Col. 1:7

V. **WHY** be a Disciplemaker?
    John 15:16   2 Cor. 5:14-15   1 John 3:16

VI. **HOW** to be a Disciplemaker
    A. By life
        1 Tim. 4:12   Titus 2:7-8   James 3:13-17
    B. By heart
        Ps. 78:72   Phil. 1:7   John 13:1
    C. By prayer
        John 17:20   Col. 4:12   2 Thess. 1:11
    D. By the Word
        Ezra 7:10   Acts 20:32   1 Tim. 4:13-16
    E. Attitudes
        Phil. 2:7   Acts 20:24   Phil. 2:20-21
    F. Actions
        Acts 20:28   1 Peter 5:2   Prov. 27:23
    G. Goals
        Col. 1:28   Eph. 4:12-13   2 Tim. 3:17

VII. **REWARDS** for a Disciplemaker
    1 Thess. 3:9   1 Peter 5:4   1 Thess. 2:19-20

Note: These two pages of verses on being a disciple and making disciples were developed by Ruth Homsten, a Navigator staff person in the Philippines. Thanks Ruth!

appendix 5

how to lead a small-group
bible discussion

1. The Preparation

Whether you are using published materials or creating your own Bible studies, you will want to be fully prepared to lead your study. Be diligent to accurately handle the word of truth (2 Timothy 2:15) as you do your original investigation of the passages you'll be discussing with your group. As you make your observations, interpretations, and applications of each passage, you'll want to try to discover what I call the three T's:

Then Meaning » **T**imeless Principle » **T**oday's Application

2. The Objective

As you look at two or three main points you've discovered in your personal study of the passages, pick out one major point that matches up with a critical need your group has. This becomes your main objective of the discussion (i.e., the one major thing that dominates their minds as they leave the study). Most small-group discussions (along with most sermons) send people away with a whole host of points. No wonder most of us cannot even remember what last Sunday's sermon was about!

3. The Questions

In this type of study, the format is discussion, *not* teaching! Jesus was a master at asking questions, and the key to good discussion will be the questions you design in advance. All the questions you create should inch your group members closer and closer to discovering the objective of your study. Good questions should create self-discovery, so never tell anyone *anything* that they could discover themselves as a result of your well-worded questions. No matter how great a question you might craft, if it doesn't push your group toward the prayed-through objective you've set for the study, throw it out! The three kinds of questions you'll want to create are:

A. The discovery question (asks *"what"*)
    An open-ended, well-worded question introducing a new topic and seeking to gather facts.
    Example: From this passage, *what* does Jesus teach us about love?

B. The understanding question (asks *"why"*)
    A more narrow, well-worded, follow-up question, seeking to find the relevance and relationship of those facts.
    Example: *Why* would Jesus say there is more reward in loving our enemies than our friends?

C. The application question (asks *"how"*)
    A direct, well-worded, final question challenging the participants to make those relevant facts a reality in their lives.
    Example: Think of one hard-to-love person in your life right now. *How* can you specifically show love to this person this week?

Instead of allowing a participant to just give a nebulous response like "My application is that I want to be a better Christian," help them to SPAM it instead. Gently guide them to make it **S**pecific, **P**ersonal, **A**ttainable, and **M**easurable.

The common denominator in these three questions is the little phrase, well-worded. This will require a lot of prayer, thought, and creativity. You'll know whether it's a good question the very moment it leaves your mouth! As you design each question you'll want to anticipate what your group's answers might be. Always evaluate each question as to whether it helps them discover the truths from the Scriptures that you have discerned they need. The Navigators have developed "The Package Principle" where you bring more questions into the study than you have time to ask. View *each* question as a beautifully prepared present that you lay in front of your group to carefully unwrap. Be sure to end the study on time, always carting out a few unopened presents (i.e. questions) with you. You'll pique their curiosity and make them want to come back the next week!

4. The Phases

There are three phases to each of the well-worded questions you ask in your group. If you follow these three steps each time you throw out a question, you will truly be leading them in an exercise of self-discovery.

A. The launching phase

In a conversational tone, use one of your well-worded, open-ended questions to launch the discussion. Like a boat that's on the shore waiting to get out into the water, you have to push off the group discussion. Ask the question with enthusiasm and anticipation, but after you ask it, zip the lip! As hard as it might be the first few times, be quiet and *wait* for an answer. Don't be afraid of silence! Don't try to repeat or reword the question—give them time to think and reply. If they understand that this study is truly a discussion and the ball is now in *their* court, their minds will get in gear to think through responses.

B. The guiding phase

Get excited about the responses you get. Affirm your group's answers, but make sure you keep them on track. Ask questions like, "What does someone else think?" or, "Julie, how would you respond to Katie's answer?" Remember, you are not the authority as much as you are the facilitator. Imagine the discussion is like a beach ball and your job is to keep it up in the air, trying to involve as many people as you can, especially the quiet ones. Keep good eye contact with everyone. Ask follow-up questions, seeking to get the group into the Scriptures and headed toward the objective you've set up for that session.

C. The summarizing phase

Once you have gathered the quality and quantity of information you were looking for, it is time to wrap it up and draw some conclusions. This is not a time for you to teach but rather to restate what group members shared. You might even keep a pen and pad handy during Bible study so that during the summarizing phase you can refer back to comments that were shared, including the person who shared it. Everyone wants to feel included, and this will make your group members feel like they contributed. You want them to not only leave the study excited but come back next week too!

The diagram below shows how the phases fit into each stage of questioning to help your group discover the biblical principle or objective you have prayed and planned for.

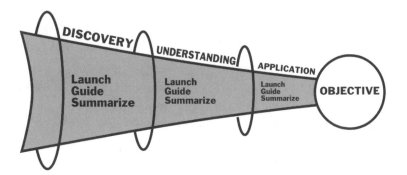

appendix 6

powerful questions to make students spiritually hungry

Jesus was a master at asking questions. Sometimes He would even answer someone's question with a question! Proverbs 20:5 teaches us "the purposes of a man's heart are deep waters, but a man of understanding draws them out." Never tell anyone something when you could ask them a question that would help them discover it themselves.

As Christian workers we are trying to recruit believers to become even more devoted to Jesus Christ and His purposes here on earth. We are also trying to recruit non-Christians to trust Jesus alone as their Savior and Lord. How do we recruit others? By *telling* them what they *ought* to do? That, many times, is the least effective way to motivate someone to go in a particular direction.

One definition of recruiting is *helping someone see their need to the point where they're willing to do something about it.* Asking others questions can peel back their defenses one layer at a time until they have to admit to themselves (and to you!) that maybe they do have a need. If they see their need and are willing to admit it, then maybe they will also be open to allowing you to meet their need. Usually, before others will take action, you must first pray and ask them grace-seasoned questions to expose their needs and make them spiritually hungry.

Questions to Make Christians Hungry

When was the last time you did something and felt as though God was in it?

What is the neatest thing the Lord has shown you lately?

Are you satisfied with the progress you've made since becoming a Christian?

What are you believing God for these days?

What is your life objective?

How would you tell another person how to become a Christian?

College equips us to make a living: what are you doing to equip yourself to live a meaningful life?

Would you like to have a part in God's plan to reach the world for Christ?

How has God used you to help others since you became a Christian?

What would you do if someone in your classes acted interested in knowing about Christ or growing as a Christian?

Who is helping you to grow in your daily walk with Christ?

What did you learn in your Bible study/reading this week?

What do you hope to accomplish during your lifetime?

Do you find it easy to apply the Scripture that you've memorized?

How does the Holy Spirit work in your life?

What book of the Bible are you reading now?

What is the most significant thing that you have learned since becoming a Christian?

How do you see your major fitting in with God's plan for the world?

What word would you use to describe your prayer life?

How many other Christians really know how you are doing spiritually?

What is God's calling for you right now?

How do you think Jesus would handle this type of situation?

What are your three favorite verses?

Are you satisfied with your life?

What do you think Jesus wants from you?

Questions to Make Non-Christians Hungry

If you could know God in a personal way, would you want to?

Do you ever think about spiritual things?

How do you decide what is true?

What gives you purpose in life?

What do you think motivates people today?

What is your view of Jesus Christ? What was His role in history?

Are you content with your life? Why or why not?

How do you handle stress and frustration?

What brings you complete fulfillment?

How will people remember you?

Do you like yourself?

Why try to excel? What's the point?

What implications does the resurrection have on the claims Christ made about Himself?

If Jesus rose from the dead, what does that tell us about Him?

Do you think right and wrong are absolute? Why or why not?

Are you aware of the blessings that God wants to give you?

For what purpose are we here?

What are your impressions of Jesus Christ?

What does Islam say about Jesus?

Who do you think Jesus is?

What do you think is necessary to do to become a follower of Jesus Christ?

What is the most significant thing you've done in your life?

What is your relationship to Christ? Are you a skeptic, admirer, follower, indifferent? Why?

What do you think happens when you die?

What do you think a Christian is, or what characterizes a Christian?

What does "religion" mean to you?

Who is Jesus to you, and what was His life like?

What is your main goal in life?

Do you believe in heaven and hell? Why do people go there?

What is sin? Why doesn't God like it?

If you were to die tonight and stand before God and He were to say, "Why should I let you into My heaven?" what would you say?

What do you think the main message of the Bible is?

Why would God come to earth?

Why would God die for us?

Do you ever feel guilty? What do you do with your guilt?

What do you think it means to have a "personal relationship" with Jesus Christ?

What can I pray about for you?

appendix 7

the cure for spiritual amnesia

We need to understand how God views us as believers. Dr. Neil Anderson said, "Understanding your identity in Christ is absolutely essential to your success at living the victorious Christian life." The greatest question any one can answer about themselves is also the simplest: Who Am I? These passages and statements from Dr. Anderson's books will help you remember who you are!

I am accepted

John 1:12	I am God's child
John 15:15	I am Christ's friend
Rom. 5:1	I have been justified
1 Cor. 6:17	I am united with the Lord, and I am one spirit with Him
1 Cor. 6:19-20	I have been bought with a price. I belong to God
1 Cor. 12:27	I am a member of Christ's body
Eph. 1:1	I am a saint
Eph. 1:5	I have been adopted as God's child
Eph. 2:18	I have direct access to God through the Holy Spirit
Col. 1:14	I have been redeemed and forgiven of all my sins
Col. 2:10	I am complete in Christ

I am secure

Rom. 8:1-2	I am free forever from condemnation
Rom. 8:28	I am assured that all things work together for good
Rom. 8:35-39	I cannot be separated from the love of God
2 Cor. 1:21-22	I have been established, anointed, and sealed by God
Col. 3:3	I am hidden with Christ in God
Phil. 1:6	I am assured that God will complete the work that He began in me
Phil. 3:20	I am a citizen of heaven
2 Tim. 1:7	I am not given a spirit of fear, but of power, love, and sound mind
Heb. 4:16	I can find grace and mercy in my time of need
1 John 5:18	I am born of God, and the evil one cannot touch me

I am significant

Matt. 5:13-14	I am the salt and light of the earth
John 15:1, 5	I am a branch of the true vine, a channel of His life
John 15:16	I have been chosen and appointed to bear fruit
Acts 1:8	I am a personal witness of Christ's
1 Cor. 3:9	I am God's coworker
1 Cor. 3:16	I am God's temple
2 Cor. 5:17-21	I am a minister of reconciliation for God

Eph. 2:6	I am seated with Christ in the heavenly realm
Eph. 2:10	I am God's workmanship
Eph. 3:12	I can approach God with freedom and confidence
Phil. 4:13	I can do all things through Christ who strengthens me

appendix 8

essentials for ministry: momentum, multiplication, management

Establishing the mission of your movement will determine what goals you set, what activities you engage in, and how you manage yourself and your ministry. Your mission, plus momentum, multiplication, and management, make up the essential components of ministry. Regardless of which of these areas you are strongest in, make sure you give adequate attention to each of them if you want to have a healthy, vibrant movement.

Momentum—Fueling the Movement

This is the enthusiasm factor in your ministry. In order to create a movement on your campus, you must purposely create momentum that draws in a growing number of students. Many times your higher-profile activities like weekly meetings, weekend retreats, or all-campus events can be used to generate this feeling of anticipation that all students want to be part of.

The staff or student leaders need to understand the mood, needs, and schedule of a campus to adequately plan and carry out a momentum-building strategy. A ministry doesn't just *happen* to become fun, attractive, and relevant by accident, it takes a lot of prayer, planning, and delegation. Getting the right students in the right roles is essential to beginning and sustaining a long-term momentum. Identifying and recruiting a core group of student leaders who can band together to plan events, recruit others, and create an air of excitement on campus is the key.

Not only do large group meetings and campus events create momentum, but retreats and conferences can too. You can build exciting, impactful momentum cycles around a retreat or conference, because it gives everyone something to look forward to and recruit to. Following an event like this, you can see how God has moved in the hearts of different students. Your role now becomes helping each student (and the movement as a whole) jump to the next level of commitment; so don't let those decisions grow cold because of your neglect. An increase in momentum has the potential to deepen students' commitment, which then cycles around to produce an ever growing pool of new students recruited to your ministry.

Multiplication—Expanding the Movement

If momentum is the skin of your ministry, multiplication is the vital organs. If momentum is the front door to your movement, then multiplication is the factory inside, with the personnel and equipment busy building the product. The enthusiasm and added numbers that momentum creates need to be directly funneled into a well-planned multiplication strategy. Don't allow your key leaders to be so consumed with the momentum activities that they don't have the time and energy to give themselves to the reason the ministry exists: evangelism and discipleship.

As soon as possible, students new to your momentum events need to have the opportunity to hear the gospel, plug into a small group, and get incorporated into your ministry's growing family. Thus evangelism and small-group leadership needs to be student owned and led. As the staff equips the student leaders, the multiplication chain can continue to a second, third, and fourth generation, with the goal of every student in your movement having a "Paul" as well as a "Timothy."

The key to multiplication is spending time with your key

students (including doing ministry with them). Pour into the individuals you've selected from the growing pool of new students. Many Christian workers are not able to stay focused on multiplication, because it requires a clear-cut plan, a patient commitment to the process, and time to build relationships. The bulk of your time and your energies must be invested here if you are going to see lifelong laborers raised up for Christ.

Management—Serving the Movement

You can have incredible momentum on your campus and a growing number of students who really want to minister, but if you don't take the time and effort to regularly organize and plan, it could all collapse. For the worker who doesn't feel gifted in administration, this management component can appear to be just busyness or simply a necessary evil they must endure. Either we control our schedules and to-do lists or they will control us. If you find yourself just reacting all the time, it could be you need a crash course in personal and ministry management.

Effective management always begins with the person we look at in the mirror each morning. Setting and carrying out personal goals in our time and relationship with God and family, sleep and physical exercise, financial stability and work, etc., are top-tier priorities that require our greatest attention.

Momentum management can feel overwhelming if there is a weekly large-group meeting or succession of retreats and conferences on the horizon. Getting the upper hand here means doing a lot of advance planning, recruiting leadership, delegating, and empowering students. Ideally, you are not *doing* anything but simply managing others who are carrying out their prearranged responsibilities. Along with organization, ongoing communication and evaluation will help define and refine future activities.

Managing the multiplication in your movement will be one of the most mentally and emotionally draining exercises you will perform. Spending time planning out the "strategy of the week" for each of the students you want to meet with takes prayer, time, and forethought. The key is to ask yourself three questions about *each* evangelism, establishing, and equipping appointment you're planning:

1. Where is this student spiritually?
2. Where does he or she need to go?
3. What is the next step?

In 2 Timothy 2:2 Paul tells Timothy to entrust himself to faithful men who will be able to teach others, showing us that the apostle was committed to raising up a strong third and fourth generation of believers. If we are going to do the same in our ministry, it will demand week after week, hour after hour of praying and planning for not only how to personally help our key students, but also how to equip them to win and disciple others. This is our *mission*, and to complete it we need to create *momentum*, funnel it into deep *multiplication*, and support it all with solid, ongoing *management*.

the fuel and the flame ♦

appendix 9

six steps for an effective house ministry

Having college students live with you for the purpose of discipling them is somewhat of a lost art. Most Americans demand their privacy and wouldn't dream of sharing their living space with non-family members. It's one thing to meet with a student an hour a week for a discipling appointment, but to invite them to live with you twenty-four hours a day, seven days a week? That's going *way* overboard!

This idea of using my house as a strategic ministry tool was introduced to me in the excellent biography, *Daws*, the story of Dawson Trotman, founder of the Navigators. He purchased a large, centrally located home and had four to eight men living with him and his family for the express purpose of building into their lives for Christ. When I was in college, my discipler invited me and two others to move in with him, and I was privileged to experience this life-on-life mentoring first hand. Since 1983, my family and I have had students living with us in order to prepare them to be lifelong laborers for Jesus Christ. I list six steps to think through in order to succeed in turning your house into a haven for ministry.

1. Pray

Ask God for wisdom and direction. Whether you're single or have a family, you must pray and discern if this is the right kind of ministry for you. Every believer is to make disciples, but not every one has to run a boarding house! Pray about whether you should buy or rent a facility and ask the Lord to lead you to the right students to live with you. Bathe the whole process in prayer.

2. Purpose

"Where there is no vision, the people perish" is what Proverbs 29:18 (KJV) teaches. I have seen many different housing arrangements over the years where the people are all Christians, but there didn't seem to be any vision, direction, or real purpose. There needs to be a definite leader and clear cut expectations. Sit down with the Word, a key student or two, and craft a purpose statement for your housing ministry. Then come up with some goals you hope to accomplish. Some of our annual goals are:

    A. To develop in Christlikeness (especially in speech, servanthood, hard work, excellence, and hospitality)

    B. To develop a heart for God and consistency in the basics of the Christian life

    C. To develop a vision for the campus and the world

    D. To develop a personal evangelism and disciplemaking ministry

    E. To develop an orientation to the biblical purposes of family and home

3. Place

Try to find a facility that is near the group you are seeking to reach. We have always acquired a house next to fraternity row, because that has been our ministry target. Consecrate your house for God's use. Understand it's not just a neat place to live, but a strategic tool in the hands of God. The house is a means to build laborers to reach the campus in order to reach the world. You can have a good testimony if you'll keep the house and grounds clean and well maintained. If you have a family, make sure there is a private (read: off limits!) area where you can sleep and recreate together in a place that is separate from the student's area.

Pick a facility that has enough room for a good-size dinner

table. You and your housemates need to eat as many evening meals together as possible, inviting as many guests as possible each time. Throughout your life, your dinner table will be the most effective evangelistic tool you'll have. We have had thousands of students eat with us through the years. Hospitality and relationships are extended at the dinner table, many times followed by a stirring one-on-one gospel presentation and opportunity to receive Christ. Ministries like Food for the Hungry will tell you that filling the stomach has a way of softening the heart!

4. People

Determine the number of students you want to live with you when you select your facility. Having had an incredible variety of students live with us over the years, I can attest that the biggest factors for selecting students are the two C's.

A. Character

Look at the acrostic F-A-I-T-H and evaluate the student. Are they faithful? Available? Take the initiative? Teachable? Have a heart for God and people? You're not looking for the perfect person, but ask whether he is growing in these areas. My experience has been that all of us are primarily (not exclusively!) givers or takers. We tend to spend most of our time either looking out for the needs of others or looking out for number one. A student may *look* spiritual singing hymns on Sunday morning, but check them out when the dishwasher needs unloading on a Thursday evening!

B. Chemistry

Think through the mix of your group. Each person has a distinct personality and gift set. If all are talkers and there are no listeners, you're in trouble! If everyone wants to lead and no one wants to serve, there will definitely be some issues! You don't really get to know someone until they live with you, but try to imagine what it will be like to throw this unique group of individuals into the same house for a year. Even if you do all of your evaluation and homework, there will still be struggles. It's called human nature, and by the end of your first year you will be better at conflict resolution than most professional counselors!

To be honest, I would rather have no students than the wrong students. This is true especially if you have children. Because of the students who have lived with us over the years, my children have grown up thinking it's cool to be a committed Christian college student. You can't put a price on that! Lastly, you must help the students see it is a privilege for them to move in and be part of the group. They need to understand and commit to the purpose and standards you have set. To be hazy on this is to invite disaster or have a foggy, mediocre experience at best.

5. Pace

You, as the leader, are the pacesetter. If you want your students to meet with God, memorize Scripture, share their faith, (or unload the dishwasher!) you must model it. The scariest thing about personal ministry is that we reproduce after our own kind. This is especially true in a house ministry, where your lifestyle is on display morning, noon, and night. If you have a family, you must balance time with them and the students. Your first priority is to your family, and the students need to see and respect this.

Yes, you need to have challenging goals and specific responsibilities lined out, but seek to create an atmosphere of love and acceptance. Some students might think you've set up a boot camp (occasionally one of our students will joke about living at our "compound"!), but have some fun, because years later they will look back on this experience and primarily remember the relationship you had with them and the kind of Christlikeness you modeled to them. For most, it is a pivotal year in their life, ministry, and preparation for a successful marriage and family.

6. Persevere

If you choose to engage in a ministry like this, there will definitely be a honeymoon period—probably about two weeks! Once the newness wears off and the masks come down, things can become routine, even monotonous. We meet every Sunday evening and Wednesday morning as a group to pray, study the Word, and report on our personal ministries. But during that second semester, at 6:30 A.M. on the seventh Wednesday in a row, laziness, unfaithfulness, or downright rebellion may raise their ugly heads! The measure of a leader, though, is not as much how you act, but how you react! Take the long look and realize that one act of immaturity doesn't define that student.

Conflicts will arise. Moods will change. You will be forced to get up early and stay up late many days. There isn't as much privacy as most westerners demand, and there is a lot of extra work as you trail behind students cleaning up their messes. Is it all worth it? Without question, it is. Not only will *your* selfishness be forged into selflessness, but you'll leave behind a string of fond memories, changed lives, better marriages, and more effective Christian workers. You will never know this side of eternity what impact you had on the students who lived with you while they were in college. Do I recommend it? Go for it!

appendix 10

five keys to raising your personal financial support team

"I want to serve God and be obedient to His leading in my life, but I don't want to *raise support!*" If you have said or thought these words, you are not alone. If fact, most Christian workers living a donor-supported lifestyle will admit that at one time they've had feelings much like this. Although personal support raising is not very popular in North America, where independence is highly esteemed, it is an essential part of funding the workers in many Christian ministries and mission agencies. And if that's true of you, then surrendering to the will of God in your life is not a question of whether you will raise support but whether you will be obedient. When that question is answered, support raising becomes an exciting aspect of the job God is calling you to.

Even though there are stresses and pressures involved in raising and maintaining a personal support team, I would *not* want to live any other way. The bonds that I have formed with our supporters over the years are priceless. The stories of God building my faith during difficult times could fill a book. And most of all, when I report to my ministry assignment, there is a sense of destiny and authority there. There are sixty-plus people who have paid a dear price to have me ministering there. I had better take it seriously and give it my all. That's what I call accountability!

You might be thinking about the best way to fund your ministry. Should you be a "tentmaker" and work a job while ministering, or should you raise part or all of your personal support? Both are biblical, but if you're going to raise support you will probably have some doubts, fears, and questions. *You are normal!* I still get butterflies in my stomach each time I pick up that phone to make a support appointment. If you want to be successful you're going to need some guidance. I have listed several resources at the end of this article that would be good for you to purchase and study. But just to hold you over until you can get to the bookstore, I've listed five keys to raising your personal support. This is one of the most exhilarating adventures (i.e., roller coaster rides!) I have ever experienced. So hold on tight and here we go:

The Five Keys

1. Understand the biblical basis

Take some time to study the Scriptures for yourself, so you will know exactly what God thinks about asking others to give to you and to your ministry. Some choose just to pray and trust God to bring the funds in like the great George Mueller did to support his orphanages in nineteenth century London. But it is just as biblical and requires as much or more faith to *personally* invite others to invest. Either way, we have to understand that God is the source of our funds, not the donors, our plans, or hard work. Scott Morton, of the Navigators, in his excellent book, *Funding Your Ministry: Whether You're Gifted or Not*, highlights five examples and teachings from the Old and New Testaments about the validity of God's ministers being supported by others:

A. The example of the Levites (Numbers 18:24) The Jews gave their tithe to the priests for support
B. The example of Jesus (Luke 8:2–3) Many people supported Jesus and the disciples
C. The teaching of Jesus (Matthew 10:9–10) A Kingdom worker is worthy of his support
D. The example of Paul (Acts 18:4–5) He stopped tent making to preach full time on support

E. The teaching of Paul (1 Corinthians 9:1–18) He had the right to be supported by the churches

Once you have a biblical perspective on this topic of asking for and living on the support of others, take a look at one more thing: your own giving! Before you can ask anyone else to give, *you* have to be committed to sacrificially investing in kingdom work on a regular basis. Let's practice what we preach!

2. Kill the Giants in Your Own Mind

Remember the twelve Hebrew spies who went into the Promised Land to take a peek before the whole nation was to enter and claim what God had given them? Only Joshua and Caleb came back ready to invade. The other ten spies were so terrified of the giants they saw in the land that they confessed, "We became like grasshoppers in our *own* sight, and so we were in *their* sight." (Numbers 13:33). Instead of trusting God and moving out with courage, they let fear paralyze them. How they viewed themselves affected how the giants viewed them! It is the same way in support raising. The confidence level that we have in God, our vision, and ourselves can make us or break us! All of us have different "giants" in our own minds that will keep us from beginning and persevering in assembling a full support team. These are some common "giants" we must conquer:

A. You or your family might think support raising is really just begging.
B. You might think you are not a worthy investment.
C. You might think that support raising is just a necessary evil that must be endured.
D. You might think that people are rejecting you or your ministry if they say no.

You must kill these giants one at a time as you fill your mind with the Scriptures and believe what God has said about you and your calling. Then you can courageously march in and take the land! Just as God had prepared the land for the people to go in and take it, we need to believe that God has prepared the hearts of the donors, enabling us to walk in faith and boldly ask them to join us in our vision.

3. Pray and Plan

Author S. D. Gordon said it well: "Prayer is the real work of the ministry. Service is just gathering in the results of prayer." We need to bathe ourselves and our donors in prayer before, during, and after this process. God will go before you. He will also build a love for your donors as you pray for them individually.

Create Your Budget

Include everything you need for your personal needs, giving, saving, and ministry expenses. Seek to balance a lifestyle that will allow you to maximize your effectiveness with the group you're reaching, but also be above reproach from your donors regarding the stewardship of your finances. If you happen to have school debt, simply include in your budget the required monthly amount owed and keep going. Your donors will admire you for keeping your promise to pay it back. Plan on and commit to raising 100 percent *before* you report to your assignment. Have a "*when* I raise my support" not an "*if* I raise my support" attitude!

Namestorm

Now that you have turned the whole process over to God, you are ready to begin your planning. Write down every person you have *ever* known during your lifetime. Don't play Holy Spirit by saying, "Oh, that person would never give." You will be surprised by a few who will give, and by a few who don't! Also, think of people who have a heart for student work, missions, or whatever group or area you are targeting. List churches, Sunday school classes, foundations, and corporations. The bulk of your support, though, will come from the individuals with whom you meet.

Map Out a Plan

Divide up all the names according to the cities they live in. Then label each name "hot," "medium," or "cold" depending upon whether they probably will give, might give, or are less likely to give. Next, pray and seek to attach an amount you would like to ask each to give. Don't use a one-size-fits-all plan; instead, base the amount on what you perceive they are able to give along with the kind of relationship you have with them. You might feel more comfortable suggesting a range of giving rather than a specific amount. Either way, know that the tendency for most of us is to ask for too little, not too much! Remember, there is no cash-flow problem in heaven. Americans alone give almost 300 billion dollars to charity each year. God has instilled in every person a desire to give, and you are helping them to invest in the eternal and thus build up their treasure in heaven. Go for it!

Plan Out a Map

Figure out what city you will go to first, second, and so on. Schedule it on your calendar. If you want to send a letter in advance, telling them what you are doing and that you will be calling, do it. But the key is to call each person before the trip in order to get the appointment. Don't let them say yes or no to giving while on the phone; your *only* objective is to get an appointment with them. Seek to line up all of your "hot" prospects first, then your "medium" prospects, and finally (if you have time) the "cold" prospects.

4. Ask Them Face to Face

This is the key. Jesus says "We have not because we ask not." The word "ask" is used in the gospels 113 times. God wants to teach us about asking—Him and others. I have looked at surveys as to why people give, and the number one reason is always because someone *asked* them! It is not unspiritual or fleshly to ask. It is biblical, spiritual, and faith-building to ask. Let's not hide behind our fears. Let's walk toward them and render them powerless! The worst thing they could say is no.

If you *just* send a letter out or make a group presentation, you might have a 10 percent response rate. If you send a letter and then call to ask them to join your team, you might get 25 percent of people to say yes. But, if you are willing to sit down eyeball to eyeball with others and lay out the incredible ministry vision God has called you to, usually well over half of the folks will pull their checkbooks out! I've had some tell me they have never been turned down in an individual support raising appointment! My research shows that ministries that train their staff to ask for the gift raise their full budget in less than half the time as groups that simply share the need but don't ask. We have not because we ask not. Sound familiar?

5. Cultivate the Relationship

Here are the ABC's for having a long and fruitful relationship with your supporters:

A. Remember, it's not fundraising, but "friendraising."
   You can have an incredible ministry in their lives, and *you* might be their only connection to Jesus Christ or the Great Commission.

B. Consider tithing your time to your support team.
   Pray, write, call, and minister to them.

C. Thank before you bank (when a new person or new gift comes in).
   Be prompt and professional in all of your correspondence and record keeping.

D. Regularly send supporters well-written newsletters.
   Share how their investments are paying off along with some specific prayer requests. Occasional postcards, phone calls, and visits are great too. Beware: The main reason people drop off of support teams is because they do not hear from their missionary.

E. Win, Keep, Lift.

When you *win* a donor they are now on your team. *Keep* them on the team by caring for and cultivating them. Periodically, ask them to consider *lifting* (increasing) their monthly or annual gift to you. Campus Crusade had a campaign where they were asking individuals to give $1,000,000 to their ministry. Almost 250 people said yes. Research showed, though, that the very first gift each had made to this ministry years earlier had been, on average, a mere $10! Someone had taken the time to win, keep, and (over the years) lift!

People will stick with you for life if you appreciate them and keep them informed. View supporters as vital partners in your ministry, and you will gain not only lifelong supporters but friends too! One day you will turn around and realize how blessed you have been and that you would not want to live any other way! Trust God and begin this exciting adventure today. You will never regret it!

Resources:
1. *Funding Your Ministry: Whether You're Gifted or Not* by Scott Morton, Dawson Media
2. *People Raising* by William P. Dillon, Moody Press
3. *Getting Sent* by Pete Sommer, InterVarsity Press
4. *Friend Raising* by Betty Barnett, Youth With A Mission Publishing

appendix 11

helpful campus ministry websites

Boundless Webzine	boundless.org
Campus Crusade for Christ	uscm.org
Evangelism Tool Box	evangelismtoolbox.com
Everystudent.com	everystudent.com
Greek students	4greeks.org
InterVarsity Christian Fellowship	ivcf.org
Leadership University	leaderu.com
The Traveling Team	thetravelingteam.org
Passion Network	268generation.com
Reach the U	reachtheu.com
Short Term Missions	shorttermmissions.com
Student Mobilization	stumo.org
The Veritas Forum	veritas.org
World Religions Index	wri.leaderu.com
Campus Christianity	campuschristianity.com
Watchword	watchword.org
Voice of the Martyrs	persecution.com
Discover the Book	discoverthebook.org
Chi Alpha Campus Ministries	chialpha.com
God Squad	godsquad.com
Waymore	waymore.org
The Navigators	navigators.org
International Missions Board	thetask.org
Growing Leaders	growingleaders.com

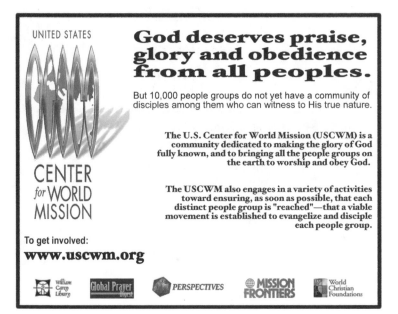
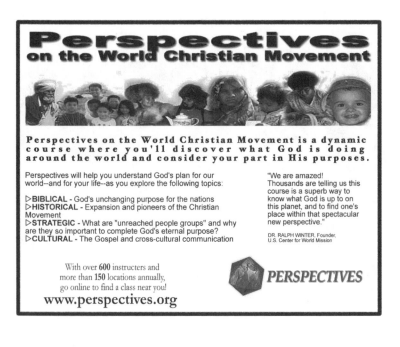

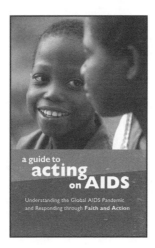

A Guide to Acting on AIDS
Understanding the Global AIDS Pandemic and Responding through Faith and Action

A Guide to Acting on AIDS is designed to equip Christian college students with a deeper awareness of the global AIDS pandemic, why their faith should inform their response, and how they can put their faith into action. This practical study examines HIV/AIDS through a variety of different disciplines and perspectives, such as the scientific, socioeconomic, political, and humanitarian impacts of the disease. Each chapter explores what the Bible says about these issues and what is being done globally to respond. The guide is designed for individuals or for groups and includes discussion questions and proposed action items for the readers.

"It is essential that the next generation understands and acts upon this crisis and the injustices behind it, as we point to the saving hope of Jesus Christ."
TOBYMAC

"In one read, we can learn about the disease, learn who is being affected, and be guided in our attempts to contribute toward a solution."
DONALD MILLER, author of *Blue Like Jazz*

1-932805-80-X   96 Pages

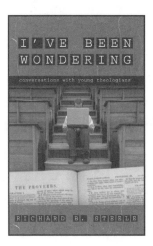

I've Been Wondering
Conversations with Young Theologians

Richard B. Steele

"Is there such a thing as 'bigger' or 'smaller' sins?"

"How important are the sacraments in worship?"

"How can there be free will and god's will at the same time?"

Good questions. In focusing on what his theology and undergraduate students are actually asking him, as opposed to what they ought to ask, Richard B. Steele gives us some very thought provoking answers to some very difficult questions.

I've Been Wondering contains a selection of email correspondence exchanged between the author and his undergraduate theology students on matters pertaining to Christian faith and ethics. Most of the exchanges were triggered by questions that occurred to the students while taking one of the author's undergraduate courses in theology, ethics, or church history.

These letters are anything but "academic" exercises, and are intensely personal to reveal what is going on in the depths of the student soul.

1-932805-44-3   256 Pages